CSCPRC REPORT NO. 4

Paleoanthropology in the People's Republic of China

A Trip Report of the American Paleoanthropology Delegation

Edited by W. W. HOWELLS and PATRICIA JONES TSUCHITANI

Submitted to the Committee on Scholarly Communication
with the People's Republic of China

NATIONAL ACADEMY OF SCIENCES
Washington, D.C. 1977

The exchange visit of the Paleoanthropology Delegation to the People's Republic of China was supported by a grant from the National Science Foundation. This visit was part of the exchange program operated by the Committee on Scholarly Communication with the People's Republic of China, founded jointly in 1966 by the American Council of Learned Societies, the National Academy of Sciences, and the Social Science Research Council. Sources of funding for the Committee include the National Science Foundation, the Department of State, and The Ford Foundation.

The Committee represents American scholars in the natural, medical, and social sciences, as well as the humanities. It advises individuals and institutions on means of communicating with their Chinese colleagues, on China's international scholarly activities, and on the state of China's scientific and scholarly pursuits. Members of the Committee are scholars from a broad range of fields, including China studies.

Administrative offices of the Committee are located at the National Academy of Sciences, Washington, D.C.

The views expressed in this report are those of the members of the Paleoanthropology Delegation and are in no way the official views of the Committee on Scholarly Communication with the People's Republic of China or its sponsoring organizations--the American Council of Learned Societies, the National Academy of Sciences, and the Social Science Research Council.

Library of Congress Catalog Card Number 77-77205

International Standard Book Number 0-309-02620-2

Available from:

Printing and Publishing Office
National Academy of Sciences
2101 Constitution Avenue, N.W.
Washington, D.C. 20418

Printed in the United States of America

FOREWORD

Two years have elapsed since the visit of the Paleoanthropology Delegation to the People's Republic of China in May 1975. The length of
time devoted to the writing of the chapters of this report and the editing by several individuals concerned with the content and format of the
chapters attest to the complexity of the topic. As noted in the introduction by F. Clark Howell, the subject of paleoanthropology was interpreted broadly in designing a delegation to visit China. Specialists
in early-man studies, archeology, Chinese history, geology, and botany
were brought together to form a group to view the subject as it was
thought to be construed in China today. As a result, the delegation's
report has taken the form of essays written by the individual delegation
members rather than a composite analysis of the field of paleoanthropology. The individual reports were circulated among the delegation members to insure adequate review of the findings of each member.

One member of the delegation served as editor for this volume: W. W.
Howells, Emeritus Professor of Anthropology and Honorary Curator of
Somatology, Peabody Museum, Harvard University. Substantial contribu-
tions to the editing process were made by Patricia Jones Tsuchitani,
Staff Officer, Committee on Scholarly Communication with the People's
Republic of China. K. C. Chang helped render the Chinese personal and
place names consistent throughout, using the Wade-Giles system of roman-
ization as a general rule. The photographs were taken by Harold E. Malde.

CONTRIBUTORS

FRANCIS H. BROWN, Department of Geology and Geophysics, University of Utah, Salt Lake City, Utah

KWANG-CHIH CHANG, Department of Anthropology, Harvard University, Cambridge, Massachusetts

ERIC DELSON, Department of Anthropology, Lehman College, City University of New York, Bronx, New York

LESLIE G. FREEMAN, JR., Department of Anthropology, University of Chicago, Chicago, Illinois

F. CLARK HOWELL, *Chairman of the Delegation*, Department of Anthropology, University of California, Berkeley, California

W. W. HOWELLS, Emeritus Professor of Anthropology and Curator of Somatology, Peabody Museum, Harvard University, Cambridge, Massachusetts

DAVID KEIGHTLEY, Department of History, University of California, Berkeley, California

ESTELLA B. LEOPOLD, *Deputy Chairman of the Delegation*, Director, Quaternary Research Center, University of Washington, Seattle, Washington

PATRICK MADDOX, Associate Director, Council on Asian Studies, Harvard University, Cambridge, Massachusetts

HAROLD E. MALDE, Geologist, U.S. Geological Survey, Denver, Colorado

H. M. WORMINGTON, Department of Anthropology, Colorado College, Colorado Springs, Colorado

PREFACE

W. W. Howells

It is only fair, to colleagues and to future delegations, to say something about our original expectations. We went to China far from fully prepared mentally, in spite of well-chosen admonitions from the Committee. To take a theme from K. C. Chang's chapter, considering how many of us had degrees from anthropology departments it is ironic that we should not have better anticipated different culture orientations. Our baggage was natural: we arrived expecting something like an international conference complete with field excursions (we had specified our ideas for these in some detail to our hosts before going). We also took along a little of our evangelical heritage. In general, we probably expected that our hosts, several of them known through literature or correspondence and a few even personally, would eagerly sit down and bandy talk about technical ideas, work in progress, and pressing problems of worldwide interest (such as human fossils or tool typology, for example) back and forth. We would come home with established communications, ready to receive visitors from China and perhaps to prepare working visits to Chinese sites.

We learned a great deal, if not along expected lines. We are used to the immediacy of events throughout the rest of the world, where a date is the same everywhere, and failed to realize that in China concerns, as always, are purely Chinese. If progress is somewhat unhinged from that elsewhere, it matters little. We were aware of other exchange delegations that must have had more immediate concern with progress, like medical problems or seismology. But paleoanthropology is doubtless a good subject to reflect other kinds of Chinese concern. We had not really grasped how, as in many fields, it is structured into the social system. And we did not realize how it is an interest that, however genuine, lacks urgency. We found that, important as they consider it, the Chinese propose to pursue it at their own pace, without reaching to borrow our equipment and without letting it be done by outsiders again. Chang especially, in his report, stresses the themes of self-reliance and serving the people, themes whose importance we had simply not understood beforehand. But now, back home, all of us would surely have been surprised if the Chinese had accepted the proffered foreign aid following the great earthquakes of 1976.

Our anticipations were probably based in part on the history of our subject, well stated by Freeman and Malde. The first third of this century was important in discoveries and information, with foreigners being prominent. After Liberation new work was done, and our delegation promised to be among the first outside scholars to have a fresh look in 40 years. The look we had was indeed enormously rewarding. But the bulk of original sites, whether newly discovered or long known, like the Ni-ho-wan basin, were excluded from our itinerary. Instead, except for visits to Chou-k'ou-tien and Ting-ts'un, we learned from discourses at institutions and visits to museums. We also learned things our hosts wanted us to learn about modern China. We had been told that visits to communes, factories, etc., were to be expected; we experienced many talks that, singly, seemed like mere propaganda. But these things were decidedly interesting in themselves and enabled us at last, on getting home, to see the whole much better and to understand the situation of paleo-anthropology in China vis-à-vis that in the United States, to say nothing of the precious personal experience of the visit. The reports of Chang and Keightley are clear about these things. Keightley notes that there *are* good books about modern Chinese life and society; nevertheless, carefully herded though we were, seeing, hearing, and touching carry a conviction without substitute.

The itinerary can hardly convey the flavor of things. The hordes of Chinese visiting the Great Wall, or the vastness of the Forbidden City palaces and the work that is being lavished on these and other monuments and museums, compel one to try to put oneself into the feelings of an individual Chinese about the past, and this too illumines the rationale of the interest in paleoanthropology. Traveling by train along the Yangtze or by boat down the Li River from Kuei-lin were intense visual pleasures, and to visit a commune was really to be in the country. (Of course, we were being taken to showpieces, but we never felt the Chinese were hiding anything from us except when they were explicit about what could not be seen.) Contrasting with these things was the formality of greetings and discourses, almost liquefying us with tea, but often followed by much more convivial dinners that surprised us by the actual variety of Chinese styles of cuisine--and most Americans think they know Chinese cooking.

As to science, the individual contributions to this report reflect the special interests and styles of the delegation members. No attempt has been made to make them into a more coherent plan or to conform to one another. Some overlapping has been removed, and some parts have been rewritten from their first forms, but that is all. The first five are primarily substantive. The last two, by Chang and Keightley, are interpretive, containing perhaps the most valuable lessons we learned about Chinese science and society. The papers by Freeman and Wormington have something of each.

CONTENTS

vii

INTRODUCTION

F. Clark Howell

In May and June of 1975 the Paleoanthropology Delegation visited China
under the auspices of the Committee on Scholarly Communication with the
People's Republic of China (CSCPRC), as part of its exchange program with
the Scientific and Technical Association of the People's Republic of China
(STAPRC). Since paleoanthropology encompasses the interdisciplinary
study of early man and related researches, the delegation reflected a
broad range of scientific expertise and included specialists in archeology, physical anthropology, geology, geophysics, paleobotany, paleontology, and Chinese history.

Arrangements for the visit were handled by the CSCPRC, who sent a
detailed program and itinerary request, formulated by the delegation
members, to the STAPRC well in advance of our arrival in China. Throughout our stay in China we were accompanied by two staff members of the
STAPRC and by a physical anthropologist from the Institute of Vertebrate
Paleontology and Paleoanthropology in Peking.

Our group arrived in Peking by air from Tokyo on May 15 and departed
from Canton by train to Hong Kong on June 14. The initial 10 days were
spent in Peking, including a day-long trip by car to Tientsin, and the
remainder of the month we were elsewhere in central, eastern, and southeastern China. We visited eleven cities in six provinces and traveled
over 6,000 kilometers, by air and rail. In spite of this substantial
exposure to China, its people, and the vastness of the country (about
a third larger than the United States), much remains to be seen--
including the northeast (formerly Manchuria), the northwest (Sinkiang
and Kansu, where foreign visitors are rarely permitted), and the southwest (particularly Yunnan and Szechwan, where foreign visitors are apparently uncommon). These latter areas of the country have numerous
paleontological sites and hence are of great potential value for early-
man studies. Teeth of fossil apes are already known from coal deposits
in Yunnan, and recently several very ancient hominid teeth have also
been found there.

The China we saw, and which many others have seen in recent years,
is a new China--post-Liberation (1949) and post-Cultural Revolution
(1966-1969). Through reading, I was broadly familiar with the more
important paleoanthropological researches there during those 15 years.
However, the lack of scientific publication in China after the Cultural
Revolution had left me largely in the dark as to the nature and results

of research activities since 1966. Chinese scientific journals again
appeared in 1973, numbered consecutively from the previous volume, even
though a 7-year gap intervened. As is now well known, the Cultural Revolution was a time of criticism, of internal change in goals and directions, and of continued and expanded rebuilding. Universities were
largely closed; students and faculty were dispersed to the countryside
or elsewhere. The effects of those events were surely far-reaching, and
their impact was felt in the general intellectual environment, in the
structure and activities of universities, and in some research institutes.

In Peking we stayed in the new, wholly modern wing of the Peking Hotel.
The original wing seemingly remained unchanged since the days when foreign and Chinese scientists met there to discuss the new hominid (*Homo
erectus*) discoveries at the famous Chou-k'ou-tien (Dragon Bone Hill) site
in the Western Hills beyond the city. As I had known both Franz Weidenreich and Teilhard de Chardin, it was an emotional experience to pass
through the rooms where they and others doubtless met over 40 years ago.

Every moment was full there--visits to institutes, Peking University,
the Peking National Library, the Palace Museum (former Imperial Palace),
the Summer Palace, the Great Wall, and the Ming Tombs. The Summer Palace is maintained as a popular park, and the vast reaches of the Palace
Museum are either open to visitors or undergoing restoration. A memora-
ble day was spent at the famous Chou-k'ou-tien site, preserved now as a
scientific resource, where a most modern museum and other facilities
have been constructed for the numerous visitors and for the renewed researches into the numerous cave fillings. The first-rate exhibits, reconstructions, and murals at this on-site museum indicated concern for
preserving antiquities and educating the masses in regard to man's place
in nature and the prehistoric development of human society.

We all gave lectures one or more times at various institutes of the
Academia Sinica, including Vertebrate Paleontology and Paleoanthropology,
Archeology, Geology, Geography, and Botany, with Chinese colleagues serving as translators. The opportunity to share our own scientific interests and experiences with our Chinese counterparts, and especially the
younger students, was among the most rewarding experiences of the trip.
Apparently word of these lectures preceded us elsewhere, for a colleague
and I were asked to discuss our work in the Omo Valley, Ethiopia, later
at the Natural History Museum in Shanghai.

Early man studies are centered in the Institute of Vertebrate Paleontology and Paleoanthropology (IVPP) in Peking. The most important and
extensive fossil and stone tool collections are housed there; those of
us principally interested in paleoanthropology were able to examine collections, so far as they were available, since the Institute was moving
into new quarters. Researches on early man were greatly stimulated in
China in the 1930's through the extensive researches on the Chou-k'ou-tien
site, which afforded fossil remains of over 50 individuals of *Homo erectus*
("Peking man"). The finds still represent the largest single population
sample of that extinct species. These specimens, as is well known, were
lost at the outset of World War II. (Sometimes it has been asserted that
the specimens were spirited away to the United States and hidden; however,
the specimens, their loss, and possible whereabouts were never mentioned

in the course of our visit.) There are fragmentary new finds from renewed work at Chou-k'ou-tien, but nothing like the wealth of material found previously. Still older, *Homo erectus*-like remains are known from the Lan-t'ien site, Shensi, where Chinese scientists carried out very extensive, thoroughly up-to-date interdisciplinary researches in the early 1960's. (We had greatly hoped to visit this locality, which is not far from Sian, but were told it was impossible to make the necessary local arrangements to do so.) Human occupation of China may well extend back to the very early Pleistocene, for in the Ni-ho-wan basin, northwest of Peking, stone artifacts have been found recently in old lake deposits much older than sites yielding *Homo erectus*. (This is another important and extensive fossil locality we greatly wanted to visit, but we were told by the Chinese that it was then impossible to do so. Recently some Australian scientists were taken there!)

Among the most interesting fossil primate remains recovered from China are those of *Gigantopithecus blacki*. This creature was first recognized in the mid-1930's by Professor Ralph von Koenigswald from a few molar teeth he purchased from Chinese "drug stores" in Hong Kong. He regarded it as a giant, extinct ape, which he named after Davidson Black, the Canadian anatomist who first recognized the distinctiveness of the human remains from Chou-k'ou-tien. In the 1950's Chinese scientists undertook to find further, more complete remains of this peculiar creature, and they succeeded in doing so in fossil-rich caves in south China. Now over a thousand teeth and three enormous mandibles are known. Only recently another cave in Hupei has afforded additional specimens, there for the first time directly associated with early human teeth, which seem to show some resemblances of *Australopithecus* in Africa. *Gigantopithecus* became extinct perhaps a million years ago but had a long evolutionary history before that, as it is known from a jaw found a few years ago in the Siwalik Hills of northern India in deposits 4-5 million years old. Unfortunately, the skull and skeleton of this creature are still unknown, and its adaptations and life style remain a mystery.

The group visited universities in Peking, Sian, Nanking, and Shanghai, where in many instances faculty and students were largely away in the countryside assisting with the harvest. In Sian and elsewhere several faculty members returned to their institution just for our visit. Museums were visited in these cities as well as in Tientsin, An-yang, Cheng-chou, and Canton. A prehistoric site of late Pleistocene age, which was especially prepared for our visit, was seen at Ting-ts'un, above the Fen River (Shansi). Neolithic sites were seen near Sian (Pan-p'o) and near Cheng-chou (Ta-ho); in each instance parts of the excavated sites were roofed over and enclosed by large, well-constructed buildings, and the major archeological features were well labeled and explained. The efforts made at preservation of these and other, more recent archeological sites we saw were most impressive. Such efforts are altogether too rare in the United States and elsewhere (I know of only one early man site in East Africa that has been preserved in a comparable manner).

Before leaving China we were fortunate to be able to visit Kuei-lin in the magnificent karstic country of Kwangi province. A nearly day-long trip downriver by excursion boat afforded us a unique opportunity to view the scenic landscape so familiar in Chinese art, as well as to obtain some idea of the kinds of situations from which *Giganto-pithecus* remains have been recovered.

Throughout China we met with the same outward friendliness, warmth, and hospitality that have so impressed everyone who has visited there. There was great concern for our comfort and convenience, and our hosts everywhere did their utmost to assure that we had an opportunity to appreciate their monumental strides forward in a difficult world situation and in spite of a trying period of internal political dissent. On the other hand, it was often recalled to us, and perhaps especially to me in my role as spokesman, that the Chinese felt dissatisfaction, anger, and hurt at the failure of the U.S. government to offer formal diplomatic recognition to theirs (a particularly sensitive matter, as the Philippines recognized the People's Republic at the very time of our visit). So long as this situation prevails, it will limit and hinder more close scientific exchange and cooperation. Hopefully it will not always be so, for there is much to be done and much to learn together.

PALEOBOTANICAL AND PALYNOLOGICAL RESEARCH IN CHINA

Estella B. Leopold

Research work in paleobotany is carried out chiefly at major research institutes of the Academia Sinica. In Peking these include the Institute of Botany, the Institute of Geography, and the Institute of Geology, and in Nanking the Institute of Geology and Paleontology. Palynological laboratories apparently also exist at several institutions that we did not have the opportunity to visit: Peking Geology College of the College of Geological Sciences; Wu-han Geological College, Wu-han, Hupei; Department of Geology and Geography at Nanking University; Shanghai Teachers College; and apparently at the Bureau of Geology in Peking.

INSTITUTIONS

Institute of Botany, Academia Sinica, Peking

The Paleobotany Section of the Institute of Botany occupies several older one-story buildings with tile roofs and a larger, also old, three-story building in the north part of Peking. Plantings around these include trees belonging to China's Tertiary history; *Metasequoia, Juglans regia,* and *Zelkova.*

   Under the Academia Sinica, this probably is the largest group of palynologists and paleobotanists in China. The Paleobotany section includes about 19 workers and is organized as follows. A name list appears in Appendix B of this report.

Paleozoic Paleobotany

Work carried out by Hsü Jen identifies a *Glossopteris* flora of late Permian age on the north edge of the Himalayas, about 35 km from Mount Everest. The locality is important, as it extends the known edge of the Gondwana continent northward.

   Mr. Ch'en Yeh has recently just published (1974) a large well-illustrated volume (130 plates) covering Devonian through Permian leaf floras of China, correlating results from 11 localities. Excellent anatomical sections of stems, etc., are included.

5

Mesozoic Paleobotany

A recent publication by Hsü Jen describes new leaf taxa from the upper Triassic of Yunnan Province (*Acta Botanica Sinica*, vol. 17, no. 1, 1975, and vol. 16, no. 9, 1974). Some work by Hsü Jen on Lower Cretaceous spores and gymnospermous pollen records a flora from Kansu Province strikingly like fossil assemblages of that age from Europe and the United States.

Cenozoic Paleobotany

Under preparation is a large new Cenozoic leaf flora covering assemblages of pollen and spores from 10 far-flung Chinese localities ranging in age from Eocene through Pleistocene. The work is a cooperative effort between Academia Sinica personnel in Nanking and Peking. The book will be comprehensive (300 species, 160 genera, 86 families), but, because all descriptions and plates are arranged taxonomically, it is hard to discern what the actual assemblages were.

In press is another important work (probably by Sun Hsiang-chün and others) on pollen and spore floras of late Paleocene through Oligocene age from Ch'in-yang of Kansu, to appear in *Acta Botanica Sinica*. The manuscript contains a large number of good-quality plates. Of particular interest is the appearance of *Parviprojectus* (*Aquilapollenites* group) in the Paleocene resembling a Rocky Mountain form from the Fort Union Formation. Noteworthy is the presence of *Anacolsidites* in the Oligocene. (It appears in Eocene beds of the United States.)

Continuing work in the Himalayas by leaf and pollen people (Hsü Jen, K'ung Chao-ch'en, and Sun Hsiang-chün) attempts to better date late Tertiary and Quaternary uplift in that mountain group. Three late Cenozoic sites are now known. One in the Mount Shisha Pangma area dated by contained plants as of probably Pliocene age records evergreen oaks and conifers at an elevation of 5700-5900 m. The assemblage, in which pollen evidence corroborates the leaf flora rather well, is thought to represent vegetation now growing at 200-2500 m today, suggesting an uplift of up to 3000 m since Pliocene time. An undescribed second site at 4200 m estimated on geomorphic evidence to be of mid-Pleistocene age, reflects a "subtropical" environment (*Quercus, Carya, Magnolia,* Ranunculaceae, Polygonaceae, *Pinus*). I would add that it could also be warm temperate in nature. Hsü Jen supposes the plants are about 1000 m above their present habitat. In still another site the same fossil assemblage was found at 4900 m.

Some of the Himalayan work ties fossil leaves and pollen to stone implements in the Yali calcareous tufa at Yali, Nyalam County, elevation 4300 m. The remains are shown but not discussed in the book *A Photographic Record of the Mount Jolmo Lungma Scientific Expedition* (Peking, Science Press, 1974).

The spectacular Himalayan Pliocene finds are described in *Acta Botanica Sinica* (vol. 15, no. 1, 1973). Similar Pliocene leaf and pollen floras have been found in steeply dipping coal beds in Erh-yüan, Yunnan Province, at elevations where the same type of flora occurs today.

We are not aware of extensive Quaternary studies by the Institute of Botany, but we were told about one major study of postglacial pollen from Kunming Lake, a large (70 km) lake in Yunnan Province in southwest China. Pollen analysis of a deep boring records a three-phase Holocene zonation: an early "cool period much like the present," a middle dry phase, and a return to cool assemblages of the Recent. No absolute dating methods have been employed as yet.

Though the people of this laboratory worked up the pollen sequences of Chou-k'ou-tien and Lan-t'ien, it does not appear that they are now engaged in further studies there.

Modern pollen studies are impressive. Aside from some short papers dealing with modern pollen morphology, this group has spearheaded the publication of a little-known but very important book, *The Pollen Grains of China* (276 pages, edited by F. H. Wong, 1960). The plates are fairly good, but not as excellent as some in their more recent publications. Another similar large book dealing with the morphology of modern fern spores of China is about to go to press. The plates seemed excellent indeed.

General Information

Upon arrival at the Institute, Li San of the Revolutionary Committee and Hsü Jen led us to the Herbarium where Tan Yen-ch'en, Director of the Taxonomy Department, showed us around. They explained that since the flora of China is known to comprise more than 30,000 species, work on such a large flora is a challenge. To meet the needs of the people and the workers who deal with the flora (vegetation description, land-use planning, etc.), the Academia Sinica has published several "popular works" on the flora of China. We asked our hosts what they meant, whereupon they produced what they explained was a "quickie" summary of China's flora--three very thick volumes, each more than 1,000 pages long, entitled *Iconographia Cormophytorum Sinicorum* (vol. 1 and 2, 1972; vol. 3, 1974). This work completes the flora from Bryophytes through Solanaceae. There are short descriptions of the geographic ranges of each species, nearly all of which are illustrated with ink drawing of good quality. We were very excited to see these fine works. Before we left, each of us was given a set inscribed with our names in Chinese. We also were shown a few volumes of a series called *Flora Republicae Popularis Sinicae*, which I think is part of a planned 73-volume series detailing flora of China. We saw only vol. 36 (on the Rosaceae) and vol. 11 (devoted to the Scirpeae section of Cyperaceae).

The Institute of Botany (the former Merrill Institute of Botany) is now staffed by 300 workers in seven laboratories, of which the Herbarium and the Paleobotany section are the only two we visited.

Equipment

The Herbarium contained at least two stereo microscopes and a typewriter that looked extremely complicated. It looked like a flat typesetter's tray with a few braces that ran on lateral tracks. One moved the braces on rollers manually to the appointed letter and then struck a key that printed on a roll of paper, much as an ordinary typewriter does. But how one knew where those appointed symbols were we could not guess. The rooms were lit primarily by windows. The Herbarium cabinets were largely of wood and looked as though they dated back to pre-Liberation days.

The Palynology Laboratory was equipped simply in comparison to Western labs. We saw two centrifuges made in Shanghai, with capacity for 15- and 50-ml tubes, and a smoky hood, chemical benches, and sinks. A research microscope was made in the USSR. The Paleobotany megafossil work area was even simpler, with a stereo microscope and a work bench.

Methodologies

Preparation procedures used here include only a few of the main steps followed by U.S. palynologists. A first step is to crush the sediment sample in a mortar and pestle (theirs was made of brass!). The sample is placed in a 10% KOH solution and brought to a boil for 3-4 min. (This step is for peat samples only.) After washing (via centrifugation), the sample is placed in an acetylation mixture of acetic anhydride/H_2SO_4 in a ratio of 9:1 and boiled in a water bath for 1-2 min. Then the sample is washed and examined as a wet mount with the microscope. At this point, if the sediment is minerogenic (all non-peat samples) they proceed to heavy-liquid flotation. But everything about this step is astonishing. First, hydriodic acid is used as a heavy liquid adjusted to a density of 1.8-2.3. (We never heard of that acid being used for this purpose.) Second, the heavy liquid separation is carried out in beakers using gravity separation! I suggested they try using a centrifuge. The hydriodic acid is reclaimed by filtering. Pollen and spore assemblages thus treated are then washed and mounted in glycerine jelly. An alternate treatment for rocks or coal samples older than Quaternary is the Schulze's solution, using potassium chlorate and nitric acid. I presume HF is used, but this was not mentioned.

I saw a few of their slides and found them sparse and having numerous pollen-sized chunks of crystalline sediments in them. Such slides would be very hard indeed to use for counting. They try to obtain 300 grains per count, which would require the use of several slides, I imagine.

There was much interest in my description of our heavy-liquid flotation procedures and also of clean-up methods using panning techniques.

Coordination with Other Institutes; Government Program

The Paleobotany section of the Institute of Botany receives a wide range of referred collections from other agencies and institutes. Geologists from the Institute of Vertebrate Paleontology and Paleoanthropology, the Institute of Geology, or the Bureau of Geology collect field material for paleobotanical determinations or pollen analysis. The Paleobotany section provides specialized service functions for these groups connected with government programs dealing with work on coal deposits, groundwater

problems, and petroleum exploration. Such service work is given by the
Paleobotany section even though the Bureau of Geology has its own palynologists and a vertebrate paleontologist. According to Hsü Jen, the
difference between the Bureau of Geology, for example, and the Institute
of Botany is that the Institute is more concerned with biological problems, evolution, environments, and taxonomy, while the Bureau is interested mainly in correlation problems. Presumably, the specialists in
paleobotany in these two groups specialize in different areas or parts
of the section and offer cooperative service to each other. At the same
time, I was rather surprised to realize how little communication occurs
between pollen laboratories in Peking, namely those of the Institutes
of Botany and Geography.

Institute of Geography, Academia Sinica, Peking

The facility is a series of older three- and four-story buildings with
campuslike grounds and brick sidewalks some considerable distance north
of the center of Peking. The Pollen Laboratory is on the second floor
of one of these buildings.

Pollen Laboratory

Within the framework of various research programs of the Institute of
Geography, pollen studies here are closely coordinated with studies on
groundwater resources. Using pollen analysis and other stratigraphic
tools, they are attempting to subdivide Quaternary strata, identify the
lower limit of the Quaternary in far-flung areas of China (e.g., Tibet
or the lower Yangtze River Valley). This institute cooperates closely
with many other institutions in studies that would identify underground
water resources and water production.
    Dr. Malde, Dr. Brown, and I spent a short half hour in the Institute
of Georgraphy Pollen Laboratory with two pollen analysts. As a major
project Hsieh Lu-lei works on a very complete and unusual Tertiary section at Lan-t'ien, southeast of Sian, Shensi Province, where rocks of
Eocene through Holocene are well exposed. The section is said to be .
300 m thick. We were not shown any of the data or assemblages, but the
studies seem to include beds of middle Quaternary age relating to Lan-
t'ien man. Miss Hsieh emphasized that she is largely trying to reconstruct sedimentary environments and determine paleoclimates. Wang Eh-hsin
carries out or directs the fossil preparation and carries out work on identification with modern pollen reference collections. She appears to be
helping Miss Hsieh on various Quaternary pollen studies.

Equipment

The laboratory has a research microscope manufactured in the USSR equipped
with 8× and 40× lenses partly for use in examining wet mounts during preparation of samples. We saw hoods, shakers, and centrifuges (manufactured

in Shanghai) with 3-inch radius holding either 4 50-ml tubes or 12 15-ml tubes with a maximum speed of 5,000 RPM. A research microscope made by Leitz of Germany is used for counting. It is equipped with a 35-mm camera (not automatic) made in China.

Methodologies

Since people in the Pollen Laboratory work with soft sediments, they described to us techniques appropriate only for Quaternary or late Cenozoic samples. When I learned that they never use Schulze's solution (nitric acid and potassium chlorate), I wondered how they managed to break up rocks of, say, Eocene age.

Samples are usually 30 g in weight and are placed first in 10% KOH for 5 min at the boiling point. After washing, they are subjected to a cold solution of 15% HCl in a beaker and put on a shaker. Several washes are done by centrifugation. The sample then goes into heavy liquid flotation in an aqueous solution of cadmium iodide and potassium iodide adjusted to a density of 2.1 or 2.2. The mixture is placed in glass tubes and centrifuged at a speed of 2,000-2,500 RPM for 25 min. The float fraction is poured off the top of the centrifuge tube, diluted, washed, and examined in wet mount.

Some samples are given an acetylation with the usual sulfuric acid and acetic anhydride and placed in a water bath for 5 min. After this step high silica samples are cleaned up with HF. Slides are then made with glycerine jelly and sealed with balsam. The cadmium solution is retrieved "by use of potassium iodide and water with heat" (I have not figured out how that works!).

These are the most sophisticated pollen preparation techniques and equipment we saw in China. People at this lab in particular were interested in our own preparation methods and said they would welcome reprints concerning techniques.

As at the Institute of Botany the fossil preparations I examined were sparse and beset with stray pieces of sediment, which they did not know how to clean up. As I commented earlier, counting such material would be a great deal of work.

Institute of Geology and Paleontology, Academia Sinica, Nanking

The Institute is set on a little hill and is surrounded by beautiful plantings of *Gingko* and leguminous trees. Narrow winding blacktop roads lead up to the place, and a long tier of stone steps leads up to the old four-story building.

This Institute, more than any other we encountered, is set up to study comprehensively all the main groups of fossil organisms in all parts of the geological section. It is in fact reminiscent of the Paleontology and Stratigraphy Branch of the U.S. Geological Survey. The structure of the Institute's six divisions includes a Paleobotany section, covering everything from algae to higher plants, and a Palynology section. Over 40 staff members compose these two sections.

The Director of the Institute explained to us that the areas of work and types of problems undertaken here depend very much on the current needs of and requests from various government bureaus (i.e., the Bureaus of Coal, Metallurgy, Oil, and Geology), and that their work is aimed directly at mineral exploration and reconstruction of China. The geological bureaus concerned send in fossils for identification of age or ask for help on given stratigraphic problems. Research at the Institute of Geology and Paleontology must be closely associated today with production needs. Some fossils brought to the Institute are from the field-workers--"the masses who are very concerned with the history of the motherland."

Though in the past more people at the Institute were engaged in Paleozoic studies, the emphasis has shifted with the developing needs during the reconstruction of China; now more efforts are needed in Mesozoic and Cenozoic paleontology and stratigraphy. This group has only recently begun to give some attention to Quaternary problems.

Fossil Exhibition

We were taken to an exhibition room displaying some major specimens and photographs of material encountered in research here. A very wide assortment of excellent specimens was set up under glass, reflecting the broad spectrum of work pursued.

In the paleobotanical displays we saw the following:

● Photomicrographs of Cambrian palynomorphs, including what looked to be primitive algae and moss spores.
● Leaves and pollen of Mesozoic age from Yunnan Province: common leaf fossils of the Triassic (pretty specimens, unpublished); ditto lower Cretaceous leaves; and lower Cretaceous pollen (many species in common with U.S. floras of that age).
● A *Glossopteris* leaf flora from the Drumalooma area of Tibet near Mount Everest (the Permo-Triassic rocks from which these came are photographed in the book *A Photographic Record of the Mt. Jolmo Lungma Scientific Expedition* [Peking, Science Press, 1974].
● Paleozoic leaves, Devonian; also Carboniferous and Permian leaves said to have been described long ago in *Acta Paleontologica Sinica*.
● Cenozoic and Late Cretaceous leaves of Drumalooma area, Tibet.
● Examples of Cenozoic leaves: Oligocene E_3 *Metasequoia*; Miocene (?) N_1 *Vitis* and *Rhus*; some Eocene and Miocene leaves from Shuntung Province.
● Precambrian (Z_1-Z_2-Z_3) algal megafossils previously thought to be of Devonian-Ordovician age.

In addition to these, we saw collections of Paleozoic fossils from all over China, especially from Drumalooma where there is a "perfect" sequence from Carboniferous through Eocene, but also various gastropods from Ordovician to Quaternary, trilobites from southwest China, brachiopods of Silurian through Cretaceous age, forams, cephalopods (Ordovician, Carboniferous, and J_2, T, J, and K from the Himalayas), stromatoporoids (P, C, D, O, T, S), corals (C, T, P), sponges (P), and Coelenterata (D, O, S).

Library

We visited the scientific library where there were current issues of such
periodicals and papers as *Oklahoma Geology Notes*; state Geological Survey
annual reports from Ohio, Maryland, Oklahoma, and Iowa; *The Geological
Journal*; *University of California Publications in Geological Sciences*;
Paleontographica; *Ecology*; *Ecological Monographs*; *Evolution*; *Geoscience
Abstracts*; *The Biological Bulletin*; *Bulletin of the Museum of Comparative
Zoology*; *American Mineralogist*; *Bibliography and Index of Geology Ex-
clusive of North America*; etc. There was a vast collection of books in
Russian, Chinese, and many other languages. It was a fine library!

Pollen Laboratory

Most of the Delegation briefly visited the Pollen Laboratory at this Institute. Personnel we met included: Liu Chin-ling (Cenozoic pollen and
spores), Chang Lu-chin (Mesozoic pollen and spores), T'ao Wu-chin (in
charge of Palynology Division), and Kuo Shung-hsing (Paleobotany).
   Mr. Liu showed us three pollen diagrams; the first was a "possible
early Pleistocene" sequence from Hujo (town) in the mountains of Kwangsi
Chuang Autonomous Region. In cool phases of this diagram *Abies* was as
high as 60 percent and *Picea* 3 percent, with small amounts of *Saxifraga,
Artemisia,* other Compositae and *Rhododendron*. A second diagram was from
Subjo Mountain at an elevation of 400 m. The age of this section was
deemed to be probably late-middle Pleistocene (no absolute dating techniques were used, so the ages were apparently estimated from other stratigraphic evidence). A third pollen diagram was a remarkable deep boring
of 282 m in depth through the Yangtze River Delta near Shanghai (long
121°15' E., lat 30°45' N.). The sequence included about 50 levels or
sample points and clearly contained four or five major pollen zones about
which we were unable to absorb the details. However, I did take down a
list of the forms plotted on the diagram. In order of their appearance
from left to right on the plot these are:

Keeteleria	*Typha*
Tsuga	Compositae
Cedrus	Total aquatics
Quercus	Polygonaceae
Ulmus	Polypodiaceae
Liquidambar	*Ceratopteris*
Fagus	*Lygodium*
Castanea	*Pteris*
Carya	*Adiantum*
Betula	*Osmunda*
Tilia	Triletes
Gramineae (two types)	*Gleichenia*

On the far right was an inferred climatic curve showing four major os-
cillations and a tentative zonation system with symbols Q_1 through Q_4.

Mr. Liu said that no absolute dating methods had been applied and that there were in fact no other fossils except pollen. When we asked if they sometimes sieve for fossil seeds in such cores, he indicated that they did not. He explained that the estimated age was based on regional surveys and stratigraphic evidence gathered by other departments. He felt that the core did not penetrate to Pliocene-Pleistocene boundary, but he did feel this sequence represented intermittent deposition through most of the Quaternary.

This diagram through the Yangtze Delta was remarkable in another way; Mr. Liu had included analyses data from three modern surface samples from the site for comparative purposes. To our knowledge this was the only institute that was using at least some modern pollen rain data for interpretation of fossil sequences. We learned that Mr. Liu is now preparing this Yangtze diagram for publication.

Methodologies

We asked questions of the young preparator in this laboratory about details of procedures, or in fact about generalities of the methods used here. She answered that the preparations were in three steps: (1) crush the sample in mortar and pestle, (2) sieve, and (3)"various steps"! We did learn that they use a heavy-liquid flotation with a solution of potassium iodide and cadmium iodide adjusted to a specific gravity of 2.2. This mixture is centrifuged with a sample for 15 min at 2,500 RPM. Acetylation (H_2SO_4 and acetic anhydride, 1:9) and $KClO_3$ are used, which could mean that the famous Schulze's solution with nitric acid is used in this laboratory. When I told the preparators a bit about our own heavy-liquid flotation and panning (clean-up) methods they seemed interested.

Slides are mounted in glycerine jelly and sealed with native balsam. We saw a few fossil slides and thought the preservation of the pollen was good, but the pollen grains were scarce and therefore hard to tally.

Modern Reference Collection

This laboratory has a collection of about 2,000 modern reference slides. I asked if they would be interested in exchanging modern reference slides with us on a slide-for-slide basis in order to complement each other's collections. It was not clear whether they welcomed this suggestion.

COOPERATIVE COLLECTIONS: COOPERATIVE RESEARCH

Between the paleobotanists at the institutes described above, cooperative research is most obvious in the team efforts to publish large atlases of modern and fossil pollen and leaves. For example, the large book now in press compiling leaf floras from Eocene to Pleistocene strata is a cooperative effort between four authors in the Institute of Botany in Peking and four authors at the Institute of Geology and Paleontology in Nanking. I gather that the fossil leaves on which these are based stay at their "home" institutions and are not traded around, at least not permanently.

A second large cooperative project was the publication of the 1960 atlas *The Pollen Grains of China*, which involved scientists at the Institute of Botany in cooperation with other institutes, possibly the Institute of Geology and Paleontology in Nanking and the Institute of Geography in Peking. The book (in press) on morphology of modern fern spores of China was spearheaded by palynologists at the Institute of Botany in Peking, but perhaps because of the book's size other institutes were called upon to help complete it.

Cooperation with other institutes such as IVPP to complete interdisciplinary studies in paleoanthropology has taken place in the past, as indicated by the papers of Hsü Jen on pollen of key early man sites at Lan-t'ien and Chou-k'ou-tien, and a few other sections, but much more effort in this direction would be helpful. Cooperation in projects with other government bureaus is vast and has already been discussed above.

Exchange of fossil plant collections between institutes is a matter I did not ask about, but, from the nature of our conversations, I presume it is very limited or for short-term loan only. For example, I did not have the impression that superior leaf or pollen collections prepared outside Peking are given to the Institute of Botany.

Exchange of modern reference collections appears to be limited. I learned that palynologists from the Institute of Geography in Peking come to the Institute of Botany herbarium and ask to make reference collections. If they do so, they "sometimes" give examples of resultant slides to the Institute of Botany.

STATUS OF LATE CENOZOIC PALYNOLOGY IN CHINA

As Hsü Jen said of Chinese palynology, "We have only just begun." I agree, and think it is a good start. I am aware that as Western scientists our views on the use of paleontology in China are influenced by our knowledge of tools that have not yet been tried in China. Therefore, it is difficult to be positive about fields that have not been developed there as yet.

In the late Cenozoic, the strongest use of palynology as a paleoclimatic tool is provided by a network of modern pollen rain "standards" that serve to identify or characterize broad regional vegetation zones using pollen alone. Conversely, the strongest use of palynology as a stratigraphic tool depends on repeat sampling across lateral horizons to show by mere repeatability the constancy of appearance of zones or units.

Chinese palynology in its present stage of development apparently has not yet explored either of the above. Modern pollen rain studies so useful in the United States since the 1960's and more recently in Europe and the USSR have not really found their way to China as a method or basis of interpretation. Much potential will come from this mode of attack in an area that holds (or in areas that once held) the world's oldest and richest floras. Based on the Chinese literature and on our conversations in China, stratigraphic sampling for pollen in any part of the late Cenozoic does not seem to have been repeated enough anywhere to lay a firm basis for correlation by pollen alone. Much more extensive use of pollen as a mere correlation tool would be of great benefit in Chinese stratigraphy.

Therefore, in my view, late Cenozoic palynology has thus far not reached anywhere close to its ultimate potential. I think the features mentioned above place Chinese late Cenozoic palynology about where American pollen studies were in 1960, at a time when Hibbard's vertebrate chronology was not calibrated in time, when a basis for ecological interpretation was botanical conjecture, and a time when the only clear pollen zonation was in the Holocene of the eastern seaboard. This means that the potentials are great.

Perhaps the greatest barrier now to the more expansive development of Chinese palynology is the lack of contact with and stimulus from outside ideas. What seems to be most needed is greater exposure to reprints from abroad, expansion of exchange programs, and increased correspondence with the outside world.

Though at least some libraries (e.g., that of the Institute of Geology and Paleontology in Nanking) are well stocked so that access to the literature may not be limited, the language barrier, especially for the young people, is clearly a problem. I was not convinced, for example, that the Nanking palynologists (mostly young people) read very much of the literature in that library.

It was clear to me that everywhere the older, pre-Liberation scientists were the people with the greatest facility in English or other foreign languages. At Peking it was they who served the function of explaining at least some foreign papers to the younger scientists. But I believe that it is not the older scientists who have the vigor to try new ideas and techniques and that the younger scientists need even more than this stimulus to try new things.

The needs for more work and better techniques are great in many areas, for example:

Stratigraphic Needs

1. Sampling is needed on basinwide deposits in order to set up a series of repeated pollen-stratigraphic sections at important selected areas such as Lan-t'ien. These can be a basis for zoning and determining lateral continuity of facies and environments.

2. Absolute dating methods. All the world is probably waiting for the Chinese to develop a more precise dating and stratigraphic tools: K/Ar, Paleomagnetism, tephrochronology.

3. Figures to document complete assemblages for inclusion in papers would always be a help to workers in China and elsewhere. For maximum usefulness, plates from assemblages should be kept together, not mixed with those from other floras.

4. Correlation of results with a broad spectrum of fossil types in the same beds should probably be emphasized more. For example, pollen sections could be run at more major vertebrate localities. Sections could be sought that include a maximum diversity of fossil types (i.e., vertebrates, pollen, clams, snails, fish, plant remains, diatoms). This

effort could serve as perhaps the best way to synchronize a vertebrate calendar with that from invertebrates and tie these in with pollen floras. A second plus from this effort would be to try and reconstruct at least a few ecosystems.

Paleoecology

1. Modern pollen rain studies. As a more precise basis for interpreting pollen diagrams a first step might be to collect modern surface samples (mud or soil) at each coring site of pollen section and plot the analysis at the top of the fossil pollen diagram for reference. Such data would tell the worker the composition of the local pollen rain today and would make a good basis for general interpretation.

As a basis for identifying altitudinal vegetation zones by pollen alone, altitudinal transects of modern surface samples can be run from rim rocks to rim rocks across a basin. The samples are taken so that each major vegetation zone is represented by several sample points. Using this approach one can see what pollen composition and numbers can identify which vegetation zones, and one can profitably apply it to the interpretation of Quaternary pollen diagrams from the basin.

2. Fossil seed studies. By sieving Quaternary core samples or sediments, American and European workers have been finding helpful megafossil evidence to accompany their pollen zones, verifying the local presence of a plant represented in the pollen diagram. It is not my impression that the Chinese are trying this. The effort necessitates building a modern seed collection for the regional flora. Results from the Quaternary section can be shown, for example, as numbers of seeds per 5 g of mud.

3. Use of diatoms for determining local water environments. Another area some American palynologists have developed to good advantage is the analysis of diatoms found in conjunction with pollen assemblages. I do not know if there are diatom experts in China, but it would seem a good idea for the Institute of Geology and Paleontology in Nanking to cooperate with them in paleoenvironmental interpretation of aquatic habitats.

STATUS OF NATURAL VEGETATION IN EAST CHINA

One of the Institute of Botany programs involves geobotany and the study of natural vegetation of China. When we left Peking my copy of Wang Chi-wu's *Modern Vegetation of China* was open and I was peering out plane and train windows watching for each of the local types that Wang described. By the end of the trip I closed my copy of Wang and decided that there wasn't any natural vegetation left in eastern China. And I began to see why Professor Hou placed such emphasis on the study of economic botany and wastelands.

Around Peking the land is completely occupied by fields. Every square inch is composed of agricultural croplands: wheat primarily and other crops are planted right up to the edges of the roads. Rows of *Populus* trees planted along roadways everywhere are the only woody plants except occasionally along roadways where *Amorpha* (?) bushes were planted.

In the Western Hills where *Thuja* and scrub oak were supposed to grow, there were no oaks at all and the *Thuja* was planted in rows along with a few scattered pine seedlings. The understory at the Great Wall was largely of weeds, and this was true on the drive through the Hills returning to Peking.

Further southwest, in the T'ai-yüan area, I was thrilled to see some giant cedars, *Trichilia* (?) and *Gingko*, planted in the tiny area surrounding the Jen Ci Temple. But the hills behind had only a few small *Thuja* planted in rows and no understory except weeds.

Outside Sian we visited a rocky hill at the tomb of Wu Tse-t'ien (Wu How). I climbed this hill with great anticipation, looking for native plant associations. On the loessial downwind slopes of the hill there was *Thuja* again, with a couple of other tree types planted in rows and the same weeds. But in the rockiest slopes (upwind parts) of the hill I logged in 24 species of herbs and shrubs, most of which appeared to be native! And they seemed in place.

Therefore, at the next opportunity to visit a large mound tomb I was looking hard for more native communities. But the tomb (first emperor Ch'in dynasty near Sian) was planted with persimmons and only about 10 species of weeds grew under them.

And so it went until we got to Nanking. There in a protected woods on a hill at the mausoleum of Sun Yat-sen we saw a nice cutover regrowth forest of mixed mesophytic hardwoods. I was ecstatic. Hills of that area and between there and Shanghai seemed to have limited amounts of regrowth woodland and some scraps of forest vegetation. I have a few notes on the mountain areas near Kuei-lin, Kwangsi Chuang Autonomous Region. The main thrust of our botanical experiences, however, was that, sadly, in east China natural communities are all but wiped out over huge areas or occur only on rocky nonagricultural areas of high relief.

The Chinese do not have a "national parks" system, but they have saved one area in which *Metasequoia* is protected and one sanctuary for the panda bear. A few historical monuments such as the one at Chou-k'ou-tien are protected but small. I was told that habitat preserves are set up by individual provinces, but no one could think of any examples.

Apparently extensive stands of native forests still occur in mountain areas of western China and in the mountains of the northeast. But what we saw is saddening when I think of the immense diversity of flora and vegetation that existed in eastern China at one time.

Tallies of the few birds and insects we saw indicate that the fauna that might be expected in a pastoral landscape has suffered badly, perhaps because of the elimination of natural vegetation and perhaps from excessive spraying.

GEOLOGY IN CHINESE PALEOANTHROPOLOGY

Harold E. Malde*

The Chinese have a long history of interest in the earth, as demonstrated by a predynastic device for measuring earthquakes (Needham, 1971) and centuries of artistic concern for landscape painting and geological objects (Cohen and Cohen, 1973, pp. 151-153, 201), but the practice of modern geology began late when considered in the perspective of its nineteenth century growth in Western countries. After a slow start in the first decades of this century, rapid progress has been made since Liberation. Today, geological work in China pursues topics that occupy geologists around the world and is part of an expanding effort to apply science and technology at all levels of local and national need. The work is done in numerous organizational units, national and provincial, bureaucratic and academic, which are surprisingly independent of each other.

The organization of geological effort has been recently reported by several observers, but probably no individual outside China fully comprehends how geological science in China has evolved. Certainly our month-long visit, which allowed only brief contact with a few geological groups and individuals, is a sparse basis for assessing China's progress in geology. Still, our conversations about geology were frequently on subjects germane to paleoanthropology, such as the stratigraphy and paleoenvironment of the Quaternary. I summarize here the matters pertaining to geology that we learned during our visit. To provide a still broader perspective, I have borrowed heavily from published accounts.

HISTORICAL BACKGROUND

Among Western geologists, geological studies in China have been often identified with the Institute of Geology, which was established in 1928 with 11 other research institutes under the Academia Sinica (National Central Research Academy) in Nanking. The first director was J. S. Lee (Li Ssu-kuang). Circumstances surrounding this event are summarized by Harland (1967), who taught at West China Union University, Cheng-tu, Szechwan Province, before 1949. He provides historical details on

---

*Francis H. Brown contributed observations on laboratory facilities and isotopic dating as seen in several institutes and universities.

18

geological administration, training, research, and learned societies for the period preceding the Cultural Revolution (1966-1969).

A division of geology was formed in Peking under the Ministry of Industry and Commerce in 1912, the first year of the Chinese Republic, and was reorganized in 1916 as the National Geological Survey of China under the leadership of V. K. Ting (Ting Wen-chiang). The Survey subsequently obtained laboratories for paleontology (1928), Cenozoic fossils (1929, with financing by the Rockefeller Foundation in China), soil study (1930, with funds provided by the China Foundation), fuels, and seismology. The Survey moved to Nanking in 1931. By 1949 the Survey had eight research laboratories, 30 senior scientists, and 200 technical specialists (Hofheinz, in Earthquake Research in China, 1975, p. 875). Geological surveys were also established in Hunan, Honan, Kwangtung, Kwangsi Chuang Autonomous Region, Kiangsi, Szechwan, Yunnan, and other provinces.

Besides the Geological Institute of the Academia Sinica in Nanking, an institute of geology was also established in 1929 under the National Academy of Peking. These academies were joined with the National Geological Survey in 1949 to become the core of the new Chinese Academy of Sciences.

Geology was taught by two German professors in the Imperial University of Peking in 1909-1912, and a school of geology reopened in 1917 at the newly reorganized University of Peking. A. W. Grabau and J. S. Lee joined the staff in 1921. Geological departments were later set up at the Central University in Nanking; Tsinghua University in Peking (1928); Sun Yat-sen University in Canton; Shantung University at Tsingtao; Chungking University, Szechwan; and Northwest University, Sian, Shensi Province (1937). Most universities had 5-year courses, but many Chinese geologists of this era received further graduate training in Europe and the United States.

During the unsettled years from 1937 to 1945, marked by civil war, the Sino-Japanese war, and World War II, the Geological Survey and all institutes and universities moved to southwest China. Further progress in geology was difficult. At the time of Liberation in 1949, China had only 200 qualified geologists.

Learned societies formed in China before Liberation remain a stronghold of expertise in science, although now administratively linked with an organization of government cadres--the Scientific and Technical Association of the People's Republic of China. Harland (1967) mentions as existing in 1965: Geological Society of China (founded 1922), Paleontological Society of China (1948), Chinese Society of Oceanography and Limnology (1949), and Geophysical Society of China (1947). The existence of other societies in fields related to earth science is indicated by several periodicals: *Acta Astronomica Sinica*; *Acta Geodetica et Cartographica Sinica 1957--*; *Acta Geographica Sinica 1953--*; *Acta Meteorologica Sinica*; *Bulletin of the Soil Science Society of China*, continued as *Acta Pedologica Sinica 1952--*; and *Journal of Hydraulic Engineering Society*.

Since 1949 the People's Republic of China has seen rapid growth in geological work under a vigorous policy of economic development. Articles describing this growth in science and technology, mainly dating before

1970, are listed by Dean (1974). The growth has been marked by changes in both administration and training. Hofheinz (*in* Earthquake Research in China, 1975, pp. 874-876) distinguishes four stages of development of Chinese science that have led to new programs of the 1970's. These stages are outlined below.

From 1949 to 1954, the groundwork was laid for a bureaucratic hierarchy in science headed by the newly amalgamated Chinese Academy of Sciences. Academic societies were allowed to flourish, and professional education continued into the graduate level. Earth scientists played a leading role during this period of consolidation, numbering 900 geologists and technicians by 1954. A Ministry of Geology was established in Peking in 1952 under J. S. Lee, with units located in all parts of China, and a major effort was applied to regional surveys of national resources. These surveys involved geological prospecting, economic geology, and regional geological mapping. Expansion within the Academy of Sciences, building on the Institute of Geology, emphasized the earth sciences in establishing five new institutes: Geophysics (1950); Oceanography at Tsingtao (1950); Pedology at Nanking (1952); Geology and Paleontology at Nanking (1950); and Engineering Mechanics at Harbin (1954). Harland (1967) notes that universities were reorganized. Geological colleges were established at Ch'ang-ch'un in Kirin (founded 1950), Peking (1952), and Cheng-tu in Szechwan (1954). The Peking College of Geology was formed as part of the reorganization of Peking University by amalgamating the former Peking University (founded 1898) with part of Tsinghua (founded 1928) and Yenching (founded 1919). Technicians and geologists received from 2 to 5 years of training (Chao, 1973). These changes were in accord with a policy since 1949 of forming large specialized colleges for specific kinds of training.

Between 1954 and 1958, coinciding approximately with the first 5-year plan (1953-1957), administration of Chinese science was closely modeled on the scientific establishment of the Soviet Union, and scientists were subject to increasing control by the Communist Party. Of the thousands of Soviet scientists who worked in China, setting up programs and installing instruments, Harland (1967) indicates that 400 were geologists. This collaboration was ended abruptly by the Chinese in early 1960. During this period, the dependence of production on earth science was officially recognized, and the Institutes of Geology and Geophysics were the most prominent among the central-level institutes of the Academy.

Harland (1967) lists several other institutions of the Academy of Sciences that seem to date from this time: Institute of Geography in Peking; Institute of Geodetics and Cartography in Wu-han; geophysical observatories in Lan-chou and Sian (additional observatories are listed in Earthquake Research in China, 1975); Coal Research Laboratory in Dairen, Liaoning Province; and the Institute of Petroleum in Dairen and Lan-chou. Harland (1967) notes that the Academy established a Committee for Quaternary Research in 1954, as well as committees for seismological work and isotope applications, but we heard nothing about them during our visit. W. F. Brace (*in* Earthquake Research in China, 1975, p. 867) mentions the Institute of Rock and Soil Mechanics in Wuhan, Hupeh Province, established in 1958 to work on tunneling, excavation, slope stability, and rock deformation. As a result of the training programs in

universities and colleges, by 1958 the geological work force had grown
to more than 20,000 (Chao, 1973). The Chinese University of Science
and Technology was established in Peking in 1957 to emphasize basic sciences (Harland, 1967). Its department of geochemistry was taught by
members of the Institute of Geology.

The third stage of development identified by Hofheinz (*in* Earthquake
Research in China, 1975), 1958-1965, which began with the call for a
"Great Leap Forward," saw scientists increasingly controlled by nonsci-
entist administrators. The Academy of Sciences was placed under a newly
formed Commission of Science and Technology, headed by Marshal Nieh Jung-
chen, and many persons from scientific institutes were assigned to productive ministries, notably the Ministry of Defense. Chao (1973) reports
that geologists looked for mineral deposits, construction materials, and
fertilizers and studied water resources (especially methods to prevent
floods). Such work was intended to make production from science parallel
with the demands placed on industry and agriculture. Because these tasks
were done by local production teams, geology became popularized through
results achieved by teams organized at the people's communes.

Still, according to Hofheinz, the reforms of the Great Leap Forward
included a commitment to increased basic research. The learned societies
continued to publish until 1965, although scientific periodicals were reorganized in about 1959. The Ministry of Geology at this time had established 26 provincial bureaus in provinces and autonomous regions of
China (Harland, 1967), as well as several institutes in Peking: Geology
(mainly involved with making geological maps); Mineral Deposits; Geophysical Prospecting; Hydrology and Engineering Geology; Geomechanics;
the Geological Museum (designed to serve the geological surveys and to
popularize geology); and the Geological Library (over 300,000 volumes).
The Ministry of Geology staff in Peking in December 1964 numbered 400
geologists and 300 physicists and chemists (Harland, 1967). The position of the Ministry in the government structure has been diagrammed by
Hofheinz (*in* Earthquake Research in China, 1975, figure 14).

For training, besides the schools previously named, Harland (1967)
mentions the existence of geological departments or foundation courses
in geology at technical colleges at Shen-yang (Mukden), K'un-ming (Yunnan), and Kuei-yang (Kweichow), and at colleges of mining and metal-
lurgical engineering at Ho-fei (Anhwei), Ch'ang-sha (Hunan), and Peking.
Geology was also taught in Peking in specialized colleges of petroleum,
steel, forestry, hydroelectric power, and water conservation. The Peking
College of Geology then offered a 5-year course in 10 specialties. The
college had graduated 7,500 by May 1965, of which 150 received higher
degrees (Harland, 1967). Schools of geology were also operated by the
Ministry of Geology in several parts of China to train technicians. As
a product of this training, the geological work force undoubtedly increased manyfold, perhaps reaching 200,000 (exact figures are not available).

Scientific work during the fourth stage, 1966-1969, the period of the
Cultural Revolution, came to a virtual standstill. Publication of scientific periodicals ceased, the Commission of Science and Technology was
abolished, and the Academy of Sciences was cut back sharply to perhaps a
fourth of its former size. Hofheinz (*in* Earthquake Research in China,

1975, p. 876) mentions internal dissension and rivalry in the Institute of Geology, observing that dissension could still be felt in October 1974. Information on activities of scientists during this period is nearly non-existent, but some continuity of scientific work can be inferred. During our visit we met two geologists of the Bureau of Geology--established in 1973 from the Ministry of Geology--whose work with the Bureau (or Ministry) dated back to the late 1950's. Also, at the South China Botanical Garden near Canton, which is about 12 years old, we met Professor Chen Feng-lura, who had been at the garden since its inception.

More concretely, we learned at the Institute of Geology in Peking, and at the Institute of Geology and Paleontology in Nanking, about investigations at Mount Jolmo Lungma (Mount Everest) in 1966-1968 in stratigraphy, paleontology, Quaternary geology, glaciology, geomorphology, geodesy, and geophysics (Anonymous, 1974a). We also inferred that many of the scientists we met, especially the older ones, had been at their respective institutes through the period of the Cultural Revolution. From visits to universities, however, we understood that university education stopped at this time. Even so, some continuity is suggested by the report of Signer and Galston (1972) that Fu-tan University in Shanghai, which we also visited, made no change in departmental structure as a result of the Cultural Revolution.

CONTEMPORARY GEOLOGY

Geological science in China is still rebuilding from the turmoil of the Cultural Revolution. Time and again we were told, as in repeating a catechism, that progress had been made but much remained to be done--meaning that more effort is needed in making geology serve the masses. Earth scientists able to observe this rebuilding have been relatively few, even counting the visit by the Seismology Delegation (Earthquake Research in China, 1975) in October 1974 and the visit by a group of meteorologists in April and May 1974 (Kellogg, 1974). Recent visits have been made by J. Tuzo Wilson (1971), Gilbert F. White (May 1972), Edward C. T. Chao (August and September 1972), Robert S. Coe (summer 1972 and September 1974), and Bruce A. Bolt (July 1973). In addition, other scientists and scholars among the hundreds who have traveled in China since 1971 have reported experiences in visiting geological institutions and individuals. Apparently, the Chinese have wished to explain their accomplishments in earth science.

Geological effort in China is currently organized at two levels, a central administration working through the research institutes of the Academy of Sciences and the Bureau of Geology, and provincial (regional) or local offices that work through brigades and production teams. Hofheinz (*in* Earthquake Research in China, 1975, figure 15) describes the administrative structure in 1974, although explaining that organizational changes are still being made. Indeed, the power struggle precipitated by the death of Premier Chou En-lai was accompanied by strong attacks in the Peking press "on unnamed 'reactionaries' accused of trying to protect the scientific sector of Chinese life from the dictatorship of the proletariat" (*The New York Times*, February 8, 1976)--words often used during the Cultural Revolution. The existing structure was not explained to us.

The geological bureau of a province operates as an arm of the central Bureau of Geology but is largely autonomous, being responsible for its own geological mapping and mineral exploration, for example. Interplay between the regional and central offices is nonetheless necessary (Chao, 1973). A geological brigade may refer complicated problems in geology to the provincial geological institute or to the central-level institutes and ministries. The aim is to have "dual-level leadership, with the locality in charge." In practice, final decisions on some matters are made solely by the central office (for example, resolution of discrepancies in mapping along provincial boundaries and selection of seismological stations). The size of the geological work force under this organization is uncertain: Chao (1973) estimated perhaps 200,000; and Hofheinz (*in* Earthquake Research in China, 1975), by including workers in counties and communes, estimated "several hundred thousand or even several million" for earthquake science alone.

Some appreciation of the importance of earth science in the science and technology program of China is given by a listing of institutes and units of the Academy of Sciences, both in Peking and the provinces. Among 36 such units, Gerwin (1975) names: Geology, Geography, Geophysics, Vertebrate Paleontology and Paleoanthropology, Meterology, Botany (includes paleobotany and palynology), and the Observatory in Peking; Geology and Paleontology in Nanking; Oceanography in Tsingtao; Oceanography of the South China Seas in Canton; and Engineering Mechanics in Harbin. For ministries with geological sections or divisions, besides the Bureau of Geology, Chao (1973) lists: Metallurgy, Fuels and Chemicals (we were told of the existence of the Bureau of Oil and the Bureau of Coal), Communications, Water and Electricity, Health (includes environmental geology and medicine), Construction Materials, Bureau of Oceanography, and Agriculture. We did not visit any offices of these ministries.

Our contact with geological research in China was largely through persons either at universities or at institutes of the Academy of Sciences. Because the bulk of geological work is done through the large governmental bureaucratic organizations, none of which were on our itinerary, we obtained only a narrow glimpse of current geological activity. Notes on what we learned are given below in summaries for each of the geological groups and individuals that we visited. In general, from discussion at the Institute of Geology and Paleontology in Nanking, we understand that regional evaluations of mineral resources are nearing completion and emphasis is shifting to petroleum, groundwater, and construction materials. Much effort is also being made to predict earthquakes (Earthquake Research in China, 1975). Accordingly, increasing work is being done on Mesozoic and Cenozoic geology. Chao (1973) was told that the program of regional geological mapping would result in a new geological map of China in early 1973 at a scale of 1:4,000,000, but this map was not mentioned to us. Rather, at Northwest University in Sian we were told that mapping at a scale of 1:200,000 is largely completed for all of China, with completion planned for 1980. Mapping at 1:50,000 has begun, and maps are also made at scales of 1:10,000 and 1:5,000 for small areas of special interest.

The willingness of the Chinese to explain their progress in geology had its limits, but we felt complimented that persons designated to receive us had seemingly been selected to include individuals trained in our specialties (Quaternary geology, geochronology, and palynology). Some of the limits were imposed by the need for translation, which made exchanges slow, formal, and comparatively shallow. Translation, however skillfully done, formed a veil that was nearly impossible to penetrate. Also, the Chinese were prepared to give a set program that seemed to take all the available time, thus preventing excursions into unprogrammed areas of inquiry. Their responses to technical questions were typically overlaid with lengthy remarks about serving the workers, soldiers, and peasants, or things explained previously were simply repeated, and we were rarely successful in evoking questions from the Chinese. In these circumstances, spontaneity of discussion was usually lacking. While being led through an institution, a few doors would be opened with someone there to receive us, but all other doors would be closed and locked.

Most frustrating to us was the lack of any opportunity to see modern geological maps of China. These are being made by the Bureau of Geology and are, we were told, not available elsewhere. Our host at the Institute of Geology, Yeh Lien-chün, explained, "We don't make maps and so have no library for maps." A few geological maps appear in Chinese geological journals, commonly without latitude and longitude, and "sample maps borrowed from the Bureau of Geology" are used in university training. To show our interest in geological maps and to foster possible future exchange of maps, our gifts included the newly compiled geological map of the United States, the national atlas recently published by the U.S. Department of Interior, and several maps representative of Quaternary geology in the United States.

Quaternary geology was always mentioned when we met paleoanthropologists, geologists, geographers, and palynologists. Each occasion was prompted by a lecture, or explanation, by the Chinese on a narrow topic of local concern: for example, stratigraphy of the Yüan-mou District, Yunnan Province, described by Chou Kuo-hsing at the Institute of Vertebrate Paleontology and Paleoanthropology; postglacial pollen in a deep boring from K'un-ming Lake, Yunnan, discussed at the Institute of Botany; sedimentary facies and clay minerals in Cenozoic deposits at Lan-t'ien, Shensi Province, mentioned at the Institute of Geography; and glacial stratigraphy and Quaternary pollen at Mount Jolmo Lungma, Tibet, described at the Institute of Geology. Such topics are representative of Quaternary research in the West, and the methods and concepts applied by the Chinese are also familiar. The presentations were well organized and easy to follow but lacked discussion of regional geological relations needed to explain the significance of the details at a site. The studies seemingly had been made by persons concerned with local matters of fossils, stratigraphy, and mineralogy, rather than with the record of Quaternary history over areas of substantial size. Thus, we did not hear from the Chinese a general summary of the Quaternary period in China. Informative reviews of the Quaternary geology of China are given by P'ei *et al.* (1965), Chang (1968, pp. 18-35), Nikiforova *et al.* (1969), and Aigner (1972).

The presentation of Quaternary topics by the Chinese was also curiously disjointed, in the sense that people at one institute seemed unaware of what work was being done at another, even though in the same specialty. Nonetheless, some past examples of cooperation between institutes were emphasized by mention of interdisciplinary study at Lant'ien and at Mount Holmo Lungma. These involved coordination between the Institutes of Geology, Geography, Botany, and others, but the administrative means by which this was arranged was not explained. Presumably, direction came from "responsible persons" in the Academy of Sciences.

Isolation in geological activities also comes from a compartmentalization of duties, at least in topics that require specialized training. Thus, we were told at the Institute of Geology and Paleontology in Nanking that all discoveries concerning human fossils were referred automatically to the Institute of Vertebrate Paleontology and Paleoanthropology (IVPP). The IVPP, for its part, if field studies are needed, makes its investigations of stratigraphy and other geological aspects with its own staff. Geological mapping, however, if done at all, is the responsibility of the Bureau of Geology. This system, at face value, does not differ from the division of work among specialized institutions in the West, but our impression was that the Chinese partake of much less give-and-take and much less communication by telephone and letter between individuals than we enjoy.

Compartmentalization, we understand, is also a hallmark of the existing bureaucratic system, in which local governmental units are individually responsible for local geological work and for some aspects of training. By such means, the Chinese believe that local incentives for production are stimulated.

INSTITUTIONS

Institute of Geology, Academia Sinica, Peking

This Institute occupies buildings built between 1953 and 1960 in the northern sector of Peking. Part of our delegation spent half a day there and later returned to give lectures.

The Institute encompasses most fields of geology with the exception of fluvial hydrology and geomorphology, which fall under the aegis of geography and are interests of the Institute of Geography, which is discussed below. Reports differ on the number of scientific and technical workers at the Institute: given as 1,000 by members of a delegation from the Royal Society of New Zealand (Anonymous, 1974b), 400 by members of the Max Planck Society (Gerwin, 1975), and 300 by the Seismology Delegation (Earthquake Research in China, 1975).

Work at the Institute is organized in eight laboratories that reflect traditional subjects:

1. Tectonics--history, deformation, and geochemistry of the earth's crust

2. Geology of the deep crust--telluric currents, terrestrial heat, relation to earthquakes

3. Modeling laboratory--magnetic geology, electronic computer, physical models, experiments

4. Engineering geology

5. Petrology and rheology

6. Sedimentation and stratigraphy

7. Isotope geology

8. Geochemistry

A slightly different list of subjects is given by Brace and Kisslinger (*in* Earthquake Research in China, 1975), perhaps reflecting only differences in translation rather than a recent change in function. The additional subjects include neotectonics and Quaternary geology.

Tectonics Laboratory

The chief task of this laboratory is to study the history of crustal deformation in China in order to understand the relation between crustal deformation and earthquakes.

Geology of the Deep Crust

Here magnetotellurics, heat flow, and heat dynamics are studied, again to investigate the relation of the deep crust to earthquakes.

Modeling Laboratory

Physical models of plates of the earth are used to determine areas of greatest stress in China, thereby identifying places where earthquakes will be most likely to occur. Polaroscopes are used as aids. In addition, methods of computing in earthquake seismology are studied.

Engineering Geology

Although we have no notes on the function of this laboratory, we assumed it fulfills the traditional functions of locating sites for buildings, roads, etc.

Petrology and Rheology

Igneous and metamorphic rocks are studied by standard petrographic techniques. Microscopes are either German or Russian. Mineralogy is studied by both microscopic and X-ray diffraction techniques. It seems that much of this work is on rocks associated with economic mineral deposits. Physical properties of rocks also come under the auspices of this laboratory.

Sedimentation and Stratigraphy

Here the normal work of grain size analysis, paleoenvironmental studies, and stratigraphic correlation is carried out. The work of this laboratory necessarily overlaps with the work of the Institute of Vertebrate Paleontology and Paleoanthropology, but the amount of exchange between the two institutes does not appear to be extensive.

Isotope Geology

Rubidium-strontium dating, potassium-argon dating, and carbon-14 dating are done in this laboratory. Also, isotopic studies are made to determine the history of igneous and metamorphic rocks.

Geochemistry

Scientific workers here carry out wet-chemical analysis of rocks submitted by other workers in the Institute and by other institutions throughout China.

Although much of the Institute's work in recent years has been on earthquake prediction, this work was not described for us. Rather, projects were described that centered on specialized studies in Quaternary geology and on a mineralogical analysis made in the service of archeology. Neither was explained in the context of applying Quaternary chronology as a means of identifying recurrence intervals of earthquakes, this being one way to predict earthquakes, but we understand this to be the main application of current Quaternary studies. Archeological chronology is also used for this purpose.

Detailed work was described on knowledge of the glacial stratigraphy and Quaternary pollen obtained by the Scientific Expedition to Mount Jolmo Lungma (Mount Everest). Pollen from lake beds on glaciofluvial deposits of the first of three glaciations (not counting a last, less widespread glaciation) and pollen from younger Pleistocene interglacial deposits indicates 1,500 m of uplift since the early Pleistocene, with a 5°-10°C lowering of temperature. The north slope, formerly in contact with warm air of the Indian Ocean, thus became an alpine steppe. This finding was explained as being important for social reconstruction in Tibet.

As an example of participation in interdisciplinary projects, Chi Sujung described her analysis of clay used to seal the coffin of a 2,000-year-old corpse dating from the Han dynasty in Hunan Province. (We learned later that 20,000 persons joined in the study of these astonishingly well-preserved remains.) X-ray analysis, differential thermal analysis, and the electron microscope showed the clay to be hydrophyllite and halloysite.

Instruments available at the Institute reflect a versatile capability for analysis of geological specimens. It is well-equipped with microscopes, X-ray diffraction equipment, differential thermal analysis furnaces, and thermogravimetric balances. An electron microprobe is available if needed. We were shown microscopes, a pollen laboratory, an optical device for measurement of rock strain, X-ray diffraction equipment, a laboratory for rubidium-strontium dating, a mass spectrometer (purchased from the USSR), apparatus for extracting argon for K-Ar dating (suitable for older, but not younger, rocks), an electron microscope with 10-angstrom resolution manufactured in 1965 by the Academia Sinica, and a Japanese "Shimadzu" thermal balance for measurement of thermal conductivity at low temperature. Differential thermal analysis of clay minerals was also mentioned. We were told than an electron microprobe is used in western China in another unit of the Academia Sinica, and the Academy expects to manufacture a scanning electron microscope.

Other facilities are described by Gerwin (1975) and by Brace and Kisslinger (*in* Earthquake Research in China, 1975): radiocarbon dating using gas counting of methane; a high-pressure, high-temperature laboratory; and a program for magnetotelluric deep sounding. Our tour included a visit to the library and its reading room. Judging from size, the library contains perhaps 150,000 volumes. Chao (1973) mentions facilities for map making, but these were not shown to us.

Institute of Geography, Academia Sinica, Peking

This Institute is located in the northern sector of Peking. Three members of the delegation visited here for half a day. Geography as practiced in China embraces the fields of physical geology and geomorphology.

A major focus of research at this Institute is on land analysis in order to: (1) determine the limits of growth according to available natural resources; (2) protect the environment by study of the origin, migration, and control of toxic elements in water bodies; (3) promote health by understanding the effect of groundwater composition; (4) determine what lands can best be used for forestry, grain, animal husbandry, etc.; and (5) maximize the use of water and maintain navigable waterways.

Work at the Institute includes numerous projects in environmental geology and applied hydrology that are designed to increase production from agricultural lands and fisheries. We met staff members trained in physical geography, cartography, fluvial geomorphology, climatology, Cenozoic stratigraphy, palynology, and statistics.

Studies were described of the following topics: (1) sediment accumulation in reservoirs and aggradation of river channels headward from reservoirs; (2) storm runoff in small basins; (3) reservoir problems in karst regions; (4) control of water pollution; (5) the effect of chemical elements on human health; (6) the geography of heart disease and bone disorders; and (7) the climatic history of China in general with the prospect of predicting problems of the future. (This is done mainly by the interpretation of pollen spectra, and the Institute has a pollen laboratory for this purpose.)

Other areas of study are hailstorms and their formation, thermodynamics, and prediction; groundwater studies; and cartographical work for regional planning. Recommendations for agricultural development are made, and the workers cooperate with other institutes on large problems such as the study of the Yangtze Valley and the Wei-Ho Valley. To forecast changes resulting from agriculture, the Institute has an agricultural experiment station.

Geomorphic work is concentrated on the valleys of major rivers and on the karst terrain of South China, the first dealing with aggradation that impairs winter navigation, the second being concerned with leakage from reservoirs. For the braided reach of the middle and lower Yangtze, discharge of sediment is considered in relation to the loess of central China. Models are tested to determine conditions for overbank and bottom aggradation and to measure the relative erodibility of the banks and the bed. Observations of change are made by repeated terrestrial photography.

The study of the Yellow River is at least as comprehensive, involving an integrated survey of the geology, geomorphology, and soils of the entire drainage basin. The Yellow River drains much of the loess terrain of central China (Liu *et al.*, 1965), which is vulnerable to erosion because of intensive use for agriculture. Special attention is given to saline soils resulting from a rising water table, which is in turn related to headward aggradation. We were shown a flume measuring 36 m by 10 m that is used to model the behavior of the Yangtze. The flume is adjustable for gradient, volume of flow, and sediment load, in the manner customary for experimental flumes in the United States. For small drainage basins, studies of storm runoff are used for engineering designs of railways. In the field of statistics, forecasts are made of droughts and floods in the Yangtze basin, and studies are underway on the distribution and frequency of damaging hailstorms. Pollen analysis is done to identify Quaternary strata as an aid in finding groundwater. Finally, much cartographic work is done for agricultural and industrial planning.

In addition to these general projects, the Institute has cooperated with other institutes and departments in several specialized projects.

Ch'ien Ling, Landscape

30

Flume model of Yellow
River, Institute of
Geography.

For example, study of the fossil pollen, sedimentary facies, and clay
minerals was completed of 300 m of Cenozoic strata (Eocene to Holocene)
at Lan-t'ien southeast of Sian, Shensi Province, as part of an interdisciplinary study of the discovery of Lan-t'ien man (middle Pleistocene).
My lecture on documenting landscape change by repeated photography, which was translated sentence-by-sentence by Professor Shen Yü-
chang, was attended by about 50 members of the Institute. The subject
was presented in perhaps too academic a manner and prompted a question
from one of the younger persons, who asked, "How does this technique
improve production?" A reply was given in terms of how knowledge of the
rates of geologic processes aids in planning optimum use of the land.
Further discussion disclosed that some of those present were using repeated photography to observe glaciers in the Tien Shan, Sinkiang.

Institute of Geology and Paleontology, Academia Sinica, Nanking

The Institute was founded in 1950 with a staff of 20 and has now grown
to a staff of 200, of which about 160 are research workers. As originally organized, the Institute did work in paleobotany, invertebrate paleontology, and vertebrate paleontology, but study of fossil vertebrates was
organized separately in 1953 to become the Institute (then the Laboratory)
of Vertebrate Paleontology and Paleoanthropology (IVPP). The remaining
functions have now been organized in six divisions: (1) palynology; (2)
paleobotany (plant macrofossils and fossil algae); (3) Lower Paleozoic
invertebrates (trilobites, cephalopods, and graptolites); (4) Upper
Paleozoic invertebrates (brachiopods, bryozoans, foraminifera, corals);
(5) Mesozoic and Cenozoic invertebrates (pelecypods and gastropods); and
(6) sedimentary rocks.
Research is centered on ways to apply paleontology and stratigraphy
in practical matters of geological surveys, mineral prospecting, and
engineering works. Accordingly, specimens for examination are received

widely from the general populace as well as from academic institutes and government departments. Mention was made of cooperative work, sometimes involving mutual field investigations of stratigraphy, with the Bureaus of Geology, Coal, Oil, and Metallurgy. Cooperative work on Quaternary stratigraphy was mentioned with the Institute of Archeology and the IVPP but was later said to be nearly nonexistent because of a lack of strength (presumably meaning a lack of personnel with the required training).

In current research, particular mention was made of the stratigraphic paleontology of Mount Jolmo Lungma (Mount Everest) where the depositional sequence of geologic strata is considered to be unbroken from the Cambrian to the Tertiary. Research on the Precambrian of Southwest China was also mentioned.

The results of work by the Institute are published in Chinese (*Institute of Geology and Paleontology Memoirs, Journal of Paleontology Sinica, Scientia Sinica*) as well as in major foreign journals. To facilitate this work, scholarly exchanges of information are made with institutes of foreign countries, and correspondence is carried on between individuals. For example, Mu En-chih, a specialist on graptolites, mentioned exchanges with Reuben J. Ross, William Berry, and Marshall Kay of the United States.

Over the past 20 years work done by the Institute has shifted emphasis from former stress on Paleozoic stratigraphy to an increasing emphasis on Mesozoic and Cenozoic stratigraphy. This was explained as stemming from needs arising from new construction. Expressed differently, this changing emphasis perhaps reflects progress in completing exploration for metal deposits and a growing interest in petroleum, groundwater, and construction materials. A shortage of strength is still felt in Cenozoic stratigraphy, however, especially the Quaternary. We learned, for example, that no work is done on the paleontology of ocean cores. Still, Chang Lu-chin described the detailed palynology of cores from Quaternary deposits in the Yangtze delta, which reach a depth of 280 m southwest of Shanghai. On the other hand, the Institute lacks a collection of molluscan fossils from the famous lower Pleistocene deposits at Ni-ho-wan.

The library of the Institute is quite comprehensive and includes a diverse range of current technical journals from around the world. Many of these are in the original covers, but some (for example, *Geological Society of America Bulletin, Journal of Geology, American Journal of Science, Scientific American*) are copies reprinted in China by photo-offset. Current journals on the reading shelves were several months old.

Nanking University, Nanking

The Geology Department at Nanking University is 50 years old and has trained many of the geologists now working in China. With the Department of Geography, it occupies a building of three floors and enrolls 500 students. Courses are offered in four specialties: (1) regional surveys, including mineral exploration; (2) geochemistry; (3) hydrogeology and engineering geology; and (4) paleontology and stratigraphy. Teaching of geology is done by 100 teachers with assistance from a staff of 50. As at Northwest University (see below), an annual recess is taken to work on geological mapping for the Bureau of Geology. The faculty and students from Nanking University do this mapping in several provinces.

Teaching since the Cultural Revolution is done without printed text-books. New texts are being compiled, and we saw a paste-up version in use in a laboratory for studies in mineral crystallography. These text-books are being written by teams composed of representatives from several provinces, and students participate by making comments as the new writing is put to use in the classroom. Revisions are then made. At Nanking University, as at other universities, the preparation of a new text in geology is an individual responsibility of the university, but guidelines are provided by the provincial Bureau of Education and the provincial Bureau of Geology. In addition to such temporary texts, a library is used for assigned reading. We did not learn whether or not students have freedom to browse at will in the library.

The older teachers, many of whom retain their pre-1949 title of "Professor," are reaching retirement age, and we asked how new teachers are trained. It appears that the training of new teachers is just now beginning. Educational reforms since the Cultural Revolution have eliminated graduate students and reduced the curriculum, but plans are underway to enroll "research students" who will become teaching assistants and eventually full-fledged teachers. Because the established teachers are still able to pass on their acquired learning, some of it having been obtained by education in Western universities, the continuity of higher education in China will depend on the success of this approach to teacher training.

To learn about the level of knowledge expected of geology students, we asked about the courses taught and received a detailed outline of the curriculum. Some exchange of students between the Departments of Geology and Geography exists, geology students taking courses in geomorphology and Quaternary stratigraphy in the Geography Department, for example. A list of courses for a student of paleontology is given below.

First year: introductory geology, tectonic geology, general paleontology, petrology, mineralogy, and crystallography (each allotted 100 hours); mathematics, physics, and chemistry (each 60 hours); foreign language (typically being reading of English); physical training; and political studies in current affairs.

Second year: historical geology, geodynamics, petrology, sedimentary geology, and ore deposits; foreign language (5 hours per week); physical training; and political studies. Paleontology students also take a course in zoology in the Biology Department, and some students have a course in vertebrate paleontology.

Third year: specialized topical courses (trilobites, graptolites, brachiopods, cephalopods, pelcypods, gastropods, ostracods, pollen and spores, plants, and corals); and foreign language (technical literature). All students complete special research assignments as members of geological teams.

Instruction for other specialties involves different sets of courses in the second year. Students who are being trained for regional surveys have courses in ore deposits, geophysical prospecting, geochemical prospecting, mining geology, heavy mineral analysis, opaque minerals, and laboratory experiments. Students of geochemistry have courses in ore

deposits, optical crystallography, X-ray analysis, differential thermal
analysis, the Federov stage, silicate analysis, optical spectrography,
analytical chemistry, and physical chemistry. No courses in geochronology are offered, but this is a subject of interest to some of the teachers. Examinations are given in each course, and a research paper is
required using a foreign language as background to the research. The
actual content of these courses was not explained.

Besides these classroom studies, students have 2 months of field
geology to learn surveying methods and to learn to recognize field relations of geologic formations. They participate with geological teams
in making maps and in some instances use aerial photographs. These
activities presumably extend into the third year when research projects
are done with geological teams.

Students who complete these 3 years of university training either become members of a provincial Bureau of Geology or may have work assigned
to them in an institute or a university.

The university has a potassium-argon dating laboratory. The extrac-
tion lines are similar to those at the Institute of Geology in Peking;
the mass spectrometer was not seen. Again, as at the Institute of Geology, no provision is made for baking out the lines. ^{38}Ar is obtained
from a laboratory in Peking.

The only other laboratory seen was for optical spectrography. Its
equipment is up-to-date and apparently is under heavy use.

Northwest University, Sian

Our visit to this university was at a time when the teachers and students
were doing work in the countryside, but several of the faculty returned
to meet us. These included Wang Yung-yen (Quaternary Stratigraphy) and
Huo Shih-ch'eng (Invertebrate Paleontology). Upon questioning, we learned
that the teachers of geology and their students were then doing geological mapping with the Geological Bureau of Shensi province, an arm of the
Bureau of Geology. Such fieldwork is considered to be part of the labor
done annually with the workers, soldiers, and peasants, which is expected
of every able person in China. Our tour included visits to the library
and the museum of the Geology Department.

TING-TS'UN ARCHEOLOGICAL SITE

Our visit to this Paleolithic site (see Appendix D) was our principal
opportunity to observe geologic stratigraphy. The site is a group
of fossiliferous localities that stretch several kilometers along
the east bank of the Fen River, 37 km south of Lin-fen, Shansi Province. All are in alluvial sand and gravel that rise about 20 m above
the river and are in turn buried by several tens of meters of loess,
now strongly dissected by gully erosion. West of the river the loess
rises abruptly to the high loess plateau of Hsiang-ning. Inter-
stratified in the loess are seven or eight buried soils that change
from brownish hues in the upper section of loess (7.5 *YR* on the Munsell

Ting-ts'un.

scale) to redder hues in the lower part. Because of the red soil,
which resembles red clay at Chou-k'ou-tien and which is widely present
in middle Pleistocene deposits of North China (Nikiforova *et al.*, 1969;
Aigner, 1972, pp. 47-48, table 4), Chinese paleoanthropologists at first
considered the age of the underlying fossiliferous sand and gravel to be
middle Pleistocene. Subsequent excavation yielded many modern mammalian
species--including *Coelodonta antiquitatis* (woolly rhinoceros), *Elephas*
cf. *indicus, Bos primigenius,* and *Equus hemionus*--and the deposits were
then assigned to the earlier part of the upper Pleistocene (P'ei *et al.*,
1958). In the Quaternary nomenclature of China, the Ting-ts'un deposits
belong to the Loessic Stage. Aigner (1972, table 5) correlates Ting-
ts'un with the Eemian Interglacial and Amersfoort interval of Europe
(110,000-70,000 B.P.), making it questionably older than the Ordos sites
of Inner Mongolia.

We briefly visited Localities 90 and 98, where details of the fossiliferous deposits are now poorly exposed, and spent a longer time at
Locality 100, which is famous among paleoanthropologists as the place
of discovery of three human teeth. At Locality 100, the geologic sequence described below is exposed.

Beginning at river level, intermittent outcrops expose as much as 3 m
of cemented sand and gravel. Correlative deposits on the west bank of the
Fen have fossils of early Pleistocene age: the freshwater clam, *Lamprotula; Equus sanmenensis;* and *Proboscidihipparion*. The fossils compare with those found at San-men on the Yellow River, 120 km south.
These conglomeratic deposits of the Ting-ts'un area are reported as
resting on an undulating erosion surface of the Tang-hsien stage, which
is formed on Permo-carboniferous shale (P'ei *et al.*, 1958). The name
Paote red clay, which is applied to a fossiliferous residuum indicative
of early Pliocene weathering, is also synonymously used for this erosion
surface. The Fen River is said to be incised into this surface, but
this aspect of the regional physiography was not pointed out during our
visit.

Disconformable on the cemented sand and gravel are about 20 m of non-

Ting-ts'un site,
Location 100.

indurated alluvial sand and gravel in uneven lenticular beds, mingled with loesslike silt. The lower part has abundant *Lamprotula* shells and scarce mammalian fossils inadequate for dating. The upper part has yielded the human teeth, Paleolithic artifacts, and most of the mammalian fossils (12 species). The beds of silt preserve freshwater mollusks such as *Melanoides, Plannorbis,* and unioidids. Remains of five species of cyprinid fishes (especially *Mylopharyngodon piceus*) indicate a riverine environment such as now found in South China, in which the Pleistocene Fen River was deep, calm, and constant. The same inference is drawn from the contemporary distribution of *Lamprotula*. Two species of turtles, widely distributed in North and South China, are also reported. These fossiliferous deposits are overlain gradationally by 5 m of unstratified, loesslike, yellowish silt and fine sand, which is considered to be material deposited in calm water. The total sequence forms a narrow terrace on which Ting-ts'un village is located.

Conformably above these deposits are the thick layers of loess that are assigned to the Ma-lan Loess (upper Pleistocene) of North China. The lower part forms a loessial terrace 1.5-2 km wide and 100 m above the west bank of the Fen. The land then climbs westward 10 km to the foot of the Houshan mountain range, where loess forms a layer 3-5 m thick on 10 m of red loessic material identified as "Pontian" (Paote red clay). We saw these regional relations only from a distance.

From this brief visit to Ting-ts'un, our impression was that the sedimentary sequence, excepting the cemented layers at the base, can be matched in degree of consolidation, color, and state of weathering with upper Pleistocene sections in North America and Europe.

VISIT WITH PAI MING-HUEI, GEOLOGICAL BUREAU OF HONAN PROVINCE

Pai Ming-huei traveled more than 100 km from his place of work to show us the stratigraphy of loess at Mang Shan, a bluff about 100 m high on

the south bank of the Yellow River near Cheng-chou. He explained, in
English, that he had worked with the Bureau of Geology 18 years since
completing his degree at Ch'in Ling University (now Nanking University).
As a specialist in engineering geology and hydrogeology, he is now making a geomorphological map of Honan Province at a scale of 1:500,000.
The map units, which emphasize fluvial features, are classified according to origin and form, presumably being modeled on geomorphological maps
made in Europe. He is also mapping the stratigraphy of the loess, using
the buried soils as stratigraphic markers. Drill cores are available
that reach sand, gravel, and lake sediments below the loess.

  With Mr. Pai, we climbed through 86 m of the loess, the height of the
upper canal at the Mang Shan Pumping Station, briefly examining some of
the buried soils. These have horizons of brown or red clay underlain
in some instances by horizons rich in small aggregates of carbonate nodules. None of the nodules are ferruginous, and mottled or pisolitic
zones (as in red-yellow podzolic soils) do not exist. These soils grade
upward more or less abruptly into ordinary loess, the transition being
attributed to an increase in rate of deposition of eolian silt as compared with a much slower rate during the episode represented by the soil.
At Mang Shan, and elsewhere in this Province, the loess is considered to
be no older than middle Pleistocene, although no methods of absolute
dating have been applied. The dating is based on the presence of buried
soils that have adjoining nodules of calcium carbonate. Lower Pleistocene loess is identified in Shansi Province.

  The excursion to Mang Shan was through fertile farmland irrigated
with water pumped from the Yellow River. Water from the pumping station

Pumping station, Mang Shan.

serves 100,000 mou (6,140 hectares). After days of travel, the opportunity to climb among outcrops was delightful, especially in the company of another geologist.

VISIT WITH CH'EN WEN-CHÜN, GEOLOGICAL BUREAU OF
KWANGSI CHUANG AUTONOMOUS REGION

Ch'en Wen-chün joined us for a visit to Lu-ti Cave, a limestone cavern at Kuei-lin, and later traveled with us on the Li River, this being a 5-hour excursion by boat that took us through some of the karst terrain near Kuei-lin. Karst topography forms in massive, well-jointed limestone in regions where percolation of rainwater enlarges the joints by solution. In an advanced stage of development, which is characteristic of much of the limestone region of South China, a fantastic landscape of steep-walled pinnacles results. The finds of *Gigantopithecus* in Kwangsi have been made in caves widely present in the karst terrain.

Mr. Ch'en graduated from Chang Chan Geological College in 1959 and came to Kuei-lin in 1962 after doing geological work in North and West China. He described some aspects of his geological work in the karst terrain and his approach in dating stages of development of this unusual topography. These investigations comprise his current work.

The geological mapping is done at a scale of 1:200,000 by a team of three: Mr. Ch'en, a second geologist who has completed university training, and an apprentice in training who has completed middle school. A typical daily traverse covers a stretch of 20 km and is done on foot, carrying a packsack. In this way, fossils are collected and the limestone formations are traced. (Because of misunderstanding during translation, such mention of lengthy traverses may pertain to Mr. Ch'en's earlier work in North China rather than to the karst terrain.) The geomorphic history is deduced by identifying former erosion surfaces from the height of limestone remnants.

River Life,
Li Chiang, Kuei-lin.

Mr. Ch'en was curious about methods of geologic mapping in the United States. From his questions, we understood that maps in China are compiled from aerial photographs, but instruments for stereographic plotting of geological formations are not used. A pantograph for adjusting the scale of geological maps and for transfer of information from field sheets, however, is commonly used. We were not able to learn how much field time is needed to produce a geological map in the karst terrain.

As in our conversation with Mr. Pai at Mang Shan, we found the exchange of information with Ch'en Wen-chuan to be easy, direct, and friendly, although Mr. Ch'en did not speak English. Despite the impediment of translation, our mutual familiarity with general geological principles undoubtedly enabled each of us to mentally enlarge on concepts expressed in only a few words.

REFERENCES

Aigner, J. S. 1972. Relative dating of north Chinese faunal and cultural complexes. Arct. Anthropol. 9:36-79.

Anonymous. 1974a. A photographic record of the Mount Jolmo Lungma scientific expedition (1966-1968). Science Press, Peking. Unpaged.

Anonymous. 1974b. Visit to China by delegation from the Royal Society of N.Z.. R. Soc. N. Z. Proc. 102:85-93.

Chang Kwang-chi. 1968. The archaeology of ancient China. Yale University Press. New Haven and London. 483 pp.

Chao, E. C. T. 1973. Contacts with earth scientists in the People's Republic of China. Science 179:961-963.

Cohen, J. L., and J. A. Cohen. 1973. China today and her ancient treasures. Harry N. Abrams, Inc., New York. 399 pp.

Dean, G. C. 1974. Science and technology in the development of modern China, an annotated bibliography. Mansell, London.

Earthquake research in China. 1975. EOS Am. Geophys. Union Trans. 56: 838-881.

Gerwin, R. 1975. Als Gast der Academia Sinica in Peking und Shanghai. Naturwissenschaften 62:290-295.

Harland, W. B. 1967. The organization of geology overseas--China. Geol. Soc. London Proc. No. 1633: pp. 102-107.

Kellogg, W. W., et al. 1974. Visit to the People's Republic of China: A report from the A.M.S. delegation. Am. Meteorol. Soc. Bull. 55: 1291-1330.

Liu Tung-sheng et al. 1965. Collected works on China's loess soil--A translation of the Chinese language publication entitled Chung-kuo Te Huang-t'u Tui-chi, pp. 1-243. Science Press, Peking. U.S. Joint Publication Research Board.

Mark, H. F. 1974. Visit to China in June, 1972. Naturwissenschaften 61:157-163.

Needham, J. (with research assistance of Wang Ling). 1954-1971. Science and civilization in China, 5 vol. Cambridge University Press, Cambridge.

Nikiforova, K. V., V. I. Gromov, and E. A. Vangengeim. 1969. Boundary between the Lower and Middle Divisions of the Anthropogen and the classification of the Anthropogen of northern Eurasia, pp. 6-9. *In* H. E. Wright, Jr., ed., Quaternary geology and climate. International Association for Quaternary Research (INQUA), 7th Congress Proceedings, vol. 16. National Academy of Sciences, Washington, D.C.

P'ei Wen-chung, *et al*. 1958. Report on the excavation of Palaeolithic sites at Tingtsun, Hsiangfenhsien, Shansi Province, China. Inst. Vertebra. Paleontol. Acad. Sinica Mem. 2. 111 pp. (In Chinese with English summaries.)

P'ei Wen-chung, Chou Ming-chen, and Cheng Chia-chien. 1965. China's Cenozoic group--A translation of the Chinese-language publication entitled *Ch'uan-kuo Ti-ts'eng Hui-i Hsueh-shu Pao-kao Hui-p'ien--Chung-kuo te Hsin-sheng-chieh* (Report of the National Congress on Stratigraphy--China Cenozoic Group). pp. 1-31. Science Press, Peking. U.S. Joint Publication Research Board. 61 pp.

Signer, E., and A. W. Galston. 1972. Education and science in China. Science 175:15-23.

VERTEBRATE PALEONTOLOGY,
ESPECIALLY OF NONHUMAN PRIMATES, IN CHINA

Eric Delson

INTRODUCTION

As will be abundantly clear to all readers of this compilation of reports,
there was an extensive overlapping of interests and competence among the
delegation members. This tended to bind the delegation together by increasing our professional interactions but made division of labor more
difficult. Formally, I was designated the vertebrate paleontologist,
but my main interest was in nonhuman fossil primates (in addition to
other fossil vertebrates), fossil man, and his Paleolithic cultural remains. Therefore, it seems wisest to divide my report into two major
aspects--a brief review of Chinese vertebrate paleontology as I saw it
and a more formal section commenting on specific primate fossils seen
there or elsewhere. Parts of the former section concerning the IVPP
have been grouped with comments of other delegation members in Appendix
B, and some of this material has previously appeared elsewhere (Delson,
1976). Additional information on various aspects of Quaternary research
in China may be found in the report of the Australian Quaternary Sciences delegation (*Australian Quaternary Newsletter*, April 1976).

NOTES ON VERTEBRATE PALEONTOLOGY IN THE PEOPLE'S REPUBLIC OF CHINA

Institutions Supporting Research on Fossil Vertebrates

Institute of Vertebrate Paleontology and Paleoanthropology, Peking

The main center of vertebrate paleontological research in China is the
Institute of Vertebrate Paleontology and Paleoanthropology (IVPP). (It
is of minor linguistic interest that after delegation members kept referring to the Institute as the IVPP for several days, I was told by
Chou Ming-chen that the Chinese began to do so also, which they had
never done previously.) As indicated, most of the delegation's information about the IVPP is presented as a unit in Appendix B, but some additional notes are included here as specifically related to vertebrate
paleontology. Several additional centers appear to support active,
long-term interest in the subject, including: the Shanghai Natural
History Museum; the Tientsin Natural History Museum; the Department of
Geology of Northwestern Univeristy, Sian; and possibly the Kwangtung

Provincial Museum, Canton. Other centers may exist, but we were not informed of them--they may have a passing interest in vertebrate pale-ontology, as when a local brigade makes a restricted discovery, not followed by long-term research in a region.

The personnel of the IVPP is assigned by the central manpower authori-ties, as is the case with all of China's work force. Before the Cultural Revolution, members of the research staff taught formal (undergraduate) courses at Peking University and worked with graduate students. Formal graduate training and Ph.D. exams (and theses) were abolished after the late 1960's, however. It now appears that younger research workers are assigned to the IVPP from one of a small number of colleges offering training in geology and anthropology: Fu-tan, Peking, Nanking, and Northwestern Universities are the main sources. There may be some nego-tiating by IVPP leaders with the state authorities in order to acquire promising candidates (perhaps recommended by their universities).

New permanent personnel of the IVPP are trained in all aspects of technical and research procedures, assisting senior colleagues until they are assigned projects of their own, individually or, more commonly now, in teams. Among technical services, I can indicate as an amateur mold and cast maker that work in this area is of the highest quality. Many molds appear to be made in plaster, from which both plaster and plastic casts can be pulled, although the latter lead to rapid mold deterioration. I demonstrated the use of both polysulfide and silicone rubber molding compounds and left some for experimentation by IVPP per-sonnel, but these materials may prove too expensive for standard use. The IVPP prepares casts both for Chinese museum exhibits and research purposes and for foreign colleagues, based on international equality as well as political contact between the nations involved.

Most of our time at the IVPP (5 full days in my case) was spent at a newly occupied building in two large rooms; we did not see any offices or other facilities in the building. In one room we were formally re-ceived, heard some introductory presentations by our hosts, and several of us presented lectures about aspects of our own research, illustrated with slides and semisimultaneously translated by either Wu Hsin-chih or Chou Ming-chen. In the second, smaller room we heard reports by staff members about specific paleoanthropological localities and remains and were able to examine and photograph specimens. Two large safes in this room housed fossil human and *Gigantopithecus* remains, while casts and some vertebrate fossils from paleoanthropological localities were stored in cases along two other walls.

The IVPP and People's Republic of China in general have good reason to be proud of not only the important recent finds in vertebrate pale-ontology but also the close and excellent relations between IVPP inves-tigators and local informants and inhabitants. Because of the impressive program of museum exhibits on evolution and paleontology and a network of local and regional antiquities commissions, the majority of major finds are due to the transmission of information and fossils discovered by farmers and other workers to the IVPP, which may then send a field team to work together with regional institutions and local people in the recovery of larger collections. Some of the important recent work, especially that relating to paleoanthropology, will be discussed below.

Institutions Outside Peking

In addition to the IVPP, at least four other institutions are engaged in
vertebrate paleontology research. The Natural History Museum in Tientsin
was visited by almost the entire delegation. The one vertebrate paleontologist there, Huang Wei-yung, was a fish specialist at the IVPP before
being assigned to Tientsin. Most of his work now deals with mammals,
which form the bulk of the collection. About 25 percent of the 300,000
specimens in the museum are fossil vertebrates, of which some two-thirds
are from the Huangho-Paiho Museum of prewar days; among the new material
are fossil fish from Ni-ho-wan. A small building houses these collections, mostly from four main regions: Ni-ho-wan, Sjara-osso-gol (Ordos),
Ch'ing-yang, and Yü-she. Although Teilhard had reported an important
specimen of *Procynocephalus* (associated mandible and partial skull) in
the Tientsin museum, it could not be located, nor was the museum staff
aware of it. It appears to have suffered the same fate as those in
Peking (see p. 51). This collection does not appear to be the subject
of active study, but it is a major source of fossil documentation.

More concerted research efforts are under way at the (newly reorganized) Shanghai Natural History Museum. This museum was begun in 1956 in
the old Mercentile Exchange. Of a total staff of over 200, more than
100 are scientific workers. Current exhibits deal with modern animals,
paleontology, and human evolution: "from ape to man." It is planned
to add botany, geology, ethnography, and human biology as well as adding
to the invertebrate halls (only insects are included now) while moving
some exhibits to a second building. Over 1.6 million visitors have come
through since 1972, about 2,000/day, of whom 60 percent are students and
children. Three paleontologists deal with all phases of the field, both
research and exhibition (Ts'ao K'o-ch'ing, Hsieh Wan-ming, and Wang
Hsiang-wen). At least two main projects appear to be under way, both
in cooperation with the IVPP: the early Cenozoic of the Nan-hsiung
Basin in Kwangtung and the "late" Pliocene of the Ling-t'ai area, in
Kansu near the Shansi border. Specimens from Ling-t'ai include rodents,
artiodactyls, and proboscideans.

After discussion of preparation methods, we were shown several specimens from Kwangtung being cleaned in a small room lit mostly by one win-
dow (this may have been merely a room chosen to let us see an example,
not the actual lab). Material included a late Cretaceous chelonian and
a Paleocene anagalidan mandible, and the technique was indicated to be
mostly manual grain removal with needles and small hammers, although the
scientists were acquainted with both acid and airbrasive techniques.
One large hall was devoted to paleontological exhibitions, with displays
dealing with the origin of life and the history of the vertebrates and
especially the mammals found in China. Many casts were exhibited, including several large dinosaur mounts. One of the two mammalogists who
were also on the staff of the museum noted that collecting teams study
ecology and behavior of the animals they seek. Mention was also made of
about 10 nature preserves controlled by the Ministry of Agriculture and
Forestry. These include one in Szechwan for pandas (and neighbors) and
one in the northeast especially for Siberian tigers.

At Northwestern University in Sian, Hsüeh Hsiang-hsi is a vertebrate paleontologist trained in Peking. Her teaching duties include field collection trips with students, and she also has some time devoted to research. Two rooms contained paleontological specimens. One was mainly for students' study purposes, with fossils exhibited inside glass-topped cases that were not normally opened. A wide range of fossil materials and some casts were on display here, including both vertebrates and invertebrates. In a second room were exhibited specimens collected by the University teams. Among the localities represented were: Ho-huan, a late Pleistocene site in Kansu, with some paleolithic artifacts, rhinoceros, megaceros, and "*Cervus* cf. *canadensis*"; and Wu-tu, a Kansu site listed as "early Pliocene." The fauna from this site included a schizotherian chalicothere, *Megantereon, Eomellivora* (according to labels), and *Macaca* (see nonhuman primates below). Hsüeh also indicated that in the first year of undergraduate geology training a student takes courses in mathematics, physics, chemistry, and general geology; historical geology, petrology tectonics, and paleontology are taken in the second year (especially by paleontology students?); and mineralogy and "new methods" are studied in the third year. In addition, foreign language is taken in all three years. Unfortunately, this discussion was not completed.

Several small collections of Pleistocene fossil mammals were displayed and later shown to us at the Kwangtung Provincial Museum in Canton. These were mostly collected in association with the search for archeological materials, but it does indicate that such small collections may be found in other local museums.

Some Specific Notes on Recent Research

Many studies, both in the field and in the lab, have been undertaken by IVPP personnel in the past decade. Most of these are published after completion in *Vertebrata PalAsiatica,* and there is no necessity to comment on them here. However, three segments of paleontological research discussed during our trip are relevant to this report. I will first summarize recent work on Paleocene and some Pleistocene mammals and stratigraphy, and comments on Eocene to Pleistocene local faunas yielding primates will be included in the following section.

Early Tertiary Localities

In terms of mammals, the most exciting work in recent years has been the study of an ever-increasing number of Paleocene sites in various Chinese provinces. Few of these fossils have been studied in any detail as yet, but eventually perhaps 50 new taxa may be described. The dominant element of the assemblages appears to be the order Anagalida, but Edentata, Condylarthra, Tillodontia, and Pantodonta are also represented. Unfortunately, no primates have yet been identified, despite the reports of "middle Paleocene lemuroids" by Chao (1973) and Lisowski (1974). I assume that these writers were told of the presence of anagalidans but did not realize that this group has long been removed from the primates. During the course of our visit, Chou kindly summarized these finds stratigraphically for me; in the months after we left, he undertook further field studies on the Paleocene of Inner Mongolia. Among the regions that have yielded Paleocene mammals are: the Nan-hsiung Basin of north Kwangtung, with middle and perhaps early Paleocene (see Chou *et al.*, 1973); the Ch'a-ling Basin of southeast Hunan, with middle and perhaps later Paleocene ("Kao Hung-hsiang," 1975); the Ta-yu area of southwest Kiangsi with middle or later Paleocene (and early Eocene at Hsin-yü, near the center of the Province); and the Ch'i-shan and Hsüan-ch'eng regions of southeastern Anhwei producing middle Paleocene to early Eocene (Chou and Feng, 1973). In addition, early Eocene has been found in Shantung, while later Eocene and Oligocene mammals have been found in the T'ien-tung and Pai-se areas of western Kwangsi (Tang *et al.*, 1974b) and the Hua-ning area of central Yunnan. In the Junggaar Basin of Northern Sinkiang, deposits range in age from Permian through Pleistocene (although Paleocene has not yet been identified).

Pleistocene Localities

In the course of lectures and discussions at the IVPP, we received summaries of current interpretations of several Pleistocene paleoanthropological sites or "fields" which might usefully be repeated here, although most are already published. Some additional information reported by the Australian delegation is included also. Notes on the human fossils and artifacts from these localitites are presented in other chapters and will not be repeated here. Tedford and colleagues at the American Museum of Natural History are now preparing annotated faunal lists of the numerous Chinese localities represented in the Museum's collections made during the Central Asiatic Expeditions of the 1920's, which will be a most useful reference in this field.

In northern China, the Chou-k'ou-tien fissures and caves range in age between Pliocene (possibly Late Miocene) and latest Pleistocene. Hope (1976) reported a date of 18,400 B.P. for the Upper Cave, just recently published (Laboratory of IA and IVPP, 1976). No new work appears to have been done on the older localities, but work at Locality 1 has continued, especially in 1959 and 1966, and the New Cave (continuous with Locality 4) has been almost entirely excavated. We were informed that perhaps two-thirds of Locality 1 remains to be excavated. Some studies have been undertaken of the stratigraphic differences in fauna within the cave levels (Kahlke and Chow, 1961), but more such work, along with further interdisciplinary investigations, might be profitable in the future. Chinese workers now consider the age of Chou-k'ou-tien Locality 1 as probably interglacial, perhaps equivalent to the Holstein or "Mindel/Riss" of Europe, a view generally shared by Western authors. The topic of Chinese Pleistocene glaciation was not formally discussed with our group, but the data shown in Table 1 were presented by Jennings (1976, p. 17) as a summary and amplification by Hsüan T'ien-ch'in of work published by Li Yung-chang *et al.* (1972).

TABLE 1 Chinese Glacial Stratigraphy

Stage	Type Area	Tentative Correlation with the Alps
Ta-li Glacial	Ta-li Lake (Yunnan)	Wurm
Lan-t'ien Igl.	Lan-t'ien (Shensi)	
Lu-shan Glacial	Lu-shan (Kiangsi)	Riss
Chou-k'ou-tien Igl.	Chou-k'ou-tien Locality 1 (Hupei)	
Ta-ku Glacial	(None given by Jennings)	Mindel
Yüan-mou Igl.	Yüan-mou Lake beds (Yunnan)	
Po-yang Glacial	Po-yang Lake boreholes (Kiangsi)	Gunz

Jennings (1976, p. 21) further commented on the origin of Locality 1 that:

> A 'cap travertine' with bat bones in it is the evidence for the inference that it is the fill of a cave and not of an open cavity in the limestone. Much cave breakdown is included in the fill as is to be expected of the ruin of a cave but there was also much bedded gravel and sandy clay which were waterlaid. It is easier to understand the emplacement of these beds if they accumulated when the plain stood at a considerably higher level than now.... The New Cave is at much the same level as the main *Homo erectus* excavation. The front of this cave was almost blocked by angular rock debris from cave entrance collapse or from the slope above it. The sediments on the floor of the cave include flowstone and some fine sediment, neither of which imply river flow in the cave. They could have formed with the plain outside at a much lower level than that of the New Cave.

The longest continuous sequence of later Cenozoic rocks in the north is at Ni-ho-wan, some 200 km west of Peking. We requested but were denied permission to visit this region, although the Australian delegation did so later (see Section of Ni-ho-wan Cenozoic, 1974; Hope, 1976; Jennings, 1976). In a lecture during our visit to the IVPP, we were informed that at least 600-700 m of silts and clays with some sands and gravels occur in the basin, dipping toward the center. The section probably ranges in age from late Pliocene to late Pleistocene with gaps and would be a most profitable region for paleomagnetic sampling and general interdisciplinary study. As yet, no hominid or other primate fossils are known from Ni-ho-wan, but some tools of early Paleolithic typology have been reported, and large collections of mammals exist in China and elsewhere.

The Lan-t'ien area, near Sian, was a second region that we had hoped to see at first hand but that proved inaccessible. Like the Sanmen Gorge region, it is important in linking North and South Chinese Plio-Pleistocene deposits. Lan-t'ien is most famous for its mid-Pleistocene hominid fossils and associated fauna and artifacts, but recently both early and late Pleistocene faunal assemblages have also been reported

(Chi, 1975 and 1974, respectively), and, of course, the region was first investigated by the IVPP after discovery of the underlying early Tertiary beds in 1963. A major interdisciplinary report on Lan-t'ien (IVPP, 1966) was published at the start of the Cultural Revolution and is almost unknown in the United States. As indicated by Howells in the next chapter, two sublocalities yielded the human faunal remains-- Kung-wang-ling and Ch'en-chia-wo. The former local fauna is larger, with 38 mammal species vs. 14 at Ch'en-chia-wo (of which 11 occur at both sites). The two were considered by Wu Hsin-chih in his presentation to be equivalent in age, although this may in part depend on altitudinal and lithologic similarities.

The Lan-t'ien area, like the Ting-ts'un region we visited, is in the loess area of central China. Although this subject also was not discussed with our delegation and best belongs elsewhere in this volume, it may be useful to summarize work reported to the Australian delegation during their visit (Jennings, 1976), as it relates to Pleistocene stratigraphy. At one Shansi locality where the loess thickness reached 134 m, paleomagnetic studies were undertaken, and the units were subdivided as shown in Table 2. If these deposits could be correlated with the fossiliferous sequences of Lan-t'ien and elsewhere, it would be a major step in calibrating the Chinese Pleistocene. Jennings further indicated that the Ma-lan loess may overlie fluvial gravels of the Sjara-osso-gol Formation, dated by its mammalian fossils to the late Pleistocene; he also discussed the question of loess origin.

Finally, there are many karst and other isolated deposits in South

TABLE 2 Litho-, Magneto-, and Chronostratigraphy of a Shansi Loess Section

Subepoch	Loess Formation	Depth, m	Paleomagnetic Epoch	Polarity	Age, m.y.
		0			
Late Pleistocene	Ma-lan	15	Brunhes	N	
Middle	Upper Li-shih	40			
Pleistocene	Lower Li-shih	65 / 74			0.69
Early		100	Matuyama	R	0.89
	Wu-ch'eng	110	(Jaramillo)	N	0.95
Pleistocene			Matuyama	R	
	(Base of section)	134			

China, some of which are mentioned in the section on fossil primates below, as well as a single, relatively well-studied, long sequence at Yüan-mou, Yunnan Province. This area was originally located and prospected by Walter Granger of the American Museum of Natural History in the winter of 1926-1927. He spent "the better part of one day in the vicinity of Ma Kai, northern Yunnan, where in a valley there was found a rather extensive deposit containing Pleistocene fossils," which were briefly described by Colbert (1940, p. 1). The current status of work here was reported to us at the IVPP by Chou Kuo-hsing. In recent years, the area has become more widely known as a result of the discovery in 1965 of two incisors referred to *Homo erectus* (see Howells) by Ch'ien Fang, of the Academy of Geological Sciences, Ministry of Geology (Hu, 1973). It is interesting that these are apparently the only human fossils of significant antiquity that are stored at the institute that discovered them instead of the IVPP. In 1967-68, during the Cultural Revolution, field teams of the IVPP made large collections of mammalian and other fossils (mollusks, pollen, and spores), butno further hominid remains were reported.

The Yüan-mou sequence is located in an oval basin about 1,100 m in elevation, some 30 km long north-south and 7 km wide east-west. The west flank, 1,400 m high, is older rocks, the 2,700-m east flank being Jurassic red beds. Four formations were recognized in the basin, as indicated in Table 3. The age of the Yüan-mou Formation is variously considered as early Pleistocene or early middle Pleistocene; perhaps it spans the local boundary, with the human teeth from the younger, upper part. Mammalian fossils from this region have been discussed recently by You and Qi (1973), Liu *et al*. (1973), Tang *et al*. (1974a), and Liu and You (1974). Professor K. C. Chang has informed me that a recent newspaper article reported that paleomagnetic studies undertaken in the Yüan-mou region resulted in dating between 1 and 2 million years (Matuyama reversed epoch) and an approximate date of 1.4 million years for the Yüan-mou Formation (perhaps the upper part with the hominid fossils).

A REVIEW OF NONHUMAN FOSSIL PRIMATES FROM CHINA

In keeping with the broad interpretation of paleoanthropology underlying our visit, some study was attempted of the earliest known representatives of primates in China, as well as examination of younger forms more closely related to, or occurring in association with, early man. Fossils representing 15 genera have been claimed to occur in China, but of these one genus (perhaps a second and third) is not a primate, while two others are synonyms. Each will be discussed in turn, following a "strato-taxonomic" sequence.

Fossil specimens were made available for our examination at the IVPP and also at the Chou-k'ou-tien research station. During our visit to the old IVPP building, we were invited to indicate our interest in observing any of the many specimens on exhibit in the museum area. Here were stored the type and figured specimens of the early Tertiary primates, as well as a few pieces from Chou-k'ou-tien. At the Chou-k'ou-tien institute we were also asked if we wished to see any specific

TABLE 3 Yüan-mou District, Yunnan, Summarized Section

Formation Name	Age	Thickness, m	Contents, comments, lithology
	"Holocene"		Neolithic
Wa-cha-ch'ing	Late Pleistocene	10	Terrace deposits, overlaps others
(erosional interval)			
Lao-hung-kou	Middle Pleistocene	25	
(erosional interval)			
Yüan-mou	Early or early middle Pleistocene	126	Hominid incisors in upper clay layer; most fossils in upper 70 m of fine sands and yellow clays
			Lower 50 m coarser sands and red clays
			Basal 8 m gravels, variegated clays (compared to Pinjor and Lower Irrawady)
(tectonic activity)			
Sha-kou	Late Pliocene	30	
Pre-Cambrian basement complex			

specimens, and those available were brought out for examination. Unfortunately, it was not possible to see the collection storage facilities, a kind of "locality" where many important discoveries may be made, simply by rummaging in drawers and locating possibly misidentified or misplaced older specimens.

Early and Middle Tertiary Primates

Since Liberation, early Tertiary primate fossils have been found at three localities, including one which had been productive earlier in the century. According to conversations with Chou Ming-chen, both

during our joint examination of the fossils and in the course of our
stay in the Peking area, some revision of previous age estimates has
been made for the three localities involved. These are based on re-
interpretation of the faunal assemblages, as conveyed to me by Chou
Ming-chen.

The geologically oldest primate fossil is a maxilla fragment with
the right P^4-M^3, IVPP No. V2466, which Chou (1961) named *Lushius
qinlinensis*. The specimen was recovered from the locality of Men-chia-
p'u, in the Lu-shih district of Honan Province (Lu-shih Fm.), the age
of which now appears closely correlative with that of Irdin Manha in
Inner Mongolia, i.e., early late Eocene. As described by Chou, the P^4
is not yet fully erupted, while the M^3 enamel has been broken or eroded
off. The two molars are quite simple in construction, with three main
cusps, moderately developed conules, steep buccal faces, and no clear
hypocone or pericone. There is no concensus as to the affinities of
this primate: Chou (1961) and Gingerich (1976) considered it a tarsiiform, while Szalay (1974), the major modern student of fossil tarsii-
forms classified *Lushius* in Adapidae.

Hoanghonius stehlini was first reported by Zdansky (1930) from the
Yüan-ch'ü Formation of the middle Huang-ho Valley, of supposedly late
Eocene or early Oligocene age. The type mandible and an isolated
upper molar (now in Uppsala, Sweden) were found in the same horizon as
the supposed primate *Adapidium hoanghoense,* now identified as a tillo-
dont (Gazin, 1953). In 1953 Chou collected additional specimens that
were referred to *Hoanghonius* by Woo and Chou (1957). These fossils
were recovered from a locality on the north bank of the Huang Ho River
in Yuanchu district, southern Shansi Province, which is slightly
younger than the type locality (Jen-ts'un, south bank of the Huang Ho
River, Mien-ch'ih district, Honan Province). The two localities are
of similar age, broadly correlative with the site of Shara Murun
(Inner Mongolia), which is later late Eocene. Of the new material, one
specimen is a maxilla fragment with the right P^4-M^1, two are partial
mandibles, and the last is an isolated lower molar. Previous examination of the illustrations in Woo and Chou (1957) had suggested to me,
and to Malcolm McKenna, that the lower teeth referred to *Hoanghonius*
were not primate, but probably artiodactyl. My suggestion of this to
Chou, while we were studying the specimens together, was well received.
We compared the two mandibles to other artiodactyl jaws from this
region, but could not find any which seemed to represent the same taxon.
On the other hand, the maxilla certainly appears to be primate; the M^1,
with clear pericone and hypocone, as well as three main cusps and two
conules, is similar to adapids such as the European late Eocene *Peri-
conodon*. Gingerich (1976) has recently voiced the same opinion, after
study of the type specimen, and Szalay (1974) concurred in a probable
allocation to the Adapidae.

The third of the recently collected early Tertiary Chinese fossil
primates is the most questionable. Chou (1964) described a partial
maxilla with right P^2-M^3 (IVPP No. V2933) as *Lantianius xiehuensis,*
a possible adapid. The specimen was collected from the early Tertiary
horizons underlying the *Homo erectus* locality near Ch'en-chia-wo, in
the Kung-kou-wan ravine locality, Hsieh-hu commune, Lan-t'ien district,

Shensi Province. The age was uncertain; it was suggested to be late
Eocene, but recent work has revised this to early Oligocene. The morphology of the anterior premolars had suggested to me, McKenna, and
Szalay that this specimen might be artiodactyl, but in discussion Chou
and I could not be certain either way. More recently, Gingerich (1976)
has written a convincing interpretation of *Lantianius,* based on Chou's
figures and descriptions, in which he argues it to be a dichobunid
artiodactyl because of premolar morphology and large infraorbital foramen. There thus remain only three or four Eocene primate specimens
from China: *Lushius,* represented by a single maxilla, either an adapid
or a tarsiiform; and *Hoanghonius,* represented by the type mandible, a
new maxilla and perhaps the originally referred upper molar, a latest
Eocene adapid. It is greatly hoped that the newly reported Eo-Oligocene
deposits from the Pai-se and Yung-lo basins in Kwangsi Chuang Autonomous
Region (Tang *et al.,* 1974b) will yield some primates, especially as they
are similar in faunal content to the Pondaung Formation of Burma, which
includes the lemuriform *Amphipithecus* and the possible haplorhine
Pondaungia.

Turning to the middle Tertiary, no undoubted primate occurs in the
Oligocene or early to middle Miocene, but two specimens that might belong to the order have been reported from the region of Taben-Buluk in
western Kansu (Bohlin, 1946). An edentulous and damaged mandibular
symphysis and a fragment, possibly of the distal quarter of a lower
molar crown, were described by Bohlin and identified as "Kansupithecus,"
a specific name being omitted "to emphasize that the name at present
must be regarded merely as a term comparable with the local names given
to geological formations" (p. 238). This specimen has been returned to
the IVPP from Uppsala, but unfortunately it could not be located for my
examination in Peking. A cast and Bohlin's figures suggest the possibility of catarrhine relationships in the *Pliopithecus*-sized animal,
but, although the canine caliber seems large, there is no sign of the
long mesiobuccal "flange" on P₃ for honing C´ usually seen in catar-
rhines. Conroy and Bown (1976) have recently commented on various
earlier Tertiary Asian primates, concentrating on the age, rather than
the morphology, of "Kansupithecus." Their conclusion was that the
association of a small mastodont, as well as possibly a lagomerycid deer
and a rhinocerotid cf. *Aceratherium,* with "Kansupithecus" combines to
suggest an age of later middle Miocene for this collection, much younger
than Bohlin's suggestion of late Oligocene. No more recent Chinese work
on these deposits was reported to us, although several parties have
collected important specimens in various areas of Kansu.

Old World Monkeys

Procynocephalus

The cercopithecid monkeys are represented by specimens of three genera
in the late Pliocene and Pleistocene deposits of China, and it was in
hope of studying several reported collections of this group that I
first applied to join the delegation. The correlation of Chinese

Plio-Pleistocene fossil assemblages, both within China and beyond, is currently in flux, as much new data have been assembled but not fully interpreted as yet. This is especially true for the older collections, if they have not been resampled or if the fossils were bought rather than obtained *in situ*. The latter appears to have been the case for the first new genus of fossil primate found in China, *Procynocephalus wimani* Schlosser, 1924. The type of this taxon is a female mandible and possibly associated fragments of maxilla from Hsin-an County, Honan Province (Locality 54). The teeth of this specimen(s), studied in Uppsala, are clearly of macaque or baboon type, indicating a representative of the Papionini, but the muzzle and remainder of the skull, so important in generic identification, are lacking. This locality was originally thought to be part of the *"Hipparion*-fauna," that is, late Miocene of modern interpretations, but it is more probably late Pliocene. Of probably similar age is the maxilla fragment from Ku-ti-ts'un, near Ch'ing-shih-ling, Ch'ing-hsing County, Hopei Province, reported by Young and P'ei (1933).

More important, however, are the fragmentary teeth and partial post-cranial material described by Teilhard (1938) from Chou-k'ou-tien Locality 12, again of late Pliocene or early Pleistocene age. The similarity of the damaged teeth to those from the two mentioned sites, as well as the low probability of occurrence of two such similarly sized primates in one region, supports Teilhard's identification of the bones as *P. wimani*. The collection includes complete or partial humerus, ulna, radius, tibia, and various wrist and ankle bones, but no phalanges. Jolly (1967) recognized that Teilhard's two "forms" more probably represented the two sexes of a dimorphic species and further emphasized the strongly terrestrial adaptations of the foot and elbow. Teilhard (1938) further noted the presence of a nearly complete mandible and associated maxilla from Yü-she, southeast Shansi, giving measurements, but this specimen has never been published. Despite attempts by Chou Ming-chen and other members of the IVPP, none of these specimens could be located during our stay in Peking. It is possible that, with the advent of the war, their inherently more "valuable" nature as primates caused the fossils to be given special treatment, resulting in their eventual loss or misplacement. Similarly, we inquired about the Yü-she specimen in Tientsin, where Teilhard indicated it was stored ("Hoangho-Paiho Museum"), but it was not located.

No specimens of *Procynocephalus* have been recovered in China since Liberation, and thus the shape of the skull is still unknown. Jolly (1967), however, assigned to this genus the female partial maxilla, probably from the Pinjor-equivalent levels of the Indian Siwaliks, as *P. subhimalayanus* (von Meyer, 1849), and, more recently, Verma (1969) has described a female mandible from Pinjor as *P. pinjorii*. Verma did not attempt comparison with the older specimen, but there seems little doubt that they represent a single species, although they do not occlude perfectly (being from different individuals). Jolly (1967) and Simons (1970) also suggested that *Procynocephalus* might prove congeneric with *Paradolichopithecus* from the European early Pleistocene. This question is now under study, but a decision is difficult at present because of the lack of relatively complete cranial material from Asia for comparison with the excellent specimens from Europe (see Delson and Nicolaescu-Plopsor, 1975). Both taxa certainly include large terrestrial animals probably descended from macaques, rather than *Papio*-like baboons, but they may represent such a development in parallel. The report by Trofimov and Reshetov (1975) of a nearly complete skull of a similar form in central Asia may be an important link between the two named genera.

Macaca

Several forms of macaque have also been reported from the Chinese Pleistocene. Young and Liu (1950) even named the new taxon *Szechuanopithecus yangtzensis* from the Ko-lo-shan area near Chungking, Szechwan; Koenigswald (1954), however, correctly showed that this genus was based on a wrongly identified dp_4 of a macaque. The first macaque specimen to be reported from China was a male facial fragment described by Schlosser (1924) in the same paper in which he named *P. wimani*. This face was collected (bought?) by Andersson in Mien-ch'ih County, Honan, which may indicate a slightly different age; V. J. Maglio (personal communication, 1971) suggested it to be later early Pleistocene. The specimen is clearly of a macaque, and Schlosser named it *M. anderssoni*, citing only minor differences from other fossil and living species.

A few years later, Zdansky (1928) described fossils from Chou-k'ou-tien, including two human teeth and one lower molar of a cercopithecid. Young (1934) reported a large number of mostly dental specimens of macaque from Chou-k'ou-tien Locality 1, to which he gave the name *Macaca robusta* (*Macacus robustus* in the original). This sample included several mandibles and maxillae, isolated teeth, and a partial humerus (discussed but not figured) but no more complete cranial material. Some years later, P'ei (1936) noted the presence of a nearly complete skull from Locality 1, which to him indicated close relationship with *M. anderssoni*, but this specimen was never described.

Additional specimens of macaque, mostly fragmentary, have been reported from: Chou-k'ou-tien, Locality 2 (Young, 1932); Ch'ing-shih-ling, Ch'ing-hsing County, Hupei Province (Young and P'ei, 1933; age probably later middle Pleistocene); drugstore specimens thought to be from late or later middle Pleistocene caves in Kwangsi (P'ei, 1935); Chou-k'ou-tien, Locality 3 (P'ei, 1936); Hei-ching-lung-ts'un rock shelter, Ch'iu-pei, Yunnan Province (Bien and Chia, 1938; age probably later middle Pleistocene); Tan-yang cave, Kiangsu Province (P'ei, 1940; age later middle Pleistocene); Chou-k'ou-tien Locality 13 (Teilhard and P'ei, 1941; age similar to basal layers of Locality 1); Ho-shang-p'o, near Chungking, Szechwan Province (Young and Mi, 1941; age ?later middle Pleistocene); Ko-lo-shan, near Chungking, Szechwan Province (Young and Liu, 1950 [including "*Szechuanopithecus*"]; age later middle Pleistocene); Liu-ch'eng, "*Gigantopithecus*-caves," Kwangsi Chuang Autonomous Region (P'ei, 1963, and personal communications from IVPP personnel; age ?later early Pleistocene); all levels of Chou-k'ou-tien Locality 1 except 10 and 11 (near the base--the fauna of levels 12-13 is unpublished; Kahlke and Chou, 1961; three caves (Localities 6146, 6148, 6151) in northeast

Kwangsi (Wu *et al.*, 1962; age ?later middle Pleistocene); Shu-an cave, N. Kwangtung (Liu, 1962; age ?later middle Pleistocene); Hsien-jen cave, near Wan-nien, Kiangsi (Huang and Chi, 1963; "Holocene"); Kung-wang-ling, Lan-t'ien district, Shensi Province (Chou *et al.*, 1965; age ?early-middle middle Pleistocene); Wu-ming, Kwangsi Chuang Autonomous Region (Chang *et al.*, 1973; age ?mid-middle Pleistocene); Pa-ma district, Kwangsi Chuang Autonomous Region (Chang *et al.*, 1975; age ?mid-middle Pleistocene); and Ch'ai-yen-shan in Yung-an, Fukien Province (Young *et al.*, 1975; age probably later middle Pleistocene). The macaque tentatively identified at Ho-shang-tung cave, Yunnan Province (Young, 1932; Bien and Chia, 1938) is probably better identified as a *Rhinopithecus* (see below).

During our stay in Peking, I requested permission to examine any of the above material that was available (the Yung-an find had not yet been published). Unfortunately, much of the older collections, especially from Chou-k'ou-tien, appears to have suffered the same fate as did *Procynocephalus*. Despite searches by the IVPP personnel, I was shown only one mandible (C1822) and one maxilla (C1817) from Chou-k'ou-tien Locality 1 and the male partial maxilla reported from Kung-wang-ling (uncatalogued, Locality V67306). While at the Chou-k'ou-tien site, I was permitted to examine a mandible from Locality 1 (51:8:H1, collected in 1951) and a mandible and somewhat damaged skull, perhaps of a single individual, from Locality 13 (55.5.10, collected in 1955). On the other hand, in the collections of the Department of Vertebrate Paleontology of the American Museum of Natural History, I have located casts of a subadult slightly crushed female mandible (36:62 C-2) and what must be the skull mentioned by P'ei (1936), damaged somewhat but essentially undeformed (34:13:1).

Having examined briefly the specimens now available in China, I am at present studying these casts and will compare them with the type facial fragment of *M. anderssoni* (studied in Uppsala) and with the skull from Tung-Lang, northern Vietnam, which Jouffroy named *Macaca speciosa subfossilis*. Preliminary examination suggests similarities with the living *M. thibetana* and/or *M. arctoides* (ex-*M. speciosa*). In his original paper, Young (1934) did not formally designate a type specimen of *Macaca robusta,* but the female maxilla C1817 was well figured, has the first (lowest) catalog number in the syntype series, and is among the few extant specimens from this series. I therefore suggest designating that specimen as the lectotype in a more formally systematic publication. Today, macaques range in China as far north as the Yangtze, with small enclaves just north of the Yangtze in Szechwan and in northern Hupei, southwest of Peking (P'ei, 1963; Hill, 1974). The known fossils suggest continuity over this range and perhaps habitation further north along the coast (Tan-yang, near Nanking), but the probability of a different species-group.

It is also of some interest to mention a specimen seen in the collections of the Department of Geology, Northwestern University, Sian, Shansi Province. While looking at fossils on exhibit from a number of sites, we noticed a partial mandible of a primate which Hsüeh Hsiang-hsi was kind enough to permit me to examine briefly. The jaw was eroded and the teeth were quite worn; the jaw was broken distal to the right P_4

and the left M_3; and the left C_1-P_4 and M_{2-3} were at least partly present. The specimen was certainly of a cercopithecine monkey, best tentatively identified as cf. *Macaca* sp. (neither very large nor very small for the genus). The specimen was in a case with (and stated to be associated with) specimens identified as *Megantereon, Eomellivora,* and a schizotherine chalicothere, with an age of "early Pliocene" (late Miocene) given for the locality (Wu-tu, in Kansu Province). If the jaw is indeed that old, it is the oldest known monkey anywhere in Asia, perhaps anywhere outside Africa. Otherwise, the oldest known cercopithecid in Asia is ?*Presbytis sivalensis* (*Cercopithecus* or *Presbytis asnoti* and *Macaca sivalensis*) from the Dhok Pathan of Hasnot, Pakistan. The oldest Asian cercopithecine on present evidence is ?*Macaca* (ex-*Semnopithecus*) *palaeindica*, apparently from the Tatrot Formation, India. It is interesting that the Wu-tu jaw was the only fossil primate we saw outside the IVPP, except for several teeth of *Gigantopithecus* (at least one possibly in fact an orang) in the Department of Anatomy of Fu-tan University on teaching exhibition. I understand that Hsüeh plans to describe this fossil and others in due course.

Rhinopithecus

A third monkey is also present in some Chinese Pleistocene fossil faunas, but rarely. This is the colobine *Pygathrix* (*Rhinopithecus*) sp. (see Groves, 1970, on subgeneric rank). Matthew and Granger (1923) first named *Rhinopithecus tingianus* from the (earlier) middle Pleistocene fissure of Yen-ching-kou (I), Wan Hsein (county), Szechwan Province, on the basis of a partial juvenile skull and several jaw fragments (American Museum of Natural History, New York). Colbert and Hooijer (1953) later suggested this form to be a subspecies of *R. roxellanae,* while Groves (1970) has considered it as *P.* (*R.*) *brelichi tingianus,* referring it to the living species closest in geographic distribution. *P.* (*Rhinopithecus*) sp. has also been reported from the Liu-ch'eng "*Gigantopithecus*-cave" and perhaps other Kwangsi caves (P'ei, 1963) and from T'ung-tzu in Kweichou Province (Wu *et al.,* 1975; age ?later middle Pleistocene), while the specimen figured as *Macaca* sp. from Ho-shang-tung cave, Yunnan Province by Young (1932; also noted in list by Bien and Chia, 1938; ?mid-middle Pleistocene) is most probably *P.* (*Rhinopithecus*) on size and morphology. According to P'ei (1963; see also Groves, 1970), the distribution of *P.* (*Rhinopithecus*) today includes that known from the sparse fossil record, limited to southern China.

Fossil Hominoidea

Gibbon and Orangutan

A number of hominoid (but nonhuman) primates are also present in Chinese fossil faunas, including two living and four extinct genera. Of the former, *Hylobates* is the rarer. Matthew and Granger (1923) reported a partial mandible from Yen-ching-kou (I), Szechwan, which they named

Bunopithecus sericus. Groves (1972) has suggested it to be a subspecies of *H. (H.) hoolock,* but it is best considered as merely *Hylobates* sp. until more material permits specific (and subgeneric) identification (see also Colbert and Hooijer, 1953). More recently, Lin *et al.* (1974) have discussed and figured a single upper molar of *Hylobates* sp. cf. *H. concolor* from a possibly later middle Pleistocene locality in Kwangsi; Chang *et al.* (1975) reported some teeth from the Pa-ma *Gigantopithecus* site in Kwangsi (mid?-middle Pleistocene); and Wu *et al.* (1975) indicated *Hylobates* sp. in their faunal list from T'ung-tzu, Kweichou Province (?later middle Pleistocene). Groves (1972) indicates that, while gibbons (*H. concolor*) today are restricted to southern Yunnan, there is evidence that they existed along the Yangtze in Szechwan and perhaps Hupei, in southern Kwangsi, Kwantung, and perhaps northern Kiangsi in historical times, thus including the range of the known fossils.

The prehistoric distribution of the orangutan (*Pongo pygmaeus*) has recently been reviewed by Kahlke (1972), who summarizes most of the previous reports for China as well as southeastern Asia. Hooijer (1948) termed some Chinese material *P. p. weidenreichi,* but Kahlke doubted the distinction of this subspecies from evidence so far available. Orang remains have been reported to date from the Ho-shang-tung cave, Yunnan Province (Young, 1932; Bien and Chia, 1938; ?mid-middle Pleistocene); Hsing-an cave E, near Kuei-lin, Kwangsi Chuang Autonomous Region (P'ei, 1935; later middle Pleistocene); Shao-ch'un (Shao-hsin) cave, Kwangtung Province (Chang, 1959; ?later middle Pleistocene); Liu-ch'eng (*Giganto-pithecus*-cave," Kwangsi Chuang Autonomous Region (Kahlke, 1961; P'ei, 1963; ?later early Pleistocene); Niu-shui-shan, Ta-hsin (*Gigantopithecus* site), Kwangsi Province (Kahlke, 1961; ?mid-middle Pleistocene); Chai-ts'un cave, Kwangsi (Wu *et al.,* 1962; age uncertain, probably later middle Pleistocene--Kahlke [1972] includes this site and the next two in the late Pleistocene, along with all the others except Liu-ch'eng, while the Chinese consider some of these to be of even earlier middle Pleisto-cene age); Shu-an cave, N. Kwangtung (Liu, 1962; age as above); Fei-shu cave, Kwangsi (unpublished, noted in Kahlke, 1972); Pa-ma district (Kwangsi) *Gigantopithecus* site (Chang *et al.,* 1975; ?mid-middle Pleisto-cene); and T'ung-tzu, Kweichou Province (Wu *et al.,* 1975; age ?later middle Pleistocene). Today, of course, the orangutan is restricted to Borneo and Sumatra, but it extended in the middle (and early?) Pleisto-cene into southern China, probably contracting its range south through the late Pleistocene--Kahlke (1972) reported some "postglacial" teeth from northern Vietnam, so it remained on the mainland at least that long.

Miocene Hominoids

Among extinct Chinese hominoids, the most questionable is Schlosser's (1924) report of *Pliopithecus posthumus* from the probably Pliocene deposits of Ertemte, Mongolia. I have studied the single worn upper molar (in Uppsala), but I must follow previous workers in questioning its identification at present. It could possibly represent a suid, a hominoid, or some other mammal.

More interesting are two lots of associated lower teeth from the Hsiao-lung-t'an lignite, K'ai-yüan district, Yunnan Province. The most recent review of the Hsiao-lung-t'an fauna (Chang, 1974) suggests a later middle Miocene, pre-*Hipparion* date, comparable to the Chinji "zone" of the Siwaliks. The primates were first reported by Woo (1957), who described five lower cheek teeth as *Dryopithecus keiyuanensis,* comparing them mainly with Siwalik *D. punjabicus;* five more teeth were reported later (Woo, 1958), with a larger size attributed to sexual dimorphism. Chou (1958) and later Simons and Pilbeam (1965) considered that the first set was indistinguishable from *D. punjabicus,* which Simons (1964) had transferred to *Ramapithecus,* while the larger teeth might be of *Dryopithecus* cf. *sivalensis.* Given the present state of our understanding of intraspecific variability of *Dryopithecus,* I consider it doubtful that the two lots of teeth are conspecific, their size differences being larger than that due only to sexual dimorphism. Instead, I would concur with earlier workers that two species are present. Professor Woo (Wu) Ju-kang was aware of these arguments, but perhaps more prudently he preferred to recognize only one species for the finds.

Only brief notes might be added to Woo's excellent descriptions: the set of larger teeth (catalogued as PA 82, not An-612, the cast number used by Simons and Pilbeam, 1965) includes the right P_3-M_3, probably of a single individual, with cingulum almost nonexistent; these teeth are most similar in size and morphology to those now termed *D. indicus* (a cast of American Museum of Natural History no. 19413, the "type" of "*D frickae,*" was used for comparison), except that P_4 is somewhat shorter and broader; I would thus identify this specimen as *Dryopithecus* cf. *indicus.* The original lot of teeth (PA 75/1-5), the type of *D. keiyuanensis,* consists of the damaged right and left P_4 (75-1 and 75-2) and the complete R M_2 (75-3), L M_2 (75-4) and R M_3 (75-5), presumably of a single individual of unknown sex. The teeth compare favorably in size and form with those of *R. punjabicus* from the Siwaliks, being rather larger than those of *D. laietanus* and somewhat smaller than those of *D. sivalensis,* as well as rather straight-sided as in *Ramapithecus.* This association of *Dryopithecus* cf. *indicus* and cf. *Ramapithecus punjabicus* is mirrored to the west in the Siwaliks and in sites of roughly equivalent age in central Turkey. These specimens represent the farthest eastward extent of the two genera now known and demonstrate once again an association with a forest fauna. Newspaper reports (indicated to me by Professor K. C. Chang) announced the recent recovery of numerous additional specimens whose publication is eagerly awaited.

Gigantopithecus

The most fascinating of Chinese nonhuman primates (and perhaps of all Chinese fossils) is, of course, *Gigantopithecus.* As is by now well known, von Koenigswald (1935) found the first reported specimen, an isolated M_3, in a group of "dragon bones" bought in a Chinese pharmacy in Hong Kong in 1935 (see von Koenigswald, 1952, for a brief history). He recovered numerous other isolated teeth in his "drugstore fauna" and described all those in his possession (eight) in 1952. In 1955 (see P'ei,

1957), the IVPP began an intensive campaign to discover the exact source, age, and affinities of *Gigantopithecus blacki,* which had previously been considered everything from an aberrant giant ape to the ancestor of man. The source of the fossils was traced to the southern provinces of Kwangtung and Kwangsi, and in 1956 three molar teeth were found *in situ* in a cave variously termed the Hei-tung (Black cave) on Niu-shui-shan Hill in Ta-hsin district of southern Kwangsi.

The next year, P'ei led the Kwangsi working team back to explore other regions of the province. A farmer digging for fertilizer in a cave in Liu-ch'eng district in central Kwangsi "discovered a quantity of fossil bones and, being persuaded by a governmental employee, presented all the fossil bones to Academia Sinica for investigation" (P'ei, 1957, p. 66). This cave, now termed *Gigantopithecus*-cave number 1, is located about 90 m above present ground level in an isolated hill or karst tower known as Leng-chai-shan about 0.5 km south of Hsin-shüeh-chün-ts'un village. The plan of the cave and an interpretation of its formation were presented by P'ei (1957, 1965) and most recently by White (1975). Between 1956 and 1960, three partial mandibles and 984 isolated teeth of *G. blacki* were found in this cave. A second cave (number 2) yielded an additional 22 teeth in 1959-1960, while 48 teeth were recovered from the Kwangsi and Kwangtung drugstore supply houses. All of these specimens were described, many illustrated, and all original measurements were given by Woo (1962). Eckhardt (1973) has recently summarized the measurements and provided some statistics that Woo did not calculate.

Three additional small collections of *Gigantopithecus* teeth have been reported in recent years, and these materials were discussed with us in Peking by Chang Yin-yün. In 1964-1966, an IVPP team found 13 teeth in the Wu-ming district of Kwangsi Chuang Autonomous Region (Chang *et al.,* 1973). An additional M$_3$ was found in a karst cave in Pa-ma district in 1973 (Chang *et al.,* 1975). Most interesting of all is the association of five teeth of *G. blacki* with four molars of a smaller hominid primate (see below) in Dragon Bone cave, Chien-shih district, western Hupei Province (Hsu *et al.,* 1974; "Gao Jian," 1975).

The precise age of these faunal assemblages has been discussed by many workers, but the current opinion in the IVPP seems to follow Chou (1958) in assigning a (later) early Pleistocene date to the Liu-ch'eng cave(s). *Mastodon, Tapirus (?Megatapirus), Doracabune, Hystrix magna, Ailuropoda microta,* and *Stegodon praeorientalis* are all present in Liu-ch'eng but absent in typical middle Pleistocene sites in southern China, including Ta-hsin, Wu-ming, and Pa-ma (see also Kahlke, 1961). Of these, only a mastodont appears to be present at Chien-shih (Hsu *et al.,* 1974), but Chang and Chou both indicated that the latter was of intermediate age, and Chou suggested it would be close to the local early-middle Pleistocene "boundary."

As to the fossils themselves, they have recently come back into the spotlight as several authors have tried to suggest that *G. blacki,* or at least *G. bilaspurensis* (=? *giganteus*), might have been ancestral to later hominids. Corruccini (1975), Delson and Andrews (1975), and others have echoed Pilbeam (1970) in rejecting this view, arguing that *Gigantopithecus* possessed a number of fundamental adaptations demonstrating it to be far removed from relationship with the ancestry of *Homo* (see discussion in Delson *et al.*, 1977). As to the argument that if size alone is considered, *G. blacki* might well have reduced its dentition to the size seen in *Australopithecus* or *Homo* in the time allowed with only a small change per generation, this is essentially irrelevant. Following such an argument, it could be suggested that *Hyracotherium* of the early Eocene was in fact the ancestor of *Homo* (or any other mammal one chose), as the size changes required would be infinitesimal per generation. This view completely ignores morphology and its indication of adaptations and relationships in favor of a dependence on "might have beens" and simplistic analysis of measurements.

One point can be emphasized about the measurements of *G. blacki*, and that is the great variability to be seen in the Liu-ch'eng specimens. It is difficult to accept that a single species could have had such a spread of size as that observed. On the other hand, I plotted a histogram of P_4 length and width as given by Woo (1962), finding that there was no clear indication of polymodality, only a smear of both dimensions. It is possible that two similarly sized taxa are present, so that their overlap produces high but reasonable coefficients of variation (around 10), and in fact Woo grouped specimens into two lots, thinking they were sexes; it is also possible that a long interval is represented, with size varying over time. Only more detailed study of the range of *morphological* variation will allow a further comment on this problem.

It can further be mentioned that the teeth from Pa-ma and Wu-ming appear somewhat larger than those from Liu-ch'eng, suggesting to Chang *et al.* (1975) that the species may have increased in size, rather than decreasing with time, although the small younger samples do not permit confident assertions. As they noted, this is another argument against the idea of Weidenreich (1945) and others that *G. blacki* might have been ancestral to *Homo*. The apparent complete lack of cranial and postcranial elements is a final most perplexing aspect of the taphonomy of *Gigantopithecus*.

SUMMARY

In this chapter I have tried to indicate the main locales of vertebrate paleontological research in China and their interests; to summarize some of the most important recent results, concentrating on Paleocene mammal finds and Plio-Pleistocene faunal and stratigraphic studies; and to review all known occurrences of nonhuman primates. The first section draws heavily on what I and other delegation members actually saw and were told in China, while the second includes much from the literature and also from the report of the Australian Quaternary delegation, which visited China in late 1975. The detailed discussion of fossil primates is based on both literature and first-hand studies, in China and elsewhere. By way of further summary of this latter section, I have prepared a tentative correlation chart of late Pliocene and Pleistocene localities yielding nonhuman fossil primates (Table 4) and a brief classification of known taxa, with localities indicated for pre-Pliocene forms (Table 5).

TABLE 4 Outline Stratigraphic Distribution of Chinese Plio-Pleistocene
Nonhuman Fossil Primates

Age	Localities and Included Primates[a]
"Holocene"	Hsien-jen (M)
Late Pleistocene	
Later middle Pleistocene	Ch'ing-shih-ling (M) Fei-shu (P) Hei-ching-lung-ts'un (M) Ho-shang-p'o (M) Hsing-an Cave E (P) Ko-lo-shan (M) Kwangsi Cave localities 6146, 6148, 6151 (M) Shao-ch'un (P) Shu-an (M,P) Tan-ying (M) T'ung-tzu (H,P,R) Yung-an (M) Chai-ts'un (P) [??Kwangsi Cave (H)]
Mid-middle Pleistocene	Chou-k'ou-tien localities 1 (M) 2 (M) 3 (M) 13 (M) Kung-wang-ling (M) Ho-shang-tung (P,R)
Early middle Pleistocene	Pa-ma (G,H,M,P) Ta-hsin (G,P) Wu-ming (G,M) Yen-ching-kou I (H,R) Chien-shih (G)
Early Pleistocene	Liu-ch'eng (G,M,P,R) Mien-ch'ih (M)
Late Pliocene	Chou-k'ou-tien 12 (Pc) Hsin-an (Pc) Ku-ti-ts'un (Pc) Yü-she (Pc)

[a]Key to abbreviations for primate fossil taxa: G = *Gigantopithecus*,
H = *Hylobates*, M = *Macaca*, P = *Pongo*, Pc = *Procynocephalus*, R = *Pygathrix (Rhinopithecus)*.

Note: Localities grouped in a single age range are approximately the
same age, except where separated by spacing. Thus, Ch'ing-shih-ling
and Chai-ts'un are roughly the same age, but Chien-shih is older than
Yen-ching-kou.

60

TABLE 5 Outline Annotated Classification of Chinese Fossil Primates

Taxon	Localities	Stratigraphic Age
Adapidae		
Lushius qinlinensis	Men-chia-p'y	Early late Eocene
Hoanghonius stehlini	Jen-ts'un, new locality	Late late Eocene
Cercopithecidae		
Procynocephalus wimani	see Table 4	Late Pliocene-early Pleistocene
Macaca spp. (incl. *M. anderssoni, M. robusta,* etc.)	see Table 4	?Early Pleistocene-modern
?*Macaca* sp. indet.	Wu-tu	?Late Miocene
Pygathrix (*Rhinopithecus*) sp.	see Table 4	Pleistocene-modern
Hominidae (*sensu* Delson and Andrews, 1975)		
Hylobates sp. (incl. *Bunopithecus sericus,* etc.)	see Table 4	Middle Pleistocene-modern
Pongo pygmaeus	see Table 4	Pleistocene
Dryopithecus (*S.*) cf. *indicus* (= *D. keiyuanensis* partim)	Hsiao-lung-t'an	Late middle Miocene
Gigantopithecus blacki	see Table 4	Early middle Pleistocene
cf. *Ramapithecus punjabicus* (= *D. keiyuanensis* type)	Hsiao-lung-t'an	Late middle Miocene
?Anthropoidea incertae sedis		
"Kansupithecus"	Taben Buluk region	?Middle Miocene
?Artiodactyla		
Lantianius xiehuensis	K'ung-kou-wan	Early Oligocene
Order incertae sedis		
Pliopithecus posthumus	Ertemte	?Pliocene

REFERENCES

Bien, M. N., and Chia Lan-po. 1938. Cave and rock-shelter deposits in Yunnan. Bull. Geol. Soc. China 18:325-348.

Bohlin, B. 1946. The fossil mammals from the Tertiary deposit of Taben-buluk, western Kansu. II. Simplicidentata, Carnivora, Artiodactyla, Perissodactyla and Primates. Paleontol. Sinica, New Series C, (8b)1-255.

Chang Y. P. Pleistocene mammals from Shaoshan, Kwangtung. Paleovert. Paleoanthropol. 1:141-144. Peking (In Chinese), no summary.

Chang Yin-yun, Wu Mao-lin, and Liu C-j. 1973. New discovery of *Gigantopithecus* teeth from Wuming, Kwangsi. Kexue Tongbao (Science Bulletin) 18:130-133. (No summary).

Chang Yin-yun, Wang Ling-hong, Dong Xing-ren, and Chen Wen-chun. 1975. Discovery of a *Gigantopithecus* tooth from Bama district in Kwangsi. Vert. Palas. 13:148-154. (English summary).

Chang Yu-ping. 1974. Miocene suids from Kaiyuan, Yunnan and Linchu, Shantung. Vert. Palas. 12:117-125. (English summary).

Chao, E. 1973. Contacts with earth scientists in the People's Republic of China. Science 179:961-963.

Chi Hung-xiang. 1974. Late Pleistocene mammals from Lantian, Shensi. Vert. Palas. 12:222-228. (English abstract).

Chi Hung-xiang. 1975. The Lower Pleistocene mammalian fossils of Lantian district, Shensi. Vert. Palas. 13:170-177. (English abstract).

Chou Minchen M. 1958. Mammalian faunas and correlation of Tertiary and Early Pleistocene of South China. J. Pal. Soc. India 3:123-130.

Chou Minchen M. 1961. A new tarsioid primate from the Lushi Eocene, Honan. Vert. Palas. 5:1-5. (English summary).

Chou Minchen M. 1964. A lemuroid primate from the Eocene of Lantian, Shensi. Vert. Palas. 8:256-262. (English summary).

Chou Minchen M., and Chang Feng. 1973. Notes from IVPP. Vert. Palas. 11:229-230.

Chou Minchen M., Hu Chang-kang, and Lee Yu-ching. 1965. Mammalian fossils associated with the hominid skull cap of Lantian, Shensi. Scientia Sinica 14:1037-1048.

Chou Minchen M., Chang Yu-ping, Wang Ban-yue, and Ting Su-yin. 1973. New mammalian genera and species from the Paleocene of Nanhsiung, N. Kwangtung. Vert. Palas. 11:31-35. (English summary).

Colbert, E. H. 1940. Pleistocene mammals from the Ma Kai Valley of southern Yunnan, China. Am. Mus. Novit. 1099:1-10.

Colbert, E. H., and D. A. Hooijer. 1953. Pleistocene mammals from the limestone fissures of Szechuan, China. Bull. Am. Mus. Nat. Hist. 102:1-134.

Conroy, G., and T. M. Bown. 1976. Anthropoid origins and differentiation: the Asian question. Yearb. Phys. Anthropol. 18:1-6.

Corruccini, R. S. 1976. Multivariate analysis of *Gigantopithecus* mandibles. Am. J. Phys. Anthropol. 42: 167-170.

Delson, E. 1976. Aspects of vertebrate paleontology in the People's Republic of China. News Bull. Soc. Vert. Paleontol. 106:39-43.

62

Delson, E., and P. Andrews. 1975. Evolution and interrelationships of the catarrhine primates, pp. 405-446. *In* W. P. Luckett and F. S. Szalay, eds. Phylogeny of the primates: A multidisciplinary approach. Plenum Press, New York.

Delson, E. and D. Nicolaescu-Plopsor. 1975. *Paradolichopithecus,* a large terrestrial monkey (Cercopithecidae, Primates) from the Plio-Pleistocene of southern Europe and its importance for mammalian bio-chronology. Reports, VIth Congress Regional Committee of Mediterranean Neogene Stratigraphy, Bratislava. pp. 91-96.

Delson, E., N. Eldredge, and I. M. Tattersall. 1977. Reconstruction of hominid phylogeny: A testable framework based on cladistic analysis. J. Hum. Evol. 6:263-278.

Eckhardt, R. B. 1973. *Gigantopithecus* as a hominid ancestor. Anthropol. Anzeiger 34:1-8.

"Gao Jian." 1975. Australopithecine teeth associated with *Gigantopithecus*. Vert. Palas. 13:81-88. (English summary).

Gazin, C. L. 1953. The Tillodontia: an early Tertiary order of mammals. Smithson. Misc. Collect. 121(10):1-110.

Gingerich, P. D. 1976. Systematic position of the alleged primate *Lantianius xiehuensis* Chow, 1964, from the Eocene of China. J. Mammal. 57:194-198.

Groves, C. P. 1970. The forgotten leaf-eaters and the phylogony of Colobinae, pp. 557-587. *In* J. R. Napier and P. H. Napier, eds., Old World Monkeys. Academic Press, New York.

Groves, C. P. 1972. Systematics and phylogeny of gibbons. Gibbon Siamang 1:1-89.

Hill, W. C. O. 1974. Primates, comparative anatomy and taxonomy. VII. Cynopithecinae: Cercocebus, Macaca, Cynopithecus. John Wiley & Sons, New York.

Hooijer, D. A. 1948. Prehistoric teeth of man and the orangutan from central Sumatra, with notes on the fossil orangutan from Java and southern China. Zool. Meded. Rijk Mus. Nat. Hist. Leiden 29:175-301.

Hope, J. 1976. Quaternary vertebrate palaeontology. Aust. Quat. Newsl. 7:22-27.

Hsu Chun-hua, Han Kang-xin, and Wang Ling-hong. 1974. Discovery of *Gigantopithecus* teeth and associated fauna in western Hopei. Vert. Palas. 12:293-309. (No abstract).

Hu Cheng-chih. 1973. Ape-man teeth from Yuanmou, Yunnan. Acta Geol. Sinica 1:67-71. (English summary).

Huang Wan-po, and Chi Hung-xiang. 1963. Note on Holocene Hsienjen cave deposit Wannian, Kiangsi. Vert. Palas. 7:263-272. (English summary).

IVPP. 1966. The Cenozoic in Lan-t'ien, Shensi. Science Press, Peking.

Jennings, J. N. 1976. Quaternary stratigraphy. Aust. Quat. Newsl. 7:10-21.

Jolly, C. J. 1967. The evolution of the baboons, pp. 23-50. *In* H. Vagtborg, ed. The baboon in medical research, vol. II. University of Texas Press, Austin.

Kahlke, H. D. 1961. On the complex of the *Stegodon-Ailuropoda*-fauna of southern China and the chronological position of *Gigantopithecus blacki* v. Koenigswald. Vert. Palas. 5:83-108. (English summary).

Kahlke, H. D. 1972. A review of the Pleistocene history of the orangutan (*Pongo* Lacépède 1799). Asian Perspect. 15:5-14.

Kahlke, H. D., and Chou Ben-shun. 1961. A summary of stratigraphical
and paleontological observations in the lower layers of Choukoutien,
locality 1, and on the chronological position of the site. Vert.
Palas. 5:212-240. (English summary).

"Kao Hung-hsiang." 1975. Paleocene mammal-bearing beds of Chaling
basin, Hunan. Vert. Palas. 13:89-95. (English abstract).

Koenigswald, Gustav Heinrich Ralph von. 1935. Eine fossile Saugetier-
fauna mit *Simia* aus Südchina. Proc. K. Ned. Akad. Wiss. 38:872-879.

Koenigswald, Gustav Heinrich Ralph von. 1952. *Gigantopithecus blacki*
von Koenigswald, a giant fossil hominoid from the Pleistocene of
southern China. Anthropol. Papers Am. Mus. Nat. Hist. 43:291-326.

Koenigswald, Gustav Heinrich Ralph von. 1954. Status of *Szechuanopith-
ccus* from the Pleistocene of China. Nature 173:643-644.

Laboratory of IA and IVPP, Academia Sinica. 1976. The carbon-dating of
bone specimens. Kaogu 1976:28-30.

Li Y-c., Pan C-y., Tsao C-y., Hu C-k., Chou M-l., Chen M-n., Wang S-f.,
and Chang C-l. 1972. Further notes on Quaternary Glaciations in
China. Peking. 7 pp. (Cited by Jennings, 1976).

Lin Yi-pu, Gu Yu-min, and He Nai-han. 1974. Pleistocene gibbon's upper
tooth from Kwangsi, China. Vert. Palas. 12:231-232. (English
abstract).

Lisowski, F. P. 1974. Vertebrate palaeontology and museums in China:
a visitor's view. J. Hong Kong Archaeol. Soc. 5:66-73.

Liu Chang-zhi. 1962 Quaternary mammalian localities of N.-Kwangtung.
Vert. Palas. 6:202-203. (No abstract).

Liu Houyi, and You Yü-zhu. 1974. New materials of *Equus yunnanensis*
in Yuanmou, Yunnan--On diagnosis of *E. yunnanensis* and phylogeny of
Equus in Asia. Vert. Palas. 12:126-136. (No summary).

Liu Houyi, Tang Ying-jun, and You Yü-zhu. 1973. A new species of *Stegodon* from Upper Pliocene of Yuanmou, Yunnan. Vert. Palas. 11:191-200.
(English summary).

Matthew, W. D., and W. Granger. 1923. New fossil mammals from the
Pliocene of Sze-chuan, China. Bull. Am. Mus. Nat. Hist. 48:563-598.

Meyer, Hermann von. 1848. *In* H. G. Bronn, ed., Index Palaeontologicus,
part 1, Nomenclator paleontologicus, second half, N-Z. Schweizerbart,
Stuttgart.

P'ei Wen-chung. 1935. Fossil mammals from the Kwangsi caves. Bull.
Geol. Soc. China 14:413-435.

P'ei Wen-chung. 1936. On the mammalian remains from locality 3 at
Choukoutien. Paleontol. Sinica, C, VII(5):1-120.

P'ei Wen-chung. 1940. Note on a collection of mammal fossils from
Tanyang in Kiangsu province. Bull. Geol. Soc. China 19:379-392.

P'ei Wen-chung. 1957. Discovery of *Gigantopithecus* mandibles and other
material in Liu-cheng district of central Kwangsi in south China.
Vert. Palas. 1:65-70.

P'ei Wen-chung. 1963. Quaternary mammals from the Liucheng *Gigantopithecus* cave and other caves of Kwangsi. Scientia Sinica 12:221-
229 (In Chinese, Vert. Palas. 6:211-218, 1962).

64

Pilbean, D. 1970. *Gigantopithecus* and the origins of Hominidae. Nature 225:516-519.

Schlosser, Max. 1924. Fossil primates from China. Paleontol. Sinica, C, 1(2):1-16.

Section of Ni-ho-wan Cenozoic. 1974. Observations on the later Cenozoic of Nihowan Basin. Vert. Palas. 12:99-110. (No summary).

Simons, E. L. 1964. On the mandible of *Ramapithecus*. Proc. Nat. Acad. Sci., U.S.A. 51:528-535.

Simons, E. L. 1970. The development and history of Old World monkeys (Cercopithecidae, Primates), pp. 97-137. *In* J. R. Napier and P. H. Napier, eds., Old World monkeys. Academic Press, New York.

Simons, E. L., and D. Pilbeam. 1965. Preliminary revision of the Dryopithecinae (Pongidae, Anthropoidea). Folia Primatol. 3:81-152.

Szalay, F. S. 1974. A review of some recent advances in paleoprimatology. Yearb. Phys. Anthropol. 17:39-64.

Tang Ying-jun, You Yü-zhu, Liu Houyi, and Pan Yueren. 1974a. New materials of Pliocene mammals from Banguo Basin of Yuanmou, Yunnan and their stratigraphical significance. Vert. Palas. 12:60-68. (English summary).

Tang Ying-jun, You Yü-zhu, Xü Qin-qi, Qiu Zhu-ding, and Hu Yan-kun. 1974b. The lower Tertiary of the Baise and Yungle basin, Kwangsi. Vert. Palas. 12:279-292. (English summary).

Teilhard de Chardin, P. 1938. The fossils from locality 12 of Choukoutien. Paleontol. Sinica, New Series C, 5:1-46.

Teilhard de Chardin, P., and P'ei Wen-chung. 1941. The fossil mammals from locality 13 of Choukoutien. Paleontol. Sinica, New Series C, 11:1-103.

Trofimov, B. A., and Reshetov, V. Yu. 1975. Asia as the center of mammalian development. Priroda 8(720):32-43. (In Russian).

Verma, B. C. 1969. *Procynocephalus pinjorii,* sp. nov. A new fossil primate from Pinjor beds (Lower Pleistocene) east of Chandigarh. J. Paleontol. Soc. India 13:53-57.

Weidenreich, F. 1945. Giant early man from Java and South China. Anthropol. Papers Am. Mus. Nat. Hist. 40:1-134.

White, Tim. D. 1975. Geomorphology to Paleoecology: *Gigantopithecus* reappraised. J. Hum. Evol. 4:219-233.

Woo Ju-kang. 1957. *Dryopithecus* teeth from Keiyuan, Yunnan province. Vert. Palas. 1:25-32.

Woo Ju-kang. 1958. New materials of *Dryopithecus* from Keiyuan, Yunnan. Vert. Palas. 2:38-43.

Woo Ju-kang. 1962. The mandibles and dentition of *Gigantopithecus*. Paleontol. Sinica, New Series D, 11:1-94. (English summary).

Woo Ju-kang, and Chou Minchen M. 1957. New materials of the earliest primate known in China--*Hoanghonius stehlini*. Vert. Palas. 1:267-272.

Wu Mao-lin, Wang Ling-hong, Chang Ying-yun, and Chang Sen-shui. 1975. Fossil human teeth and associated fauna from western Hupeh. Vert. Palas. 13:14-23. (No abstract).

Wu Xin-zhi, Chao Zi-kuei, Yuan Cheng-sin, and Shen Jia-yu. 1962. Report on a paleoanthropological expedition of the northern part of Kwangsi. Vert. Palas. 6:408-414. (English abstract).

You Yǔ-zhu, and Qi Guo-qin. 1973. New materials of Pleistocene mammals in Yuanmu, Yunnan. Vert. Palas. 11:66-85. (No summary).

Young Chi-cheng, Chi Kou-chin, and Wen Ben-heng. 1975. Quaternary fossils from Yongan, Fujian. Vert. Palas. 13:192-194. (No abstract).

Young Chung-chien. 1932. On some fossil mammals from Yunnan. Bull. Geol. Soc. China 9:383-393.

Young Chung-chien. 1934. On the Insectivora, Chiroptera, Rodentia and Primates other than Sinanthropus from locality 1 at Choukoutien. Paleontol. Sinica, C, VIII(3):1-160.

Young Chung-chien, and Liu P-t. 1950. On the mammalian fauna at Koloshan, near Chungking, Szechuan. Bull. Geol. Soc. China 30:43-90.

Young Chung-chien, and Mi T-h. 1941. Notes on some newly discovered late Cenozoic mammals from southwestern and northwestern China. Bull. Geol. Soc. China 21:97-106.

Young Chung-chien, and P'ei Wen-chung. 1933. On the fissure deposits of Chinghsinghsien with remarks on the Cenozoic geology of the same area. Bull. Geol. Soc. China 13:63-71.

Zdansky, Otto. 1928. Die Saügetiere der Quartärfauna von Chou-kou-tien. Paleontol. Sinica, C, V(4):1-141.

Zdansky, Otto. 1930. Die Alttertiären Saugetiere China nebst stratigraphischen Bemerkungen. Paleontol. Sinica, C, VI(2):1.

HOMINID FOSSILS

W. W. Howells

Important though hominid fossils are, their total number appears small compared to discoveries made since 1949 in Europe and western Asia. The question may be asked: Why have not four or five Chou-k'ou-tiens been found, with corresponding quantities of human remains? Various factors may have operated, such as intensive farming over millennia having obliterated sites and destroyed cave fillings in a search for fertilizer.* It may be that the main explanation is that given by the Chinese themselves: the limited number of professional workers, their preoccupation with museums and other public work, and the social system in general. Finds are made and reported by an increasingly informed peasantry, and investigation is done by professionals in cooperation with the workers. The peasants are concentrated essentially on the arable land, and many important sites may lie in territory unsuitable for farming, as they do in Africa and America. The shortage of professionals and their mission in present Chinese society act to prevent outright prospecting of the sort that has been so productive in East Africa and the kind of intensive excavation that originally produced whole suites of fossil remains at Chou-k'ou-tien (which has done the same since then at places like the La Chaise caves in France or Qafza in Israel). Many of these Western finds are fragmentary, but no more so than Lan-tien, Yuan-mou, or Ting-ts'un, and they are often made at long-known sites, not new ones alone. Only Chou-k'ou-tien seems likely to produce further fossils under systematic excavation comparable to that in the West. Otherwise, for some time to come, finds will be lucky strikes. It seems clear that excavation of sites found, or the search for others, will not be open to foreign investigators such as the Japanese, French, and Americans in Israel or the international teams in Ethiopia.

Before 1949 known hominid fossils from China (including the original *Gigantopithecus* teeth) were all recognized or excavated by foreigners or under their direction (Chou-k'ou-tien plus the Ordos and *Sinanthropus officinalis* teeth). It is a source of satisfaction to the Chinese to

---

*At least one *Gigantopithecus* mandible, as well as the Ma-pa and Liukiang specimens, was found by fertilizer collectors.

have organized conditions for the discovery of more sites, to have collected examples representing a wide time range, and to have published descriptions of them in the course of the 25 years since Liberation. Our delegation was favored by seeing the essential specimens first hand and by being given an overview of Chinese work and interpretation. This was the most complete and intimate contact with scholars and original material our delegation had, and it was most satisfactory.

Because we were not expected to do our own investigations of the materials beyond inspection and note taking (such investigation is reserved for Chinese workers), this report is an attempt to show merely the present position of such studies as seen in first-hand contact and as presented to us by various scholars at the Institute of Vertebrate Paleoanthropology (IVPP). Previous publication is not ignored herein, of course--what is presented is what we saw and heard against this background.

Over several days we met with Chinese scholars in groups or individually at the IVPP. On May 16, after a welcome by Yang Chung-chien, we were given an outline of the history of the Academia Sinica and the IVPP by Chang Li-pin, Responsible Member of the Revolutionary Committee, who reviewed the manyfold growth of the staff since Liberation, the main lines of research, and the place of paleoanthropological work in the interpretation and illustration of political and social theory. Woo Ju-kang later gave us a second introductory review, also making comparisons between pre-Liberation and post-Liberation work and presenting some of the theoretical implications of the discoveries, but mainly outlining the actual finds made, with basic facts of context, in order of geological age (approximately that followed below).

The following day, junior staff members made detailed presentations of particular sites and specimens, with the latter on display. These were made with clarity and enthusiasm (all within the limits imposed by translation), with questions being answered freely and fully, or else with the candid response that they did not have the information wanted. Unfortunately, the exposition had only got approximately through the middle Pleistocene by midafternoon. It was stopped at that point, and other, later fossils were brought out for our inspection. We were able to examine and photograph all the specimens at will in later visits (though not to measure them), but the formal presentations of the finds unfortunately were not resumed. More unfortunately, Professor Woo developed a bad case of bronchitis, and, though he attended some lectures, he was not available for much discussion. I had only a brief talk with him over the Liu-chiang skeleton.

Certain minor specimens mentioned in the literature were not produced and may not have been available. All pre-Holocene human fossils are supposed to be concentrated at IVPP, but there are probably exceptions.

The Pleistocene fossils below are treated concisely, largely from what we were told and saw. Most have been published, in many cases in English in *Vertebrata PalAsiatica*. Basic details on discovery and context of all but the most newly discovered may be found in the recently issued *Catalogue of Fossil Hominids, Part III: America, Asia, Australia*, edited by Oakley, Campbell, and Molleson (1975).

CHIEN-SHIH*

Dragon-bone cave, Chieh-shih (Jianshi) district, Hupei Province. Also Pa-tung district, Hupei Province.

Found by IVPP teams in 1970 and 1968, respectively.

The Chien-shih cave contains not only *Gigantopithecus,* as indicated in the preceding chapter, but also three molariform lower teeth of a hominid, which was published as an "australopithecine" of uncertain affinity ("Gao Jian," 1975; this is a pseudonym for a team of authors, including Han Kan-xin, Wang Ling-hong, and Xu Chun-hua; the "Jian" may refer to Jianshi). The fauna of the cave is listed in Hsu *et al.* (1974; see under *Gigantopithecus* in the preceding chapter, where the age, apparently near the boundary between early and middle Pleistocene, is also discussed). One other tooth was also reported from Pa-tung district in the publication, but, while we were in Peking, this point was not really mentioned and only Chien-shih was discussed. "Gao Jian" also indicates that at least one tooth from Kwangsi may also pertain to this taxon.

The three teeth from Chien-shih could well come from a single individual, as two of them (probably left and right M_2, PA 502 and 503, respectively) have similar occlusal patterns, reflecting what may be pathology involving enamel flaws and formation of an extra crest across the talonid. A good summary in the publication indicates morphological details, while the size of the teeth falls in the overlap zone of South African "robust" and "gracile" australopiths, but somewhat smaller than the largest *Homo erectus* (measurements from Wolpoff, 1971). It is also of interest to note that von Koenigswald (1957a, 1957b) named the new genus and species *Hemanthropus* (ex-*Hemianthropus*) *peii* for a number of "drugstore" hominid teeth probably from south China. These specimens are somewhat larger than the Chien-shih and Pa-tung teeth.

LAN-T'IEN†

Locality 63709, near Ch'en-chia-wo village, ca. 10 km northwest of Lan-t'ien, Shensi.

Found by IVPP team, July 19, 1963, in middle Pleistocene deposits (beginning in the lower Pleistocene) of reddish clay containing many buried soils. Human fossils were found in the lower part of the uppermost of three general members of the whole deposit.

Mandible with almost complete dentition except for some damage. Both M3's were missing, confirmed as agenesis by X-ray. The mandible is believed to be that of an aged female and gives evidence of peridontal disease. Its characters are like those of Peking man except for differences in detail, e.g., level of mental foramen.

*Notes by Eric Delson.

†Based on a lecture by Wu Hsin-chih.

Locality 63706, Kung-wang-ling Hill, 15 km east of Lan-t'ien, Shensi, in the same general level as Lan-t'ien 1. Isolated tooth (M^2) was found in May 1964, and the forepart of a cramium, containing matching M^2 of the other side, was found in excavated material brought back to the laboratory.

The skull is probably that of a female about 30 years old. It is described by Woo Ju-kang (1966) in *Vertebrata PalAsiatica*. With a lower frontal squama and very large and heavy supraorbitals, exceptionally thick vault bone, and missing frontal sinuses, this hominid is considered to be clearly related to but more primitive than the Chou-k'ou-tien population. Woo named it *Homo (Sinanthropus) erectus lantianensis*.

Note: Aigner and Laughlin suggested that the mandible was of younger age than the skull. According to the Chinese this is not the case, since the faunas of the two sites coincide except for a few species and contain a species of elephant unique to both; also the formation is the same at both localities and has been mapped across the interval between them.

YÜAN-MOU*

Yüan-mou District, Yunnan.

Found in 1965 by geologists doing field investigations in a hill site along the bank of the Lung-ch'uan River, at 4000 above sea level. This contains many fissures with mammalian fossils, known for some time. Following the find of human fossils, and during the Cultural Revolution, intensive supplementary excavations were carried out with local support. The stratigraphy was reported to us in some detail. It comprises four formations, the human teeth being recovered from the uppermost part of the Yüan-mou formation, third from the top.

The fauna and stratigraphy suggest a date equivalent to Locality 1 at Chou-k'ou-tien, but the Chinese have suggested the date here to be late early Pleistocene.

Note: in August 1976, the news agency Hsinhua announced a date for Yüan-mou of 1.5 million years, based on paleomagnetism but without amplifying details. (Information from K. C. Chang.)

The hominid remains consist of two teeth, I^1 and I^2, of the left side. The crowns are robust and well preserved. The root of I^2 is thick but not particularly robust. The crowns are thick labiolingually at the base, but, for the size of the teeth, appear to be only moderately thick at the occlusal edge. Shoveling of the lingual surface is marked, with a slight central ridge on this face as well. Wear is distinctly sloping, in a lingual-labial direction, i.e., not edge-to-edge. There are marked wear facets at the central-lateral contact but slight if any wear on I^2 for contact with the canine.

Morphological primitiveness is rated by the Chinese as equivalent to Chou-k'ou-tien *Homo erectus*.

*Based on a lecture by Chou Kuo-hsing.

CHOU-K'OU-TIEN, LOCALITY 1 (EXTENSION)*

Found in 1966 by IVPP excavations of a "fissure" that is separated by a gap from Locus H of Locality 1. The deposit contained Strata 1-4 of the main deposit. The human fossils and some artifacts were found in Stratum 3, and the excavation showed that Locus H belongs to this Stratum, something not previously known.

The stratum and remains suggest a slightly later age than most of the prewar fossils of the main deposit. In general, Strata 1-3 are thought to have been deposited after the roof collapse (Oakley *et al.*, 1975).

The hominid remains consist of: (1) most of the frontal, including the squama and apparently a portion of postcoronal parietal, and the supraorbital torus on both sides; (2) the right half of the occipital, extending to the left beyond the midline, incomplete in the foramen magnum region but apparently including a portion of the parietals above lambda; (3) a premolar tooth. These parts were not in immediate association, being mutually separated by distances on the order of 60 cm.

The vault parts are designated as Skull 5, since they can be associated with parts given this number by Weidenreich, found by him in Locus H. The new occipital fragment articulates perfectly with a cast of the left temporal-parietal-occipital fragment found by Weidenreich in 1934 (PA 74) and also nearly fits the smaller, somewhat eroded right temporal fragment found in 1936 (PA 86 [PA 68 in Oakley *et al.*, 1975]). Weidenreich assigned these parts to the same individual, as Skull V in his Table 1 and elsewhere (1943). He also referred to it as H III, or Skull III Locus H, here and in other publications.

Although the new frontal fragment is separated from the other parts by an apparently narrow gap on the left side and more broadly on the right, the vault has been reconstructed with what seems like a satisfying result. The vault is large. Chiu *et al.* (1973) give a glabello-occipital length from his reconstruction of 213 mm and a biauricular breadth of 148.5. Weidenreich also sketched a reconstruction from the original parts (1937) and estimated values of 206 (or "at least 205" [1943]) and 148 or perhaps 155, respectively. Capacity is estimated (by water measurement of a model) at 1,140 cc. This is higher than the highest of the more complete prewar skulls, although less than Weidenreich's estimate of 1,225 cc for Skull X; however, Weidenreich thought Skull V was large, "perhaps reaching the 1,300 cc mark," and used this figure in giving the total range for Sinanthropus in 1943.

According to Ku Yu-min, who presented the new material, the individual is believed to be male, judging from size and the development of the temporal lines. The vault is asymmetrical, sloping less steeply to a more laterally extending auricular region on the left side. The skull is viewed as more progressive than the other known individuals, from the cranial capacity and various other features. The bone of the frontal is thinner. The occipital torus is less developed than in most (Skull XI excepted) and does not extend all the way to asterion. The frontal sinuses are larger than in all others, except Skull III. The vault as

*Based on a lecture by Ku Yu-min.

Chou-k'ou-tien, Location 1.

reconstructed is higher. From this assessment of status (see also Chiu *et al.*, 1973), the Chinese believe that the morphology of later Peking man is thus established, as showing evolutionary development within the Peking man phylum.

MA-PA

Shih-tzu-shan Hill, Ma-pa village, Shao-ch'un Municipality (formerly Ch'ü-chiang District), Kwangtung Province.

   Found June 1958, by farmers digging fertilizer in a limestone cave in the hill.

   From fauna (*Ailuropoda, Stegodon*, with *Paleoloxodon namadicus, Felis tigris,* other genera unnamed as to species), the site is believed to be late middle or early late Pleistocene.

   The skull is represented by several fragments which join well but not tightly (from erosion ?): frontal, most of right side and part of left including supraorbitals to this extent, also lateral margin of orbit, nasalia, and adjoining parts of maxillae, especially on right; major parts of the parietals, joining frontal on right side; with parts of sphenoid and temporal on right, and extending to or beyond the lambdoid suture.

   The specimen has been described in detail by Woo Ju-kang (1959)

with measurements, all of which lie within the ranges reported for
Neanderthals. Woo makes comparisons with Sinanthropus, Solo, and Neanderthal morphology, finding Ma-pa intermediate in some ways, filling
the gap between Sinanthropus and other "Paleoanthropic fossils found in
China" and says it "probably belongs to the early Paleoanthropic stage
in human evolution." Some Neanderthal-like traits are the following
(which include some slight supplementing of what Woo said from observation of the original and Woo's photographs). The vault is ovoid in
vertical view, with the characteristic Neanderthal posterior placement
of greatest breadth. The supraorbitals are somewhat arched over each
orbit, and thickness is greatest near glabella, in contrast to Solo.
In vertical view the supraorbitals are somewhat retreating laterally,
as is the lateral orbital border, though not as much as in some Western
Neanderthals. The frontal sinuses (exposed by rodent gnawing) are
larger than in Sinanthropus and Solo and are in fact substantial,
occupying both the glabellar and part of the supraorbital spaces. The
supraorbitals are separated from the frontal squama by a slight sulcus
only. There appears to be no medial frontal notch in the upper orbital
margin. The interorbital space is wide.

Comment: The likeness in morphology to Neanderthals (sensu stricto)
is perhaps more marked in viewing the actual skull, or at any rate the
difference in impression from *Homo erectus* (e.g., Sinanthropus, Solo,
Broken Hill). If found in Europe in 1950, the skull would very likely
have been called a "classic" Neanderthal, if anything veering to the
"progressive" side. One slight departure from classic Neanderthals is
the nasal region. There is a somewhat more definite profile angle at
nasion than appears typical in "classics." Also, the nasal bones are
difficult to interpret because of poor definition of naso-maxillary
sutures. Woo believes that nasalia are wide (minimum breadth 13.3 mm)
as in Neanderthals; this is so if the lines evident on the surface are
the actual sutures as they appear to be. On the other hand, the con-
formation is elevated near the midline, as with narrower, raised nasals
seen in some modern populations. These narrower nasalia are bounded
laterally by possible but barely discernible sutures.

The phylogenetic position of Ma-pa suggested by Woo would accord best
with the date presently assigned, i.e., early late Pleistocene at latest.
Viewed as a really Neanderthal-like fossil (far removed in space from
any other known), an early date would seem anomalous.

A cast was presented to the Delegation, and it is now in the Peabody
Museum, Harvard.

CH'ANG-YANG

Lung-tung cave, near Hsia-chung-chia-wan village, 45 km southwest of
Ch'ang-yang city, Hupei.

Founded in 1956 (discoverers unknown). Site was investigated by team
from IVPP in 1957.

Fauna is Ailuropoda-Stegodon, and investigators assign age as late
middle or early late Pleistocene, i.e., same age as Ma-pa. The site was
not described to us in detail during our visit.

Fossil is a partial left maxilla comprising the lower part of the nasal cavity and left half of the papate, with P^3 and M^1 in place; also a separate P_4 is assumed to derive from the same individual. Details of teeth are cited fully in Chang (1962) from Chia (*Vert. Palas.*, 1/3: 247-252, 1957). The maxilla is "pronouncedly orthognathous," i.e., a decidedly vertical alveolar region and fairly sharp lower border of nasal aperture, moderate nasal apine, and moderately broad nasal aperture (apparently in the high side of the modern range). We did not review the fragment with IVPP members.

Comment: Certain features, including tooth size and verticality of anterior part, plus moderately broad aperture, suggest western Neanderthal morphology and thus harmonize with the Ma-pa specimen.

TING-TS'UN*

Found in 1954 at Ting-ts'un village, Shansi, at Locality 100, one of a complex of exposures discovered since 1953 due to erosion along the Fen River. Teeth were found on a surface (since covered by slumping) in the high face of the river bank, at a level resting on 17 m of sand and gravel and under 5 m of loess or loesslike material, perhaps waterlaid.

The date is believed by the Chinese to be early upper Pleistocene; Chang (1962), following Movius, thinks the Chingshui Erosion stage (Eem of Europe) is most plausible.

Three teeth were found: right I^1, I^2, and M_2. The teeth are worn and appear to be of no more than modern size, though the molar is well developed as to pattern. Chang (1962) gives fairly full notes translated from Woo's description. Both incisors are reported to have rather pronounced shoveling formed by raised lingual margins, and a pronounced

Ting-ts'un approach.

*Based on a lecture by Ch'iu Chung-lang.

lingual tubercle on I^1 projections (ridging ?) extending downward from the last along the lingual surface. My limited observations were that the shoveling was only moderate for the size of the teeth. There is not an actual "tubercle," projecting downward, on either tooth, but rather a thickened bulb of enamel at the junction of the lateral ridges. The molar pattern, with six cusps and other details, is reported to be further removed from *Dryopithecus* than is that of Sinanthropus.

In the opinion of Woo (Chang, 1962), the Ting-ts'un individual is situated phylogenetically between Sinanthropus and modern man and is closer to Mongoloids and to Caucasoids; it is close to the Neanderthals, especially Ordos man. However, the crown diameters (see Chang, 1962), especially labiolingual breadth, are close to modern figures and inferior to those of western Neanderthals as given by Wolpoff (1971).

LIU-CHIANG

Tung-tien-yen cave, Liu-chiang County, Kwangsi Chuang Autonomous Region.
Found in September 1958 by farm workers digging for fertilizer.

The cave itself contained the Stegodon-Ailuropoda fauna found in other Kwangsi caves. The human skeletal parts and the complete skeleton of *Ailuropoda* were near the entrance embedded in different material (Chang, 1962), and thus are not to be associated with the rest of the fauna. The human material, heavily fossilized, is presumed to be late Pleistocene.

The human fossils are a skull without mandible, complete except for parts of the zygomatic arches and the crown of the left central incisor; five thoracic and five lumbar vertebrae, sacrum, right innominate (in articulation), and parts of five ribs; and also two femoral shaft fragments that may belong to another individual.

The find has been fully described by Woo (1959). The low, broad face and orbits, he points out, are seen in upper Paleolithic crania of other continents and contrast with those of Neanderthals. Woo concludes that Liu-chiang was a primitive *Homo sapiens,* an evolving Mongoloid with clear affinities in that direction.

In publication Woo diagnosed the individual as a male of middle age. However, during a conversation in Peking, he suggested that it might be female instead. The form of the innominate and virtually all individual traits of the skull (tooth size, face size, basal muscle attachments) would support this. The cranial volume is relatively large for face and skeleton, and the supraorbitals are moderate in size; other writers appear to have formed an exaggerated idea of the robustness of the cranium and have suggested Melanesian or Negrito affinities for the individual. Woo's assessment of a proto-Mongoloid nature seems well supported by the specimen, and if it is female the small size of face and postcrania give no basis for a suggestion of Negrito racial affinity.

Casts of the specimen have been made and are on display at least in the Chou-k'ou-tien museum.

CHOU-K'OU-TIEN, UPPER CAVE

We visited the cave at the top of Chou-k'ou-tien Hill. It has been completely excavated, and the skeletal material is said to have been all lost in 1941 together with that from Locality 1, so that nothing survives excepting possibly some small artifacts.

Wu Hsin-chih has reanalyzed the human fossils from casts and earlier reports. The excavation notes of Chia Lan-p'o are at IVPP: These show (as Weidenreich [1939] also noted) that the remains were found over a range of several meters of vertical depth and are unlikely to represent, in the three well-known skulls, the burial of a single family, as suggested by Weidenreich (1939) and by Hooton (1946). Wu would refute Weidenreich's idea that no. 102 and no. 103 represent an incipient Melanesoid and Eskimoid respectively, in a population still undifferentiated racially. Wu finds a number of common characters in the three skulls, especially low orbits and relatively broad noses, the first being characteristic of many upper Paleolithic crania elsewhere; the traits of all in general could be ancestral to modern Chinese via Neolithic populations. Wu has measured some 200 modern Chinese skulls and has found that the Upper Cave skulls all fall in the range of the modern. His assessment is that the Upper Cave population was proto-Mongoloid and not distant from American Indians in character.

Aigner (1972) has suggested, because of the component of warm fauna, that the Upper Cave hominids may be dated to the interval before the Würm maximum, or 27,000 to 30,000 B.P. The Chinese appear to prefer a later date, i.e., upper Paleolithic.

TZU-YANG

Bank of Huangschanchi River, 0.5 km west of Tzu-yang City, Tzu-yang County, Szechwan Province.

Found in 1951 by railway workers.

In original reports (e.g., Woo, 1958) the skull and accompanying materials were believed to be late Pleistocene, i.e., a Paleolithic specimen; recent radiocarbon dates (see Chang, 1973), however, show the find to be less than 7,500 years old.

The individual is represented by most of the cranial vault and by nasals and a maxillary and palatal fragment. We saw only casts of these. The individual was assessed as female, which seems probable. It was originally regarded as relatively primitive, as compared with the Upper Cave crania. The skull is small and smooth, though with supraorbital elements of moderate size, and mastoid processes that are large, though not for a male or some (e.g., Polynesian) females. It would be rather difficult, from inspection, to exclude from recent populations. The frontal is vertical in profile; there is some frontal and sagittal keeling. Surviving features are acceptable for a Mongoloid population: general pentagonoid vault form, absences of nasion depression, and suborbital fossa. It is possible that earlier estimates of its age allowed the skull to appear more archaic than if it had turned up in a modern series.

NEOLITHIC

Excavations of Neolithic villages have regularly produced burials, sometimes numerous. To judge from a limited sampling of the literature
(virtually all in Chinese), conditions of preservation and breakage are
varied but usually unfavorable. At Hua Hsien, Shensi (Yen, 1962), 99
burials uncovered yielded 9 skulls good enough to study; at Pao-chi,
Shensi (Yen *et al.*, 1960), 136 individuals yielded 16 complete and 21
partial skulls; at Pan-p'o near Sian, 61 adults of the first series
excavated (52 males, 10 females) yielded 3 complete and 32 partial
skulls (Yen, 1960).

According to what we learned, skeletons exposed in such excavations
meet one of three fates: (1) from some sites they are sent to Peking
(Institute of Archeology) for study; (2) others are stored locally;
(3) probably most are inspected and discarded. Publications on them do
not seem to indicate where material is kept. We saw no collections
ourselves.

Evidently because of the prevailing shortage of professionals, a
physical anthropologist is not present at excavations. (Wu Hsin-chih
did visit the important village of Pan-p'o, but between the excavation
of the first and second lot of burials, the skeletons of which were sent
to Peking). Determinations of sex or age may be made by local anatomists,
as at Ta-ho, Honan. At this site an excavation 10 m square had been
made of part of the village cemetery, exposing about 24 burials in which
the skeletons were in relatively good condition. This burial area is
destined to be roofed and enclosed for a public museum, and it was not
apparent that further excavation, here in the midst of farmed land,
would be made.

In published reports, skeletal series have been treated in standard
international fashion, using measurements as defined by Martin and giving the means of a substantial list of these. Comparisons are made
among the Neolithic series (actually few) and with some well-known
Asiatic series in the literature (e.g., Harrower's South China, Black's
North China, Morant's Tibetan, etc.). Some use is made of tests or of
overlap of ranges as a means of judging relative likeness. The groups
studied have been judged to be generally Mongoloid in cranial character;
the Pao-chi and Hua Hsien samples were all found to approximate South
Asiatic Mongoloid groups (South China, Vietnam, or Indonesia) most
closely in metric traits.

Cranial capacity is computed from formulae of Pearson. In the case
of the Ta-wen-k'ou series, artificial deformation was present in all or
almost all crania; corrections of the vault diameters were made by
Shapiro's formulae (1930) before computing capacity. Stature is also
computed from long bone measurements, using the formula for Mongoloids
of Trotter and Gleser (1968).

In the Ta-wen-k'ou series, in addition to cranial deformation, the
bilateral avulsion of the upper lateral incisors in 75 percent of 31
skulls points to diversity in tribal cultural practices. The archeological context and date of the site have been published in a separate
monograph, *Ta-wen-k'ou* (Peking, Wen Wu Press, 1974).

The effect of the present extreme shortage of workers in the osteology of the Neolithic and of the lack of facilities for storage of skeletons might be shown by a comparison with the current relative affluence, in number of workers and resources, enjoyed by the same sector of anthropology in the United States. Here, major prehistoric Indian occupations, from the Archaic on, have much in common with Neolithic China for probable local cultural diversity within broader traditions, and for the kind of pattern of biological variation among local and regional populations discernible from osteological evidence.

Recently (and only recently, except for the work of G. K. Neumann) there has been a good deal of close analysis, often using multivariate statistics as the tool, of highly specific cranial populations in a given area of America, controlled for date as well as possible. This aims to develop precise information on intragroup variation as the first step in detecting changes in morphology through microevolution or as the result of movements of peoples over the last 7,000 years. In the 1970's there have been perhaps half a dozen Ph.D. theses so far, of considerable merit and sophistication, presenting such work and reflecting mutual acquaintance of the work of others.

This is not recounted in disparagement of Chinese workers. It represents something of a recent renascence in craniology in this country, as well as special resources for, and academic encouragement of, many young workers. It is a particularly active phase and happens to contrast with what the Chinese can devote to this field just now. However, it suggests that the future might see similar intensive analysis of the period termed Primitive Society, which would specify local biological variation during the Neolithic and changes as the Chinese population formed during dynastic times. Such patterns, and descriptions of Neolithic populations, would certainly be of interest to Americans working in North American prehistory. Visits and correspondence between Chinese and U.S. students would be mutually profitable in such a development. However, this must wait until the Chinese feel able to place a number of young professionals in this kind of work and more collections from Neolithic village cemeteries exist.

REFERENCES

Aigner, J. S. 1972. Relative dating of North Chinese faunal and cultural complexes. Artic Anthropol. IX(2):36-79.
Aigner, J. S., and W. S. Laughlin. 1973. The dating of Lantian man and his significance for analyzing trends in human evolution. Am. J. Phys. Anthropol. 39:97-110.
Chang, K. C. 1962. New evidence on fossil man in China. Science 136: 749-760.
Chang, K. C. 1973. Radiocarbon dates from China: Some initial interpretations. Curr. Anthropol. 14/5:525-528.
Chiu Chung-lang, Ku Yu-min, Chang Yin-yun, and Chang Sen-shui. 1973. Peking man fossils and cultural remains newly discovered at Choukoutien. Vert. Palas. 11(2):109-131.

78

Hooton, E. A.   1946.   Up from the ape, 2nd ed.   McMillan and Co., New
    York.

Koenigswald, Gustav Heinrich Ralph von.   1957a.   Remarks on *Giganto-
    pithecus* and other hominoid remains from southern China.   Proc. Neth.
    Acad. Wet. Series B.   60:153-159.

Koenigswald, Gustav Heinrich Ralph von.   1957b.   *Hemanthropus* N.G. not
    Hemianthropus.   Proc. Neth. Acad. Wet. Series B, 60:146.

Oakley, K. P., B. G. C. Campbell, and T. I. Molleson, eds.   1975.   Cata-
    logue of fossil hominids.   III.   Americas, Asia, Australasia.   Br.
    Mus. Nat. Hist. Publ. no. 767.   217 pp.

Shapiro, H. L.   1928.   A correction for artificial deformation of skulls.
    Anthropol. Pap. Am. Mus. Nat. Hist.   30:1-38.

Trotter, M., and G. C. Gleser.   1952.   Estimation of stature from long
    bones of American whites and Negroes.   Am. J. Phys. Anthropol., New
    Series 10:463-514.

Weidenreich, F.   1939.   On the earliest representatives of modern mankind
    recovered on the soil of East Asia.   Peking Nat. Hist. Bull.   13:161-
    174.

Weidenreich, F.   1943.   The skull of *Sinanthropus pekinensis*.   A compara-
    tive study on a primitive hominid skull.   Paleontol. Sinica, New
    Series D, no. 10, Whole Series no. 127.   484 pp.

Wolpoff, M. H.   1971.   Metric trends in hominid dental evolution.   Case
    Western Reserve University Studies in Anthropology no. 2.   244 pp.

Woo Ju-kang.   1958.   Tzeyang Paleolithic man--Earliest representative
    of modern man in China.   Am. J. Phys. Anthropol.   16:459-471.

Woo Ju-kang.   1959.   Human fossils found in Liukiang, Kwangsi, China.
    Vert. Palas.   3(3):109-118.

Woo Ju-kang.   1966.   The hominid skull of Lantian, Shensi.   Vert. Palas.
    10(1):14-16.   (Abstract).

Woo Ju-kang, and Peng Ru-ce.   1959.   Fossil human skull of early Paleo-
    anthropic stage found at Mapa, Shaoquan, Kwangtung Province.   Vert.
    Palas.   3(4):176-182.

Yen Yin.   1962.   A study of Neolithic skeletal remains in Hua Xian.
    Kao-ku Hsüeh-pao (2):85-104.   (In Chinese).

Yen Yin.   1972.   Report of a study of Neolithic skeletal remains at
    Ta-wan-k'ou.   Kao-ku Hsüeh-pao.   1972.   (1):91-122.   (In Chinese).

Yen Yin, Liu Chang-zih, and Gu Yu-min.   1960.   Report on the skeletal
    remains from the Neolithic site at Bao Ji.   Vert. Palas. 4(2):103-111.

Yen Yin *et al*.   1963.   Study of skeletal remains at Pan-p'o.   *In* Hsi Pan
    P'o.   Science Press, Peking.   (English abstract).

PALEOLITHIC ARCHEOLOGY AND PALEOANTHROPOLOGY IN CHINA

L. G. Freeman, Jr.

As a member of the Paleoanthropology Delegation, I hoped to learn about current techniques of excavation and analysis of Pleistocene occupation residues in the People's Republic of China and to see the extent to which Chinese prehistorians and paleoanthropologists collaborate with other scientists in interpreting such evidence. Some Chinese sites, such as Yüan-mou and the Lan-t'ien and Chou-k'ou-tien complexes, provide unique documentation concerning early human adaptations and the course of biological and cultural evolution in eastern Asia. It has long been thought that these developments occurred in relative isolation from the rest of the world. For more than a quarter century no Western prehistorian with much familiarity with European and African Paleolithic materials, especially those from middle Pleistocene contexts, has examined the Chinese sites or collections.

I hoped to be permitted to see enough sites and materials to serve as a base for detailed comparisons with the European and African materials I know. I wanted to compare notes with my colleagues in the People's Republic concerning current terminology for artifact typology, since Chinese and Western usage have grown so far apart that type lists are no longer mutually intelligible, even to scholars fluent in the other language (I do not myself read Chinese). Having been active, over the past few years, in the development of rough-and-ready, easily understood procedures for quantitative data processing and statistical inference that may be used in the field by archeologists with shoestring budgets, I also hoped to exchange information with interested research workers concerning quantitative techniques that are now used or could be used in paleoanthropological research in the People's Republic of China.

The names of new professionals occur with some regularity in Chinese scholarly journals published after 1967, so it was evident that some means of training paleoanthropologists and archeologists continues. I was interested in discovering what alternative educational pathways those young people have followed since 1966. New releases in the world press, articles in *China Reconstructs* and *Peking Review,* and pamphlets on archeological discoveries stress the fact that archeological research in China has a broad base of support among the masses. We read that archeological research is no longer undertaken by technical personnel alone but is always shared and even sometimes originated by workers, peasants, and soldiers. The mechanisms by which technical archeological

79

skills and a necessary appreciation for and understanding of prehistoric documents are diffused to the general public are obviously of great importance in evaluating this development.

Most scholars and government officials in the United States rely for information about China on the interpretations of a dedicated handful of "China specialists." As a consequence, their interests, backgrounds, and viewpoints filter and color the information we receive. In general, their invaluable work deserves the strongest praise. Nevertheless, scholarly interpretations, like all translations, sometimes run against obstacles that make us more aware of the shortcomings of the filters used. Acquiring the necessary language facilities for scholarship in Chinese is so time consuming that it greatly limits the range of experience many China specialists can obtain outside their special fields.

The magnitude of the corpus of literature on China also demands an extraordinary investment of research time. These factors interact to produce specialists with an intensive exposure to the Chinese field but less familiarity with comparable data from other countries than they should ideally have. It seems to me, after our visit to the People's Republic, that in consequence we tend to think of China as more distinctively idiosyncratic and enigmatic than it actually is. I don't know that there is any realistic solution to this dilemma, but I do feel that any specialist in things Chinese who can acquire an additional data base in some other part of the world will be able to arrive at interpretations of the Chinese scene that are both more sophisticated and more realistic than those produced by less broadly based colleagues.

DEVELOPMENT OF PALEOANTHROPOLOGY AND RELATED FIELDS

The development of paleoanthropology in China is intimately linked with the development of the fields of geology and mammalian and human paleontology. As one might expect, Westerners played a large role in these fields. Among the earliest attempts by trained professionals to construct a corpus of systematic geological and paleontological observations in China were those of the foreigners Przewalski, Pumpelly, Kingsmill, Szechenyi, and von Richthofen. The work of the last-mentioned pioneer is basic to later investigations.

Sponsored and financed by the Shanghai Chamber of Commerce, von Richthofen spent 4 years (1868-72) in China, surveying structural geology, stratigraphy, mineral resources, and trade routes in 11 provinces. His collected observations appear in a series of reports to the Chamber of Commerce (*Baron Richthofen's Letters 1868-1872*), in his published diaries (1907) and the monumental five-volume *China* (1877-1911). Much subsequent investigation has amplified and rectified observations first recorded by von Richthofen.

Other Europeans undertook fieldwork around the turn of the century, but geological research by Chinese nationals really began after the 1911 Revolution. Before then, a few Chinese had been trained abroad in the specialty, but there seems to be no record of independent geological fieldwork by Chinese in China, and even after 1911 European participation loomed large.

In 1912, the Nanking Provisional Government included in its executive departments a Ministry of Industry and Commerce (Houn, 1957, p. 43) with a Bureau of Mines encompassing several sections, one of which was geological. H. T. Chang (Chang Hung-chao) was first director of the section (Chang, 1922, p. 6). After the government moved to Peking, Chang left the Ministry of Industry for the Ministry of Agriculture and Forestry, and the position he vacated was filled in 1913 by V. K. Ting (Ting Wen-chiang) (Ting, 1919; Furth, 1970, p. 35). Ting had received his B.S. degree with a double major in zoology and geology from Glasgow University, and Chang graduated in geology from the University of Tokyo (Furth, 1970, pp. 25, 39). Together, the two set out to create a working geological survey and an active training institute. The Geological Section, still in the throes of organization, did not really begin active research and teaching until 1913.

As early as 1910, a Department of Geology had been established at the Government University of Peking, with Friedrich Solger as department head and teacher. Geology classes in the Department had been suspended because of lack of interest. Ting and Chang persuaded Solger to join them as a teacher in a Geological Institute under the auspices of the new Ministry of Agriculture and Commerce, a fusion of the two earlier ministries (Ting, 1919; Houn, 1957, p. 43; Furth, 1970, p. 40). When Solger left in 1914 at the outbreak of World War I, he was replaced in the Institute by Wong Wen-hao, a geology graduate fresh from Louvain. In the same year J. G. Andersson, past director of the Geological Survey of Sweden, was invited by the Chinese Government to accept a post as mining advisor and joined the staff of the Institute for a year. Andersson continued his informal affiliation with the Geological Section and, later, the Geological Survey, without formal membership in either. The Institute was discontinued in 1916, having graduated 30 students, 18 of whom went directly to positions in the Geological Survey, which replaced the Geological Section of the Bureau of Mines in that year. Many of the others were sent abroad for graduate study (Ting, 1919; Furth, 1970, pp. 41-42).

The newly organized Geological Survey was headed by Ting, and during the first year of its existence it included Andersson's two Swedish associates, Tegengren and Nyström (Ting, 1919). European participation in the Survey was broken from 1917 until 1920, when A. W. Grabau became its senior paleontologist (Gregory, 1947).

Modern paleontological research in China was given its earliest impetus by the work of the German naturalist H. A. Haberer, who went to China for exploration in 1899. His trip unhappily coincided with the Boxer Rebellion and he was thus restricted to travel in the treaty ports. He nevertheless managed to accumulate paleontological collections by purchasing "dragon bones" from apothecaries. The specimens he recovered in this unorthodox fashion were sent to Max Schlosser in Munich, who published a description of the finds in 1903. However important Schlosser's work, it was flawed by the total lack of information regarding provenience and stratigraphic attribution of the bones. Nevertheless, his discovery of a hominid tooth stimulated the search for early man in China.

Although J. G. Andersson's primary responsibility to the Chinese government concerned the discovery and development of mineral resources, his interests ranged far more widely into stratigraphy, paleontology, and archaeology. His paleontological fieldwork included surveys that recognized the broad division of the Chinese faunal succession, although he seems to have been kept so busy by the many projects in which he was involved that he did not personally pursue many of his discoveries to any depth. The numerous research opportunities he generated were dispensed liberally to younger scientists.

In Uppsala, Professor C. Wiman prepared Andersson's fossil materials for study, analyzing some himself and distributing others among his colleagues and students for monographic treatment. One of these paleontologists, a young Viennese named Otto Zdansky, was persuaded by Wiman to travel to China for 2 years (1921-22) to assist in the excavation of important faunal localities discovered by Andersson (Andersson, 1973, p. 80). As it happened, he stayed longer. Zdansky collected at several localities and was present with Andersson and Walter Granger, of the American Museum of Natural History (a member of Roy Chapman Andrews' expedition to Mongolia), at the discovery of Chou-k'ou-tien Locality 1 in 1921 (Andersson, 1973, pp. 97-98).

Foreign missions played an important part in the growth of geology and paleontology. In 1914 Emile Licent, a Jesuit with a broad background in natural sciences, joined the S. E. Tcheu Ly mission. In the next years he was to undertake a thorough exploration of the Yellow River basin. In 1923, Licent's collections became the nucleus of the Huangho-Paiho Museum in Tientsin, which he founded as a headquarters for regional research in the natural sciences and as a center for their divulgation (Licent, 1924, pp. 1554-1558; Chyne, 1936, pp. 115-116). In 1923 the paleontologist Teilhard de Chardin came to China to form, jointly with Licent, a French Paleontological Mission and to join the Museum staff. In Tientsin, both Licent and Teilhard were quartered in a Jesuit institute of business and engineering, the Hautes Études Industrielles et Commerciales, founded in 1923, which was located in the same compound as the museum (Licent, 1924, pp. 1438-39, 1559; Chyne, 1936, p. 109; Teilhard de Chardin, 1968, p. 72). Teilhard left China briefly in 1924 but returned to stay, except for short visits abroad, until 1946. In China he served in several capacities, including that of advisor to the Geological Survey. Teilhard also participated in excavations of several important Chinese Paleolithic localities.

The Union Medical College in Peking opened in 1906 and was operated by the combined efforts of three Protestant missions. The college was picked for intensive development by the Rockefeller Foundation, which purchased it in 1915, restaffed it, and renamed it Peking Union Medical College. Premedical enrollments began in 1917, and the Medical School was formally dedicated in 1921 (Peking Union Medical College, 1921). Davidson Black, who had studied anatomy with G. Elliot Smith while the latter was engaged in the study of the Piltdown man, which turned out to be a forgery, was appointed to the staff as professor of neurology and embryology and accepted with the understanding that he would be allowed sufficient time to pursue investigations in physical anthropology, including periods of leave to undertake extended field expeditions.

When Edward Cowdry, Head of Anatomy, returned to New York in 1921, Black assumed that position (Bowers, 1972).

This outline indicates that Europeans were heavily represented on the staff of research organizations devoted to modern geology and paleontology in China. However, we in the West are generally less aware of the fundamental part played by the Chinese themselves in such research. Large as the figure of a Grabau or a Licent may loom, an impressive amount of basic geological and paleontological field research was independently undertaken and published by enthusiastic young Chinese scientists from 1912 onward. V. K. Ting's work in defining the Sanmenian is just one outstanding example of such contributions. Chinese scientists also founded the Geological Society in 1922, and for several decades that body was the single most important forum for the exchange of information on Chinese geology and paleontology among scholars of all nationalities (Black, 1922; Ting, 1922). Chinese also collaborated extensively in many Western-directed projects undertaken during the period between 1912 and Liberation. While most Westerners credited Chinese scientific collaboration fairly, there were a few inexcusable exceptions, which understandably contributed to bad feelings and distrust. Most Chinese scientists maintained an open, frank and amicable attitude towards their European colleagues and worked to open avenues for the free communication of information on topics of mutual interest across national boundaries.

All these diverse threads were finally woven into a single skein of paleoanthropological investigations, which united Chinese, Swedish, French, Canadian, American, German, and Austrian specialists in a productive, focused (and exciting) research effort. The event which catalyzed this happy fusion was the discovery of remains of early man at Chou-k'ou-tien.

CHOU-K'OU-TIEN DISCOVERIES AND THE
CENOZOIC RESEARCH LABORATORY

Following the discovery of Locality 1, Otto Zdansky spent several weeks there in 1921 collecting fossils (Zdansky, 1923) and returned to excavate more extensively in 1923. In the course of his study of the recovered materials in Uppsala, Zdansky recognized two teeth among the faunal remains as hominid (Zdansky, 1926, 1928; Black et al., 1933, p. 6). The great importance of this discovery of remains of early man stimulated the Geological Survey, in collaboration with the Anatomy Department of Peking Union Medical College, to undertake a 2-year (1927-28) intensive research project at Chou-k'ou-tien (financed by the Rockefeller Foundation), with the aim of recovering more hominid material.

During the first year, Li Chieh was titular field director of excavations and served as topographer and geologist (Wong, 1927, p. 335; Li, 1927). Birger Bohlin, the field paleontologist, apparently supervised most details of the excavation (Bohlin, 1927; Black et al., 1933, p. 7; Black, 1934, p. 62). In 1928, Yang Chung-chien replaced Li as representative of the Survey and P'ei Wen-chung joined the field staff

(Black *et al.*, 1933, p. 8). Towards the end of the 1927 field season, Bohlin recovered a hominid left lower molar tooth, on which Black founded a new genus, *Sinanthropus pekinensis* (now referred to as *Homo erectus*). In successive field seasons, hominid remains were recovered in quantity (Black, 1929a, 1929b; Black *et al.*, 1933, pp. 7-8; P'ei, 1929).

With the discovery of fossils of *Homo erectus* at Chou-k'ou-tien the necessity of concentrated research on the regional Tertiary and Quaternary became obvious. To undertake and supervise such research, the Cenozoic Research Laboratory was organized in 1929 as a special department within the Chinese Geological Survey. This organization included Davidson Black (who took a 3-year leave of absence from Peking Union Medical College to study *Sinanthropus*) as honorary director, Teilhard as advisor and collaborator, Yang as assistant director and paleontologist, P'ei as paleontologist and director of fieldwork at Chou-k'ou-tien, and M. N. Pien as assistant. The Laboratory thus united representatives of the Peking Union Medical College, the Huangho-Paiho Museum, and the Geological Survey in one research organization. Ties with other members of the Survey remained close. The work of the Laboratory continued to be financed by the Rockefeller Foundation, and the Geological Survey was to maintain title to all finds (Black *et al.*, 1933, pp. 3-4; Black, 1934, pp. 62-63). Davidson Black died of advanced myocardial disease in 1934 and was replaced as honorary director of the Cenozoic Research Laboratory by Franz Weidenreich in 1935. Weidenreich's appointment naturally had the full approval of the Geological Survey, and he continued to use the facilities of the Peking Union Medical College for the study of the hominid fossils from Chou-k'ou-tien (Geological Society of China, 1934; Bowers, 1972, p. 98).

It is significant that prior to 1949 there was a tendency for Westerners to monopolize the scientific study of important recovered specimens and to regard their Chinese colleagues primarily as field supervisors and research assistants, even when they were adequately trained to act independently as full partners in the scientific enterprise. Understandably, this caused resentments that still surface from time to time.

THE TOOLS OF EARLY MAN

The study of prehistoric hominid behavior is as much a part of paleoanthropology as the examination of the skeletons of early people. However, the discovery of true stone tools at Chou-k'ou-tien was sufficiently unexpected to generate quite a controversy.

For many years, it had been generally accepted in the West that China had no human occupation prior to about 5000 B.C. (de Morgan, 1925). Enormous new vistas were opened by archeological discoveries made by Andersson, Licent, and Teilhard in the twenties. Andersson recognized the first prehistoric site in China, Yang-shao-ts'un, in 1921 (Andersson, 1923a) and made several similar discoveries of importance in the next few years. Incidentally, Davidson Black participated in Andersson's work as human paleontologist and had studied the skeletal populations from several prehistoric sites before his work on *Sinanthropus* (Andersson, 1923a, p. 13, 1923b, p. 134, 1943). Licent and Teilhard found the first

Paleolithic sites recognized in China beginning in 1920 (Licent, 1924, pp. 1563-64; Teilhard and Licent, 1924, pp. 46-47). Two of these, Sjàra-osso-gol and Shui-tung-kou, have been the subject of an extensive report (Boule *et al.*, 1928). Probably the archeological interests of Andersson and Teilhard, coupled with the fact that stone tools were found at Chou-k'ou-tien, operated to keep Paleolithic prehistory in the domain of activities of the Cenozoic Research Laboratory over the following years.

The presence of fragments of quartz in the deposits of Locality 1 at Chou-k'ou-tien, noted by Andersson and Zdansky when the site was first discovered (Zdansky, 1923), seemed suggestive of human activity to Andersson at the time (P'ei, 1932, p. 110; Andersson, 1943, p. 22). From 1927 on, P'ei also noted such quartz chips in disturbed site sediments but did not find the first flaked stones *in situ* at Locality 1 until 1931. In that year, however, two convincing cultural horizons containing chipped stone implements were revealed in stratigraphic context (P'ei, 1932, p. 110). In the same year several apparently charred bones from Locality 1 were analyzed in Paris and shown to be truly burnt (Black, 1932). Apparently worked bones were also recovered from the cultural horizons (Breuil, 1932; P'ei, 1933). Announcements of these discoveries generated some controversy in the contemporary scientific world, since the cultural vestiges seemed at the time much more advanced than the hominid remains, but P'ei was abundantly able to substantiate the suggestion that the Chou-k'ou-tien deposits included residues of cultural activities of early man with many further discoveries.

THE PRESENT STATE OF THE FIELD: METHODS AND RESULTS

Techniques of Excavation and Recording

During our visit, we saw only Neolithic and Dynastic excavations in progress. However, Paleolithic excavation technique was described, and we visited two Paleolithic sites that provided data of relevance when compared against the literature.

Apparently, techniques currently employed in most Chinese Paleolithic investigations have evolved from the careful paleontological methods developed by the American Museum of Natural History and introduced to Chinese paleoanthropology by Walter Granger, of the Museum's Third Asiatic Expedition, who accompanied Andersson and Zdansky to Chou-k'ou-tien in 1921. Andersson specifically credits Granger with introducing new excavating equipment, including Marsh picks, geological pick-hammers, crochets and brushes, as well as improved procedures for the recovery of delicate specimens. In his own work, Andersson used the new methods extensively, as did Zdansky (Andersson, 1943, pp. 15-20). Items and features recognized as important in Andersson's excavations were located in space with reference to an arbitrary three-dimensional coordinate system (sometimes the reference line was a tape suspended along the ceiling of a cave), and burials were drawn at a scale of 1:10 to be reduced by half for publication. In 1930 Yang and Teilhard served several months as geologists with Roy Chapman Andrews' American Museum Expedition in Mongolia, and on their return Yang temporarily took over direction of fieldwork at Chou-k'ou-tien while P'ei briefly visited the expedition to study paleontological field technique with Granger (Black *et al.*, 1933, p. 9).

There is some precise information on field techniques employed at Locality 1 in various published sources in English, and P'ei has provided a detailed account of his practice in Upper Cave.

Estimates of the quantity of sediment moved during the first three field seasons at Locality 1 are readily available. During the 24 weeks of the 1927 season, an area that at surface measured 17 × 14 m was excavated to a depth of between 11 and 17 m in the main cave (Li, 1927, p. 339). Around 3,000 m^3 of earth were removed. In 14 weeks in 1928, 2,800 m^3 were removed, and in 26 weeks in 1929, about 3,000 m^3 were excavated. Most of the sediment was so indurated as to necessitate drilling and blasting (Teilhard and Young, 1929, pp. 176-177). P'ei (1937, p. 362) tells us that about 100 workers and 20 trained technicians were engaged in work at Locality 1 each year.

In 1927, Bohlin collected larger paleontological specimens *in situ,* threw large, indurated blocks from the "less important layers" down the slope to be crushed with hammers as time permitted, and shoveled the looser material down the slope to be passed through 6-mm mesh screens. However, sometimes there "were not screens enough." From the "very important layers," sand was sieved with more care, and all blocks were taken to Peking for excavation there (Bohlin, 1927, p. 346). No mention is made of any horizontal grid system, though some vertical measurement must have been done, at least to produce measured sections.

Compared with such practices, P'ei's later work is an immense improvement. In 1932, P'ei dug a series of 3 × 3 × 5 m excavation units. Before beginning the excavations of Upper Cave in 1933, he divided the area to be excavated into a grid of squares 2 m on a side. To judge from published photographs, this reference grid was painted on the sediments and the exposed cave wall. The grid lines on the walls were level and served as vertical reference marks. During excavation, vertical profiles were drawn along the N/S grid lines only (every 2 m). Each grid square was in turn subdivided into four excavation units of 1 m^2 each, and one technician supervised the excavation of the four contiguous units in a grid square. Although the visible natural strata are often far from level, each 1 m^2 was excavated in arbitrary 50-cm vertical spits, alternating units so that the whole 2 × 2 grid square was taken down to the same level before a new spit was begun. All important items were located horizontally within their respective 1 m^2, and plans of the horizontal distribution of recovered materials were made for each 0.5-m spit. Plans and sections were drawn at a scale of 1:50. All sediment was screened by spit and meter square. Whenever possible, P'ei had three photographs of the excavation taken from different directions each day. The excavation lasted 141 days in 1933 and 1934 (P'ei, 1934b, 1939a, p. 8). Apparently, similar techniques were employed by P'ei and Chia at Locality 1 after 1933 (P'ei, 1937, pp. 362-63).

During our visit to Chou-k'ou-tien, the information we were given, along with our own observations, suggested strongly that excavation and recording techniques currently employed are very similar, perhaps identical to those used by P'ei during the pre-Liberation excavations.

At Locality 1, vestiges of a three-dimensional reference system based on cells 2 m on a side could still be seen painted on the rock of the cave wall, and a 2-m grid system is shown in recently published diagrams. This suggests the same basic referencing system that was used in the early thirties. Whether the position of each recovered object is physically measured with reference to this system or if it serves primarily as a sort of guide in excavation was not determined. Certainly the horizontal position of some items is measured, since they are shown on published plans. I was told that horizontal plans of (at least the major) contents of 50-cm-deep arbitrary spits are made for each square, but that measurement of exact depths is noted only where it is judged important to do so. Otherwise, vertical relationships can be found by superposing plans from different spits or judged from overlap indicated in the individual plans. I saw photographs of squares that had been internally gridded with strings at either 10-cm or 20-cm intervals (the latter is probably the correct figure). This gridding may have been done to give scale to the photograph or to help the excavator draw a floor plan (I could not determine which). I did not see any of the floor plans personally. I was told that, while consolidated sediments were not screened, loose sediments were washed through fine screens to recover microfauna and other small items.

The amount of earth moved during the 1966 field season at Chou-k'ou-tien must be between 270 and 360 m^3. I do not know how many excavators were engaged in the work or how long it lasted, nor were we told how dense the finds were (I would judge from our discussions that they must have been locally abundant but generally very scarce). Because of these uncertainties it is not possible to say how rapidly earth moving proceeded. However, if the field season was at all extensive, the excavators must now be much more painstaking than those during the twenties and thirties, when it was customary to excavate from 115-200 m^3 per week of sediment so indurated that some had to be removed by blasting. (In contrast, at the mid-Pleistocene Spanish site of Torralba, our field crew of 18-25 people excavated only around 20 m^3 per week during the 1962 and 1963 field seasons.)

Keeping control of the excavation must have been a difficult task in the early years at Chou-k'ou-tien. At Upper Cave, P'ei was assisted by just two well-trained specialists, Chia Lan-p'o and M. N. Bien (P'ei, 1939a, p. 8). These three professionals had to direct the work of a mass of untrained (and probably uninterested) laborers. Now, many student trainees participate in each dig. The quality of data recovery must be improved as a consequence.

We were not shown the warehousing facilities of the IVPP, and thus I cannot say what sorts of materials were saved during the excavation or how they are stored. Many of the artifacts I saw bore inked numbers. Most of the 1966 pieces were so labeled. The designation shows level, square, year, and (apparently) the individual identifying number of the artifact (e.g., L1 A8 66:35). Some also had a supplementary number, which may be an acquisition number or an indication that the piece has been published. The labeling system represents some simplification of that in use in the thirties, where year, identification number, square, and another complex number (which may give coordinates) are shown:

36:136:A4:41L24. The fact that what I have identified as individual
artifact identification numbers are never very large, although there are
well over 100,000 stone artifacts from Locality 1, suggests either that
numbering begins anew with each level in each square or that I was shown
a highly unrepresentative sample.

The great value of paleontological remains for archeological interpretation is certainly appreciated by IVPP personnel, and the fact that
reexamination of old collections has resulted in the recognition of
important specimens that were not identified earlier suggests that many
fragments whose nature is uncertain are collected and preserved for future
study.

Chou-k'ou-tien was prominently mentioned as a focus of interdisciplinary
and interinstitutional collaboration in research. Personnel from the Institute of Archeology apparently assisted in the excavation, and pollen
samples were taken and analyzed by Hsü Jen of the Institute of Botany.
However, it was surprising to find that this is evidently the extent to
which interdisciplinary research has been carried. There is considerably
less interest in the potential of sedimentological, mineralogical, and
chemical analysis of the cave deposits than I had anticipated.

The age of the hominid-bearing sediments is still open to some question. Other than uranium series dating, which is certainly not ideally
suited for this purpose, new dating techniques have not been tried.
Since collaboration with foreign scholars is not possible at the present
time, it will probably be a long time before we learn whether those
techniques might provide reasonable dates for the deposits.

At the Ting-ts'un sites, the excavated areas have been filled, and
aside from some general details concerning topographic setting and
stratigraphic sequences, there was little to be seen. Apparently, many
of the finds from most localities are casual surface discoveries of
items eroding out of the Pleistocene strata. We were told that over 100
surface finds have been turned in by the masses since 1966. Other
casual discoveries were made by production teams during construction.
(This was the case with Locality 92, where an elephant tusk was found
by farmers digging a trench.) When such finds are made, work is
stopped and district governmental and Cultural Relics officials are
notified. Known find localities are examined every 15 days and cleared
of newly eroded specimens at least once a month.

Finds were first made at Ting-ts'un in 1953. Workers reported the
discovery of artifacts and fauna to the provincial Cultural Relics
bureau, and the site complex (which follows the Fen River for 11 km)
was surveyed in 1954 by the IVPP. More than 15 localities were discovered, which to date have produced around 2,000 implements, a large
faunal series, and three human teeth, said to be intermediate in form
between *Homo erectus* and *H. sapiens*. Nine of the localities have been
excavated, including Locality 100, which yielded the human remains (P'ei
et al., 1958).

The excavations themselves are long since filled, but we were shown
several of the major localities. From the visible stratigraphy, the
nature of the fauna, and the artifact typology, a late Pleistocene age
for this complex seems most probable, although that diagnosis disagrees
with the opinion of some Chinese scholars who have favored a middle

Pleistocene attribution (Movius, 1956). A late Pleistocene age was suggested by P'ei Wen-Chung, Chia Lan-p'o, and Chou Ming-chen, the original investigators, and is generally accepted at present.

At Locality 100 the human remains and associated fossils were said to have been recovered in the upper part of a 17-m-deep series of sands and gravels overlying sandstones of Sanmenian age and capped by 5 m of waterlaid loess. The approximate find spot, a gravel seam whose height was given as 17 m above the present Fen River drainage, was still visible in the section at Locality 100, although some slumping obscured the levels in adjacent areas. I measured the section with a Brunton compass used as a hand level and found the true height of the fossil-bearing gravel seam to be only ca. 9.9 m above the Fen River (the base of the derived loess is only ca. 11.7 m above drainage at this point). Since the Fen River was not in flood, these figures suggest that the section was originally measured with much less care than I expected.

We also visited a site museum at the Neolithic village of Pan-p'o. Untangling the complex stratigraphic superimpositions of houses, pits, and postholes at this multicomponent village required no mean technical sophistication. Published photographs of the excavation show painted grid lines and measuring devices, demonstrating that considerable care was probably exercised in recording finds.

We witnessed two excavations in progress near Cheng-chou with An Chin-huai of the Cheng-chou City Museum. In most cases only important or difficult excavations are entrusted to the provincial museums; other digs are handled at the local level.

At the Shang Palace site we saw 10 to 12 workers and students trowelling out the contents of a late Shang trench cutting through earlier palace buildings. The fill from this trench, including large decorated potsherds, was simply thrown away. There were no screens and we were told that they are not used. There was no evident grid system, and I learned that "area excavation" is the rule. None of those excavating had notebooks and we saw no measurements made, but we were told that they do record observations "as necessary."

A site museum covers a large trench crammed with cut human bone, including parts of skulls, broken ceramic, and stone. Later we were shown a plan of the trench, on which only certain items were numbered. We were told that identification numbers are given only to human and animal skulls or pottery fragments that the field excavator knows can be reassembled to form essentially complete vessels. These "restorable" sherds are collected, but the rest are thrown away. Similarly, the best-preserved human skeletons are chosen for display, but other human remains and fauna are simply discarded. One of our informants from the Revolutionary Committee of Honan Provincial Museum was wryly amused at the idea of saving the discarded materials: the museum staff would soon be up to their ears in junk were that to be tried.

The sexing and ageing of skeletons is done by the field archeologists; anatomists from Honan provincial medical school are called in to help with specimens whose age or sex is difficult to diagnose ("manlike women and womanlike men"). Our guides from the museum gave the impression that ageing and sexing can be done with virtually complete accuracy given such professional assistance. In the West we find the problem somewhat more difficult.

Ta-ho village is a multicomponent Neolithic site about 300,000 m^2 in area. Cultural layers, usually 4 to 6 m deep, include materials from two major divisions of the Neolithic: Lung-shan (later) and Yang-shao (earlier). Five staff members from the Cheng-chou City Museum are permanently stationed at the site, and assistants are hired from nearby villages. We saw several excavators at work with trowels (often using them as hand-held picks, a technique we did not see at the Shang Palace, and one that entails some risk of damaging artifacts or bones before they are exposed to view). The area excavation took place in an ungridded square ca. 10 m on a side. Excavators were clearing several features, and pottery from each feature was "level-bagged" separately. No measurements were being taken at the moment, but one of the excavators held a notebook and a plumb bob; a tape and a pad of millimeter paper were close at hand against one wall of the excavated area.

A nearby cemetery, evidently opened some time previously, held more than 20 adult skeletons (two with grave goods) and some infant burials in jars. Due either to rain or irrigation, the uncovered individual graves holding the skeletons had filled with standing water, partially or completely immersing most of the skeletons and associated artifacts. No one seemed especially concerned with the fate of the burials, perhaps because the finds had already been photographed or drawn for publication. The lack of concern was remarkable, since alternate soaking and drying will destroy the bones. It can only be explained as a consequence of the policy of discarding most human skeletal material after excavation.

I asked whether the preservation of skeletal series might not permit future studies of pathologies, population vital statistics, epidemiology, and similar subjects that the archeologist is usually not trained to deal with. I was told that such studies are regularly done and was given references to publications. All the supplied references are concerned with dentition--tooth wear, caries, and tooth loss, for example.

Ta-ho-tsun Site,
Chenchou.

Other types of skeletal evidence of pathology, especially postcranial evidence, are not mentioned in those publications, and, even though I am not familiar with the literature, I expect that all but the grossest evidence of this sort may ordinarily be overlooked.

Other relevant information came from our visits to the Yin Hsü archeological station at An-yang and the Honan Provincial Museum in Cheng-chou. At the former institution we saw a storeroom where there were stacks of uncovered brim-full bushel baskets piled one atop the other, each containing a mixture of broken pots, animal remains, and human skeletal material. Some items in each basket were labeled with the same identifying number, and all the baskets in a single stack seem to have held material with a single identification. We were told that the labels identified different storage pits, that the pits are ordinarily both large and deep, and that the contents of each pit are removed as a unit, without attempts to differentiate levels within a pit.

Our guides told us that their excavation procedure is similar to that we saw in Cheng-chou. No preliminary grid is established. Areal excavation is the rule. A series of regular test pits or trenches are sunk into a site, and recovered materials from a single test are labeled the same way and stored together. When an interesting structure, pit, or other feature is encountered, further excavation of the test pit is abandoned and the excavation is extended to encompass that feature. Then, the feature itself becomes the spatial reference unit and all items from a single feature are given a single identifying designation and stored together. What we saw in storage were the cleaned but otherwise unprocessed bulk contents of several such features.

At the Honan Provincial Museum the process of acquisitioning finds was demonstrated for us. Items arriving from the field are accompanied by forms that list the number of pieces in each container, the site name, a designation of the locality where found (house 1, pit 52, etc.), the name of the finder, and a date. Predictably, the form has no provision for listing depth or coordinates of the find(s). In the museum warehouse a registrar checks the contents of the consignment against the list and affirms the list with his signature. It is at this point that each item is given a number, which is inked on each piece; before, only the container was numbered. Next, the piece is measured and studied. Only then is it formally acquisitioned by giving it a museum number, which is recorded on a special form, along with the description, measurements, and typological characteristics of the piece. This information is later abstracted on a summary sheet that seems to be part of the general museum catalogue.

It will be recalled that only items judged important by an excavator are numbered. If the identifying numbers are not painted on the find until it reaches the museum, and if all items that reach the museum receive numbers (as seems to be the case), it is clearly implied that most finds judged unimportant by the field excavators never get as far as the museum: they are discarded in the field. Such exclusive reliance on the opinion of the field archeologist must give the sophisticated field director qualms, to say the least. The burden thus placed on the shoulders of cadres whose formal preparation is limited is tremendous. Only a very naive archeologist has such confidence in his own omniscience.

It seems to me that this degree of concentration of responsibility is inadvisable and unnecessary.

Near Sian we visited one western Chou site at Chang-chia-p'o. West of the Chang-chia-p'o village, a site museum preserves evidence of two horse-and-chariot burials excavated by the Institute of Archeology. Though the horse skeletons were well preserved, the wooden chariots had disintegrated, leaving earthen casts or pseudomorphs of the wagon wheels, bed, tongue, and yoke. Their recovery required excavation of the utmost virtuosity, as did the development of casts of the harnesses, richly decorated with small cowries. Obviously, China has some technically superb excavators.

In overview, the evidence we saw, though scanty, was illuminating. Chinese techniques of excavation and recording are variable, as one might expect. Paleolithic research comes closest to meeting contemporary standards of good archeological investigation and, in general, excavations at the Shang Palace were furthest removed from those ideals. Individual field directors differ considerably in the standards they apply, and this is true for specialists in every period. There is much less interdisciplinary collaboration in data collection than there should be, which is regrettable but understandable given the prior demands placed on the natural scientist's time by expanding production in a developing socialist economy.

Despite the critical observations presented above, this is not a negative evaluation of current Chinese practice. If excavation and recording procedures do not usually meet ideal standards, neither does average Chinese practice fall below the average practice in most of the West. In Western archeology there are also great differences between the recovery techniques used by better Paleolithic prehistorians and those used by better excavators of the Western centers of classical urban society, and those differences offer point-for-point analogies with the Chinese case. Data recovery must be improved in the People's Republic, but it must also be improved elsewhere.

Similar observations can be made about techniques for archeological data analysis. Several minor points deserve brief mention. In the first place, there is, once more, far too little cooperation for analytical purposes with specialists from other disciplines. Strangely, Institute of Archeology personnel seem more keenly aware that this a failing than do some members of the IVPP. Furthermore, statistical techniques, which are proving so useful in the West, seem not to be part of the Chinese analytical battery, though they should be. In this case there is no difference between IA and IVPP.

Some Pleistocene prehistoric archeologists and paleoanthropologists seemed rather naive about the significance of geological strata. Unwarranted attention was paid to sediment color as a basis for chronological correlation. For example, it is still sometimes believed that all bluish-grey, green, yellowish, or white lacustrine clays in North China are "Ni-ho-wan" (= lower Pleistocene) in age and that all reddish clays date from the mid-Pleistocene. Fortunately, recent discoveries of late Pleistocene fauna and tools in blue-grey clays in the Ni-ho-wan basin itself are now forcing Chinese scholars to reevaluate this tenet.

For a brief period, artifact and fossil-bearing localities at Ting-ts'un were tentatively assigned a mid-Pleistocene age by a few scholars, because immediately above the Sanmenian sandstone the clay at the base of the artifact-bearing fluviatile deposits at Locality 99 was reddish. This interpretation is abundantly contraindicated by the data from the fossil-rich horizons, but we were told that a very few geologists still believe it.

At the Kwangtung Provincial Museum I was told that South Chinese grey clays are ordinarily thought to be Neolithic (Holocene) in age. That interpretation was followed in discussions of archeological finds in the province; what is more, some suspiciously Neolithic-looking aceramic collections were apparently attributed a Paleolithic age because they occur in yellowish (or other nongrey) deposits.

Although some of these ill-founded assumptions are now under scrutiny and have been abandoned in specific cases, they nevertheless persist in the practice of at least some professionals. They could be shown to be generally ill advised, and the relative chronology of Chinese Pleistocene sediments could be put, once and for all, on a firmer foundation if the stratigraphic sequences and geographic settings of key Pleistocene localities were studied in detail by well-trained geomorphologists and stratigraphers, and if a concerted attempt were made to collect sample suites from these localities and subject them to suitable relative and absolute dating techniques.

L. H. Morgan's classifications of the stages of social evolution provide the primary model for the reconstructions of prehistoric social life and customs produced by Chinese scholars (Morgan, 1963). This leads to interpretations entirely without foundation in the recovered archeological evidence.

NOTES ON ARTIFACT TYPOLOGY AND A
CLASSIFICATION OF SOME COLLECTIONS

General Observations

Any Pleistocene prehistorian familiar with the English or Russian summaries of Chinese articles dealing with Paleolithic stone tools will be aware that the equivalents chosen for typological designations by the translators are often terms that are difficult for Western specialists to understand. Often, artifact illustrations, when they are provided, are just ambiguous enough to leave the issue unresolved.

I had expected to be permitted to examine Paleolithic artifact collections in the company of Chinese Paleolithic specialists and to discuss typology with them simultaneously. In that way we could each use the artifacts themselves to illustrate our terminology. I had hoped that this might lead to the development of a bilingual glossary of terms used in artifact classification, but in the course of our visit that hope was largely unrealized.

Good typology depends on three basic principles. The categories used should be mutually exclusive, they should not overlap, and they should exhaust the variability in the artifact collection. Virtually all pieces should be classifiable, although a few pieces in any collection will elude diagnosis. No matter whether the typology used be a set of arbitrary *a priori* definitions or whether it be generated from the statistical study of artifacts in a single collection, these principles should hold.

I soon learned that type names used in the Chinese literature (and this is true for the Chinese terms as well as English translations in abstracts) do not conform to these principles. As an example, there is no strict definition of items called "pointed implements": they include fortuitous pointed flakes, retouched implements that are vaguely pointed, blunt-nosed pieces, squarish utilized flakes, trihedral picks, end scrapers, and even some irregular (but unpointed) cores. Some items called scrapers are indistinguishable from others called choppers or chopping tools, and sometimes pieces in both these categories (and some of the "points") are really denticulated and enough like each other so that they belong in a single category. Deliberate retouch, minimal nibbling due to utilization, and geological crushing are frequently confused.

One (translated) category in the literature had especially puzzled me. Retouched pieces of the greatest variety of shapes are called "round scrapers" in English. I asked Li Yen-hsien and Ch'iu Chung-lang to show me examples of this type, and they did. At first I still failed to grasp the reason for the type name, but I eventually realized that the pieces all showed more or less continuous circumferential retouch. "Round scrapers" means "scrapers all-around," not "circular scrapers." Li and Ch'iu were as amused as I by this inadequate translation, once the difference between the two English concepts was explained.

Lack of system in typology is by no means unique to the People's Republic of China. Systematic typological usage is still the exception in most parts of Europe, and serious attempts to put lithic typology on a rational footing really made little headway until the 1950's, when François Bordes, Denise de Sonneville-Bordes, and Jean Perrot developed the coordinated system for Paleolithic tool typology that several European specialists now use. Although Chinese typological usage must eventually change, it would not be true to say that the People's Republic lags behind in this respect, since its practice is at least as good as the abysmal average in most other parts of the world.

· Because of these problems, a useful glossary was only half developed. Li and Ch'iu took my "Bordes" type list for lower and middle Paleolithic collections (the upper Paleolithic type list is not really applicable outside Western Europe) and returned it with Chinese equivalents for all the terms. (This glossary is not appended since the Chinese characters will have to be transcribed by a specialist.) They told me, of course, that this list would be of little use at present because the Bordes' terms are not in current use in China. On the other hand, none of us thought an English translation of commonly used Chinese type names would be of much practical utility, either, and given the press of time we did not attempt to develop such a glossary. I think that we parted with a mutual realization that this is a serious problem area that now hinders communications between specialists inside and outside the People's Republic. I am hopeful that both sides will attempt to resolve this problem in the future.

Chinese Paleolithic Collections

Partly because of the lack of terminological comparability, the Chinese Paleolithic is something of an enigma to Westerners. As students, we learned that Paleolithic collections from China were completely *sui generis*: that as a result of a combination of intractable raw materials and local idiosyncracies in flaking techniques, the collections were incomparable with Western products. More recently it has become fashionable among some prehistorians to regard the tools from Chou-k'ou-tien and Lan-t'ien as a logical offshoot of the Developed Oldowan, and even in some cases to give the Chinese assemblages that designation. As a result of our trip I have become convinced that all such preconceptions about those collections are false.

I saw only 228 stone artifacts in China. This is a pitifully small sample. Nevertheless, it probably includes a larger number of lower paleolithic pieces than has been classified by any Westerner familiar with European and African middle-upper Pleistocene materials since Breuil. Though the number is small, the collections still permit some confident, if general, conclusions.

Chou-k'ou-tien

Before the discovery of stone tools in Locality 1, no lithic artifacts had been found in association with hominid remains of comparable age anywhere in the world (P'ei, 1932, p. 127). As a consequence, contemporary opinions concerning the correspondence expectable between the documents of biological and cultural evolution were quite misleading. Neither P'ei nor Teilhard had any extensive familiarity with earlier Paleolithic artifact assemblages outside China, and the evident great age of the sediments, as judged from the fauna, combined with the apparently "primitive" morphology of the hominid finds seem to have preconditioned both to regard the artifacts as particularly crude. From the first, the relatively great proportion of unretouched pieces in the artifact series was stressed, although nowadays we recognize that assemblages from any period, including the most recent, may have large proportions of unretouched pieces, depending on the extent to which stone knapping was actually performed on the spot in the area excavated. Much apparent retouch was explained away as the result of utilization rather than trimming. Variability in the retouched artifact series was characterized as random, capricious, ill-defined, and scarcely under conscious control. Since so many pieces were made in quartz and quartzite, some of this variability was ascribed to the intractable nature of the raw materials, and the toolmakers were said to have been dominated by raw material, rather than to have mastered it (P'ei, 1932, pp. 135-37; Teilhard and P'ei, 1932, pp. 322, 354). These supposed characteristics of the Locality 1 collections were considered to correspond quite well with expectations, given that the tools were so ancient and associated with such early hominids.

In October and November 1931, the Abbé Breuil visited Peking at the invitation of the Cenozoic Research Laboratory. At the time, Breuil was probably more familiar with lower Paleolithic industries outside China than any other person. In contrast to P'ei and Teilhard, Breuil was struck by the sophistication of the Chou-k'ou-tien artifacts. Comparing some of the quartz and quartzite pieces from Locality 1 with artifacts in similar material from such sites as Chez Pourré in the Corrèze, France, he concluded that the Chou-k'ou-tien assemblages, and particularly the quartz series, contained quite a complete range of artifact types of a degree of sophistication comparable to that displayed in quartz in some French Mousterian sites (Breuil, 1932, p. 153). Unlike Teilhard and P'ei, Breuil stressed the regular patterning observable in the retouched tools and the evident mastery the toolmakers exercised over their raw materials. Teilhard, P'ei, and Breuil all agreed that true bifaces were either rare or lacking at Locality 1, but Breuil specifically commented that he personally recovered several heavily eroded artifacts in metamorphosed sandstone (grès metamorphisé) that might have been large trihedral flakes or even amygdaloid bifaces before they were altered (Breuil, 1932, p. 152).

After his second visit to China in early 1935, Breuil's views concerning the Chou-k'ou-tien assemblages became even stronger. The list of recognizable tool types he then presented includes true blades, burins, endscrapers, sidescrapers, perforators, points, and very small ovate or cordiform bifaces. Some pieces reminded him of Levallois flakes. Although he ascribed part of this seemingly evolved series to a clever and precocious adaptation of the products of bipolar retouch, he nevertheless fell into the error of speculating, on the basis of the artifact series, that the site might be somewhat younger than had been suggested, perhaps dating to the period just prior to the late Mousterian in Europe (Breuil, 1935, pp. 742-43). Such a suggestion equates in modern terms with an earlier upper Pleistocene age for Locality 1. (The argument is unnecessary, since all the "evolved" types Breuil noted are now known to occur in assemblages even older than those from Chou-k'ou-tien.) Breuil concluded, quite reasonably, that the artifacts from Chou-k'ou-tien were really not comparable to any recognized European industrial complex, and that they should be referred to by a distinctive label: "Chou-k'ou-tienian" (Breuil, 1935, p. 744).

Breuil's views naturally provoked argument. Teilhard, P'ei, and Black went to some length to discredit them, and in reaction themselves overstated the unpatterned, rudimentary nature of the implements. Although some parallel between the best tools from Locality 1 and the cruder speciments from some French Mousterian levels was admitted, and the levels show some minor evolution in artifact manufacturing technique through time, it was stressed that, at least in the lower levels at Locality 1, "not a single highly refined implement has been found so far, which could for instance be compared with the best pieces found in the Mousterian quartz-layers in France" (Teilhard and P'ei, 1932, p. 354; see also Black *et al.*, 1933, pp. 132-33; Black, 1934, pp. 110-111). Teilhard eventually went even further, claiming that the Chou-k'ou-tien hominids were incapable of making better artifacts even in good siliceous raw material (Teilhard, 1941, p. 61).

In a more recent article, summarizing much additional material, P'ei still assumes this "primitivist" view of the Chou-k'ou-tien tools strongly.

According to P'ei (1965, p. 256) new research highlights the crude nature of the series:

> The primitiveness of the *Sinanthropus* Industry is fully demonstrated by the facts: 1) abundant utilization of flakes without secondary work; 2) all the secondary work on the Choukoutien implements is crude and irregular; 3) no definite 'types' could be recognized as noted above, etc. The primitive characters of the *Sinanthropus* Industry fit well its geological age and its morphological feature [*sic*] and indicate the first stage of the industrial development in human history.

This is essentially the viewpoint now seen in the general literature (Movius, 1944; Oakley, 1964, pp. 237-39; Treistman, 1972, p. 15). Even Breuil seems eventually to have abandoned his earlier position. The reasoned views of François Bordes (1968, p. 84), quite close to Breuil's early stand on the artifacts, constitute a minority opinion at present.

I saw 101 pieces (or casts) from key localities at Chou-k'ou-tien. One was a cast from Locality 13: the well-known chopping tool (P'ei, 1934b). Although there is room for some disagreement over the classification of this piece as a chopping tool or an amorphous core, I believe that the former (traditional) classification is correct. The other 100 pieces came from Locality 1, and all were actual artifacts rather than casts.

Pieces from Chou-k'ou-tien were seen in the IVPP, the Chou-k'ou-tien Field Station, the Tientsin Museum, the Cheng-chou City Museum (Paleontology section), the Nanking Museum, and the Shanghai Natural History Museum. The IVPP has the bulk of the collection. Many or most provinces probably have one or two pieces from Locality 1 for display. Many of these (like the collection at Cheng-chou) may not have been studied.

All but about 50 of the artifacts I saw from all sites were in the IVPP. I was not permitted to measure any of the pieces, nor did time allow it. With these restrictions, I was unable to undertake any detailed study of platform preparation or any measurement of bulb/butt angles. In a few instances, pieces were displayed in closed cases (nine of the tools from Locality 1 and several flakes), and as a result I could not classify five retouched artifacts from Locality 1: sometimes, typology was obvious even through glass.

While some of the artifacts I saw from Locality 1 were made of quartz, a far greater number than I had expected were of hornfels, fine grained quartzite, and chert, all of which are quite tractable. In fact, such pieces were more numerous than quartz artifacts in the series shown me. One tool, a chopper, was made of dolomite, which I was told was imported from at least 20 km from Chou-k'ou-tien.

The first compelling impression one receives from the Chou-k'ou-tien series is that of considerable patterning and great typological variety among the retouched pieces. Reading the published descriptions and illustrations had not prepared me to expect the variety and regularity I saw. On the other hand, this discovery is not surprising; not only did Breuil and Bordes recognize it, but, additionally, such a degree of variety is well within the expectable range for earlier mid-Pleistocene European (or African) assemblages with which I am familiar.

Of the 100 pieces I saw, 37 were unretouched flakes (31 chert, 6 quartz), and 9 were minimally retouched or utilized flakes. One other was a geologically crushed piece. There were two cores (one discoid, one rough pyramidal), three hammerstones (all with heavy battering or flaking on at least one extremity), and one double-pitted stone that bore evidence of utilization as both hammer and anvil.

Although I could not make exact counts of butt types, facetting was the exception, while many pieces had smooth or dihedral butts. An appreciable part of the smooth butts was cortical. Bulb angles are often open and there are occasional pieces with double bulbs, but the series I saw offers no proof of flaking by what has been called "anvil technique." Such features are found in other collections made by ordinary percussion. I saw only a few "bipolar" pieces.

I was somewhat surprised to find two large flakes (in the Tientsin Museum) made on prepared cores. (Both were also seen by Professor Howell.) These two pieces were perfectly good proto-Levallois or "atypical Levallois" specimens, and as far as I am aware neither had been recognized and described before, although Bordes (1968, figure 27) figures a "Levallois-like flake" from Upper Locality 1.

At Tientsin I could not classify five obvious retouched stone tools in cases. All had scraper retouch and some also were denticulated. There were 42 classifiable retouched tools, including a chopper and two chopping tools.

One piece, in quartz, was a true dihedral burin. There was 1 perforator and ten denticulated tools, a truncated flake and two notched pieces (one a double notch). The series included three core scrapers or "rabots." There were 16 sidescrapers of several kinds. Most (7) were simple lateral convex sidescrapers, while the rest include convergent convex scrapers, canted sidescrapers, double biconvex sidescrapers, scrapers on truncated flakes, scrapers with abrupt backs, scrapers on ventral surface, steep scrapers, and transverse convex sidescrapers. This was both the most numerous (38%) and the most variable (nine types, of which 7 are recognized in Bordes' system) artifact category. Denticulates make up the bulk of the rest of the collection, with 24% of the 42 pieces. Some are macro-denticulated pieces, others are normal denticulates. Besides the scraper/truncated flake, there were two "combination tools" of diverse typology: one alternate sidescraper/denticulate and one combination perforator/denticulate.

Obviously, a sample of 100 artifacts from a total of 100,000 is a pretty small lot on which to base wide-ranging conclusions. The series I saw was probably selected as representing the best pieces and undoubtedly contained more retouched pieces in comparison to flakes than would be found in any of the Chou-k'ou-tien assemblage as a whole. (That

probably explains the low incidence of quartz pieces.) But there are
reasons for thinking that even intentional attempts to bias the artifact
proportions in the series shown me would probably not have been completely successful. For example, Chinese prehistorians do not recognize denticulates as a distinct category. Instead, such pieces are lumped with
others in several types. As a result, proportions of denticulates among
retouched tools might be little affected even if the collection I was
shown was heavily biased towards what the Chinese call "scraping implements." On the other hand, given the typological variety I saw, it
seems likely that larger samples would reveal many more types--regardless
of the typology applied--than I was able to identify.

In sum, the collection shows that *Homo erectus* at Chou-k'ou-tien was
a stone knapper of about the same degree of skill and attainment as his
contemporaries in Europe and Africa. His artifacts are not so strange,
after all. The degree of patterning in the artifact series is greater
than that of any evolved Oldowan collection with which I am at all
familiar and is quite comparable with that in mid-Pleistocene Acheulean
assemblages, although the series is so idiosyncratic that it would not
be confused with any Acheulean collection I know. The idea that the
Chou-k'ou-tien assemblage is especially rich in choppers and chopping
tools may be simply a reflection of differences in nomenclature.

The apparent absence of true bifaces from the collection has been regarded as one of its most noteworthy aspects. Whether such pieces are
truly absent or are present but rare, crude, and unrecognized, remains
for some future qualified prehistorian with more access to the collections to establish. In my opinion, a completely satisfactory analysis
of the place of the Chou-k'ou-tien industry in world prehistory will
require collaboration by both Chinese and Western scientists, and I hope
that the groundwork for collaboration of this sort will eventually be
established.

Breuil also claimed that the faunal series from Locality 1 included
many pieces that were deliberately shaped or utilized as tools (Breuil,
1932, 1939). His judgment was questioned on the grounds that some of
the attributes Breuil accepted as evidence of intentional human alteration might have been due to other causes or the accidental by-products
of activities with other primary aims, and that without much preliminary
investigation (such as that outlined in P'ei, 1938) to rule out such
alternate explanations, the existence of a systematic bone industry at
Locality 1 could not be proved (Teilhard and P'ei, 1932, p. 354; Black
et al., 1933, p. 130). Now, undoubted intentionally shaped bone implements have been found in European lower and middle Paleolithic contexts (sometimes in fair numbers), and some of these pieces look strikingly similar to some flaked bones from Chou-k'ou-tien figured by Breuil
(1939, plate XVIII [3], plates XXII and XXV [3, 8, 11, 12, 13]).

Our hosts from the IVPP informed us that Breuil's identifications of
true bone tools at Locality 1 are now universally rejected, and though
we asked to see the specimens, they were not shown to us. It seems
likely that the Chou-k'ou-tien faunal materials do contain some convincing bone tools, but until the series has been reexamined their presence
cannot be verified, nor can their proportional abundance be assessed.
In a note to Breuil's 1939 monograph (p. 41), P'ei states that the
pieces described by Breuil were sent to Nanking for exhibition and lost

in hostilities with the Japanese in 1937. If the pieces were indeed destroyed, it is most unfortunate, and we must hope that new excavations will supply further specimens for analysis in the near future.

Smaller Collections Claimed to Be of
Comparable (mid-Pleistocene) Antiquity

I classified four small lots of artifacts from sites whose age may be as great as or greater than that of the Chou-k'ou-tien collections just described. All are now considered to be broadly mid-Pleistocene in age. All are housed in the IVPP in Peking.

The most interesting are the pieces from the vicinity of the *Homo erectus* sites near Lan-t'ien. Seven of these pieces came from strata at Kung-wang-ling correlated with those in which hominid remains were found. These comprise a large quartzite chopper on a cobble segment, a quartz core with minimal secondary retouch or utilization, a quartz scraper with use-denticulation, a thick quartz utilized flake, an unretouched quartzite flake with smooth (cortical) butt, and, from some "8-25 m horizontally distant from the skull fragments, and 1-2 m vertically distant," a small quartzite perforator. The artifacts would all be quite at home in the Chou-k'ou-tien collection, but quartz and quartzite pieces are very abundant in the Kung-wang-ling series.

Two kilometers from the hominid site, in a red soil of "comparable age," investigators found a large, elongate, almost triangular, partial biface with cortical butt. If this piece is really contemporary with the hominid finds, it is compelling evidence that Asiatic *Homo erectus* could and did produce true bifaces at least on occasion. The piece is usually called a "pointed implement" in Chinese publications, but its nature had been suspected by some prehistorians earlier. The last artifact I saw from Lan-t'ien was from the banks of the Lao-ch'i River. It is a large trimmed cobble, perhaps an amorphous core.

Four pieces from the K'o-ho area on the Fen River in Shansi Province are possibly mid-Pleistocene in age, judging from associated fauna. There are 11 excavated localities at K'o-ho (Chia *et al.*, 1962); I was unable to ascertain which one(s) produced the artifacts in question.

One piece is probably a prismatic-sectioned quartzite core. (It could possibly be a broken trihedral pick.) Two are chopping tools and one is an alternately retouched combination steep denticulate/side-scraper. Once again, such pieces would not be out of place in the collection from Chou-k'ou-tien Locality 1, but I saw so few that the rest of the collection may be very different.

From the Ni-ho-wan basin I saw two possible artifacts: a large, heavily rolled triangular chunk that could easily be nonartifactual (the "facetted stone" of Breuil) and a recently discovered large flaked cobble (possibly a core?) that is undeniably artifactual. The latter piece is very important since it was found in a stratum that is thought to be earlier than anything yet discussed (early Pleistocene). However, the Ni-ho-wan stratigraphic succession is now being thoroughly revised, so I prefer at present not to rely too heavily on earlier diagnoses.

Kwan-yin-tung (Guanyindong) is an artifact-yielding cave in the
province of Kwei-chou in southern China. Over 2,000 stone tools were
recovered at this locality. Associated faunal remains (more than 20
species) include *Ailuropoda, Stegodon,* and *Tapir.* Discovered in 1964,
Kwan-yin-tung is the biggest early Paleolithic site (mid-Pleistocene age)
in the southern part of China.

I saw five casts of artifacts from Kwan-yin-tung. All are retouched
flake tools and all have been subject to some crushing. One is a combination left lateral sidescraper/right lateral denticulate; the second
is a large canted sidescraper with three convex working edges that
meet at obtuse angles; the third is a transverse concave sidescraper
(on a pseudo-Levallois point); the fourth is an endscraper with two
lateral convex sidescrapers; and the last is a double biconvex sidescraper crushed at its distal extremity. All are large and, from the
casts, seem to be made of fine-grained siliceous raw material. One
flake butt is facetted; the others are smooth or removed. None of the
tools is made on a Levallois flake. Two of the pieces bear islands of
cortex (one on the butt). Judging from the size of these artifacts
and the extent of the primary flaking to which each was subjected, I
would venture the guess that the collection will prove to have some
proto-Levallois or true Levallois flakes when it is finally studied.

Ting-ts'un (late Pleistocene)

From this late Pleistocene site complex (P'ei *et al.,* 1958), I saw 41
artifacts from at least 15 localities. Some of the pieces bore no
locality designation. Almost all artifacts from these sites are made
of a black raw material identified as hornfels, but in several cases
I could detect marked granularity in the material, which suggests that
the term is being used loosely.

Uniformity in raw material selected need not indicate contemporaneity
of the collections compared. That there may be considerable temporal
spread between the earliest and the latest collections from Ting-t'sun
is strongly suggested by the fact that artifact-bearing horizons at the
localities we actually visited were at quite different heights above
the present Fen River; leveling with a Brunton compass showed Locality
98 to be considerably lower than Locality 90, for example. The fauna
from these localities is broadly late Pleistocene in age but does not
include forms that would permit much refinement of that age estimate.

The pieces I saw are described below. Four pieces without provenience
and the pick from Locality 91 are in the Shanghai Natural History Museum.
The rest are stored at the IVPP in Peking.

● *Locality 29*: Six pieces: One huge flake; one denticulate on a
retouched flake; one steep convex sidescraper; one combination denticu-
late/sidescraper; one variant tool combining a notch and a steeply retouched piece; one trihedral pick.

● *Locality 39*? (number blurred): One small asymmetrical elongate
core or very atypical biface.

102

- *Locality 41*: One transverse denticulate with adjacent retouch.
- *Locality 81*? (number blurred): One combination sidescraper/ denticulate.
- *Locality 84*: One pointed flake (not a point).
- *Locality 90*: Six pieces: One large flake used as an anvil; one large sidestruck flake; one utilized flake; one double lateral denticulate; a ventrally retouched sidescraper (convex); one double biconvex sidescraper.
- *Locality 95*: One chopping tool.
- *Locality 96*: One trihedral pick.
- *Locality 97*: Four pieces: One bola; one chopping tool on a disc-like piece; one long steep sidescraper on a retouched flake; one convergent convex sidescraper on a blade.
- *Locality 98*: Eight pieces: Two chopping-tools (one on a core); one trihedral pick; one flake; one utilized flake; two denticulates (one multiple); one more or less rectangular canted sidescraper with one bifacially trimmed edge on a disc-like piece.
- *Locality 99*: Two pieces: One utilized flake and one steep disc-like sidescraper.
- *Locality 100*: One double biconvex sidescraper.
- *Locality 102*: One denticulate.
- *Sanuguo* (some 5 km east of Tingtsun localities proper). One absolutely characteristic long lanceolate biface. This is not a "proto-biface," nor can it be called "almost a biface" or "a bifacial flake" as has been done in the literature (P'ei, 1965, p. 258; Coles and Higgs, 1969, p. 403). It is a perfectly good, typical biface without qualification.
- *Undesignated or surface pieces*: Five pieces: One bola; one polyhedral stone; one retouched flake; two denticulates.

Were it legitimate to pool these pieces, as though they constituted a representative sample from a single assemblage or closely related group of assemblages, the following summary might be in order. First, the Ting-ts'un pieces shown me are mostly retouched artifacts. That is almost certainly due to deliberate selection by our hosts of pieces they thought would give us the most information on the composition of the retouched artifact series. Many of the Ting-ts'un pieces are quite large. There were no evident Levallois flakes in the series I examined. Bolas and polyhedral stones are reasonably numerous, as are chopping tools. Sidescrapers are somewhat more abundant than denticulated pieces. However, I was most surprised at the biface series.

Most of the primary sources and secondary publications mention the "three-faced pointed implements," "large trihedral points," or "Ting-ts'un points" from these sites as though they were rather unique (P'ei, 1965, p. 260). Published drawings do not show all sides of such pieces and so it had not been possible to judge how closely they conform to true trihedral picks, which may occur with some frequency in Spanish and African Acheulean assemblages. After seeing the actual artifacts, I am convinced that they are well within the expectable range of variation within this type in good Acheulean series. With the long, lanceolate biface from Sanuguo these pieces give an entirely different impression of late Pleistocene developments in China than one normally receives from the literature. (Incidentally, in several well-excavated or completely collected Acheulean series, bifaces and picks make up only a small proportion of total retouched tools.)

Naturally, the scanty and scattered evidence at hand is insufficient basis for claims that Acheulean-like biface-bearing assemblages exist in the Fen River region. Nevertheless, "Movius' line" has proven a much less solid barrier to the interchange of tool-manufacturing techniques, at least in South Asia, than it was supposed to be. Perhaps the apparent boundary will disappear as more data are gathered. It would seem for the present well-advised to keep an open mind about the possibility that biface-bearing industries may exist in China. After having seen the Ting-ts'un collections, the discovery of true Acheulean or Acheulean-like industrial complexes in China would come as no great shock.

The Ting-ts'un collections have less in common with the Chou-k'ou-tien Locality 1 materials than I had expected. It has been rather generally held that there are both broad and specific relationships between the Chou-k'ou-tien assemblages, the Ko-ho materials, and the Ting-ts'un series. My impression is quite the contrary. The similarities between them are no greater than those between Acheulean and Clactonian industries from Western Europe and England. The Ting-ts'un picks are not, as has been suggested, simply elongated pointed chopping tools: I saw no degree whatever of intergradation in form between the chopping tools and picks in the Ting-ts'un series. It is true that there may be similarities between the Ting-ts'un artifacts and the "late Chou-k'ou-tienian," apparently upper Pleistocene artifact series from Locality 15 (P'ei, 1939b; Movius, 1944, figures 30 and 31). However, judging from illustrations (I did not see the specimens), there is little similarity between the artifacts from Locality 15 and those from Locality 1. I do not believe the two series from Chou-k'ou-tien are morphologically continuous to any significant degree.

Other Late Pleistocene Collections

I was shown artifacts from seven other collections. Concerning three of these, age is reasonably well fixed. The other four (the Shansi-Honan sites) could be as early as mid-Pleistocene, but there is no compelling evidence for such an early attribution.

Pieces from four of the collections were displayed in the Honan Provincial Museum in Cheng-chou. Although they were in display cases, the artifacts from these four sites were shown completely enough to permit confident classification. One case was opened to permit us to examine the artifacts closely. All four sites are located in a small region of the Huang River terraces in Shansi and Honan Provinces, and in each case the artifacts were primarily made of coarse-grained raw materials.

● *San-men-hia*: Nine artifacts: Three denticulates, one a flat flake blade; one large convex sidescraper with use denticulation; one flake with minimal retouch; three large flakes (two are primary decortication flakes); one globular quartz core.

- *Chia-cheng*: One more or less globular core.

- *Ling-pao*: Three tools: One notch; one double denticulate on a prismatic chunk; one flake.

- *Shan Hsien*: Three pieces: One large notched piece; one ventrally retouched flake; one chert flake.

These pieces have been studied and, except for the Chia-cheng core, were known to me from earlier publications.

The three sites that are undoubtedly late in age are Hsiao-nan-hai, dug by the Institute of Archeology, Ho-huan, in Kansu (now being studied), and Feng-k'ai, excavated by personnel from the Kwangtung Provincial Museum but still unpublished.

- *Feng-k'ai (Provincial Museum, Kwangtung)*: Six artifacts in dark, granular stone: One combination hammer/grindstone; one simple hammerstone, battered at one end, one chopper, one large convex sidescraper, one large sidescraper/denticulate combined, one large cortical flake.

A skull of fully modern *Homo sapiens* was found in grey clay near the entry to this cave, but is thought perhaps to be Neolithic. The tool level is underlain by a faunal horizon which yielded remains of *Elephas namadicus, Equus caballus, Sus,* and an apparently modern rhino. From the appearance of the fauna, the overlying artifact horizon should not be earlier than late Pleistocene, and may even be Holocene in age.

- *Ho-huan County (Northwest University, Sian)*: Nine pieces, including one small core, one large core, six utilized flakes (at least one of which may be a flake tool), and one chopper are in this series.

This collection was displayed in a case which was not opened. Fauna associated with the tools include *Cervus canadensis, Megaloceras ordosiensis,* and a rhino. There is also burnt wood from the site.

- *Hsiao-nan-hai Cave* (Institute of Archeology, Peking, Yin Hsü Museum, An-yang, and Honan Provincial Museum): Most of the pieces from this site are presently in the Museum of the Chinese Revolution and Chinese History, which was closed during our visit, probably because of revisions to displays necessitated by the Cultural Revolution and the movement to criticize Confucius and Lin Piao.

I did not count the Hsiao-nan-hai artifacts I saw at the Institute of Archeology (around 50 pieces). For that reason, I do not present exact counts here (there were 37 pieces in the other two museums). By far the largest number of them, perhaps all, were chert flakes and spalls. The other two samples contained equal proportions of chert and quartz. Chert is said to be the dominant raw material.

The artifacts from Hsiao-nan-hai were very small, and among the flaking debris were a number of flake blades. The tools I saw are a hastily made, nondescript lot, including mostly notches and denticulates, but with a few minimally retouched convex sidescrapers. In chert, there were two dihedral burins. None of the quartz pieces I counted was retouched. At the Yin Hsü, the Hsiao-nan-hai collection included abundant fragments of broken ostrich eggshell. Judging from what we saw, the Hsiao-nan-hai collection could as easily be Mesolithic as Paleolithic. We were told that there are similarities between Hsiao-nan-hai and Chou-k'ou-tien (I presume comparison with the Upper Cave collection was intended). However, judging from the 10 or so Upper Cave tools that have been illustrated, I can see no grounds to claim such resemblance. I cannot imagine that the comparison was with earlier assemblages like that from Locality 1, which are totally unlike the Hsiao-nan-hai series.

One problematical unpublished collection remains to be discussed. Although the excavators believe it to be Paleolithic, my subjective impression is that the artifacts could easily be "Neolithic" or "latest Mesolithic." The site is Yang-ch'un in Kwangtung, and the collection now resides in the Kwangtung Provincial Museum.

Yang-ch'un has been the subject of two seasons of field work, in 1964 and 1972. It is a cave, with deposits in one long (30 m), narrow (3 m) chamber. The site is known from a pit 1 m × 2 m in horizontal dimensions, 2 m(!) deep. So far, although subdivision of the cultural horizon would be possible, it has been treated as a single unit since it is not clearly stratified. Most of the fauna comes from the lower part of the level, while the upper part has only bovids, cervids, and suids.

The faunal list is extensive and quite modern. Twenty-two forms are recognized: *Rusa unicolor*, *Bandicota* sp., *Muntiacus*, *Macaca mulatta*, *Arctonyx collaris*, *Paguma larvata*, *Rhinoceros sinensis*, *Petaurista* sp., *Rattus rattus*, *Lutra vulgaris*, *Hemigale hardwickii*, *Hipposideros* sp., *Viverra malacensis*, *Ursus thibetanus*, *Presbytis*, *Hystrix* sp., *Felis lemmincki*, *Sus scrofa*, teeth of a small orang, a small muskrat or beaverlike rodent, Caprinae, and Bovidae indet. The fauna indicates that the countryside in the near vicinity of the cave was broken and densely vegetated.

The stone artifacts are eight in number. All are made in quartzite, quartz, or granular raw material. They are a denticulated scraper, three choppers, a core, a (burnt) notch, a broken cobble, and a completely perforated stone of the size and proportions of a digging stick weight.

Supplementary Observations on Paleolithic Sites

Although I did not see other artifact collections, I did hear descriptions of several during the course of presentations made to us; we also heard of some discoveries of human remains that are not yet published. Two items deserve especial attention. In the site of Chien Shih (Hupei), attributed to the late early Pleistocene age, some isolated *Australopithecus*-like teeth have been found associated with *Gigantopithecus* remains. These teeth would be the first evidence of an australopithecine in China.

In 1965, geologists found two incisors identified as *Homo erectus*

at the Yüan-mou site, near Shang-na-pang in Yunnan. The site is also
supposed to be late early Pleistocene in age. Surveys of the area were
reported to have yielded stone tools. We learned that these are from
more recent strata than the hominid remains.

Several Paleolithic finds were mentioned, but there was only one
additional site with which I was totally unfamiliar: the Ko-tze-tung
Cave in the Liaoning Province. Collections from this site were not
described, except to say that the artifacts were early Paleolithic.

Summary

The total number of artifacts I examined is extremely small compared
with the evident richness of the Chinese Paleolithic record. It would
be impossible for anyone with such a fleeting familiarity as I was able
to gain to provide a definitive description of Chinese Paleolithic
prehistory. In fact, given the current noncomparability of typologies,
it is not possible to produce a really satisfying synthesis from the
literature. However, the experience of handling a limited sample of
Chinese specimens drove home some lessons that I believe to be both
reliable and valuable.

Many of the opinions about Chinese Paleolithic materials expressed
in the primary literature are insubstantial, and their effect on contemporary Chinese scholarship has been generally deleterious. In turn,
the West has taken the evaluations at face value, without subjecting
them to critical scrutiny. Secondary sources have embellished a bad
caricature rather than correcting it. Widely used texts by usually
reliable scholars such as Oakley (1964, pp. 237-38) and Clark (1965,
pp. 32-33, 1967, p. 31) have spread the idea that most artifacts in the
Locality 1 assemblages are so formless that they are almost unrecogniz-
able as products of human activity. After having seen a tiny lot of
implements from Locality 1, I find such characterizations baseless.

One of the most important observations I can make is that the
Chinese lower Paleolithic does not have the earmarks of conservativeness
or retardation that secondary sources so frequently allege. In regularity, diversity, and technical finish the Chou-k'ou-tien artifacts are
on a par with the industrial products of hominids elsewhere in the world
at a comparable time.

Equally important is the observation that Chinese Paleolithic industries do not give the impression of a unified, homogeneous local
evolutionary sequence. What I saw indicates that even lower Paleolithic
assemblages exhibit marked regional and temporal difference. Although
there are still very few sites, the present evidence suggests that we
shall eventually find regional/temporal differences in Paleolithic
China to be as great as those we know from Europe and Africa over comparable periods. Even though I have not seen the Locality 15 material,
which seems to resemble the Ting-ts'un tools in certain typological
characteristics, attempts to trace a close family resemblance from Lan-
t'ien and Chou-k'ou-tien Locality 1 through Ting-ts'un to Hsiao-nan-hai
are unfounded. The diversity between these collections is at least

as great as that between Acheulean, Mousterian, and upper Paleolithic assemblages in Europe.

Last, it is important to note that the collections I saw suggest that the Chinese Paleolithic is not so idiosyncratic and strange, after all. In fact, Bordes made the same remark with respect to the Chou-k'ou-tien pieces and the French collection from the Mousterian site of Shui-tung-kou. The local raw materials are not so intractable as to produce un-recognizable artifact types. If the Chinese collections were accessible, I would expect to find that they are, in many ways, quite comparable to Western materials of approximately similar ages.

That realization was one of the most significant personal benefits I received from our visit. In a very real sense, I have previously been unable to deal satisfactorily with the Chinese Paleolithic or to under-stand how its relationships to developments elsewhere might best be studied. After having seen the artifacts at first hand, I am convinced that they are not simply an unusual but peripheral addendum to world prehistory; they have an integral and important position within the story of human and cultural evolution.

DIVULGATION

Municipal and Provincial Museums

The paleoanthropology delegation visited several local, municipal, and provincial museums. Others will present more complete reports concern-ing those institutions; my comments will be very general.

Most of the museums we visited were reasonably well set up, with clearly marked exhibits, dioramas, and some moving displays (flashing lights on maps, rising water in models of flood control systems, and so on). The Chinese make extensive use of paintings and sculptures of reconstructions of extinct animals, life groups, and fossil men. Most of the artists are local and have little or no experience in scientific reconstruction. Questionable reconstructions are quite universally ex-hibited--even at Chou-k'ou-tien field station some of the figures are of dubious accuracy. But such defects are noticeable only to specialists, and the impact of the artistic representations on the general public should be considerable, because the displays are both impressive and attractive. The Chinese make better use of graphics than is usual in the average Western museum.

Most (or all) of the museums we visited had staffs of guides to ex-plain exhibits to visitors. The information they offer repeats and supplements attractive and apparently clear labels on the cases or specimens.

Like the greater number of their Western counterparts, Chinese museums sometimes attempt to display too much in too little space, but the larger establishments have kept clutter to a minimum in their exhibits.

I had only two criticisms of the museum displays I saw. First, they were often inadequately lit. That is a technical problem which could easily be remedied. The second criticism is more fundamental.

So that all Chinese may become familiar with their national heritage, and with the important documents of human and cultural evolution found in China, certain assemblages have been split and disseminated across the country. This is especially true of Pleistocene artifactual materials. Almost every museum we visited had one or two original specimens from Chou-k'ou-tien Locality 1.

Disseminating collections is always bad practice, and there is no reason why casts of the specimens would not serve equally well. (The same museums display casts of the important Pleistocene hominids with great effect.) In this case it is especially bad, because some of the pieces in question have not been published or even studied. In my experience, it is often very difficult for serious scholars interested in seeing whole assemblages to examine disseminated specimens. In the first place, the responsible authorities in each museum develop their own sets of regulations controlling access to exhibited pieces; sometimes access is permitted or denied for completely arbitrary reasons. More important, the central authority that disseminates the specimens may lose track of the location of artifacts it has sent out; even when good records are kept, they cannot be sufficiently informative if the pieces have not been studied. Local institutions may regrettably sometimes mislay or discard specimens during housekeeping or reorganization. For obvious reasons, the collections from any single locality should be kept intact for future study. Whether this be done in local museums or large national institutes like the IVPP is immaterial.

The Site Museums

All paleoanthropologists would agree that one of the best ways of saving information from important prehistoric sites is to preserve crucial sections of the sites intact in some sort of shelter. There is no other way of preserving large archeological features that are fragile.

The People's Republic of China has the most impressive site museums I have ever seen. Some are small, like the brick structure covering the Chou horse and chariot burials (which only occupy about 20 m^2 of space). The Pan-p'o Museum, the size of a large aircraft hanger, covers a substantial part of a huge Neolithic village. The other two we saw (Ta-ho Village Museum and the Shang Palace Museum at Cheng-chou) are relatively small and closer in size to the Yin Hsü building. Three of the four museums included more than one building: in addition to the site building, there was at least one other structure housing displays and workspace.

China's site museums should serve as models for other nations. Light, spacious, and airy, they inform the public much better than any quantity of drawings or photos would, and at the same time they preserve and protect site sediments and features for future generations of students. If the governments of wealthy industrialized countries would invest a fraction of the money and effort in site museums that China has devoted to such installations, it would be a great step forward.

The two Paleolithic sites we visited were not preserved in the same way. Permanent monuments have been installed at important find spots at both sites. At the Ting-ts'un localities known so far, there is little point in attempting any more thoroughgoing preservation. At Chou-k'ou-tien, excavations are periodically still undertaken. The museum at Chou-k'ou-tien station is very well designed, and further expansion in that direction seems unnecessary. However, one hopes that, when excavations terminate, some substantial portion of the stratigraphic sequence at Locality 1 will be preserved intact in a sheltered enclosure. At present, erosion is not a major problem at Chou-k'ou-tien, vandalism is unheard of, and there is sufficient staff to maintain the site and protect it.

At both Ting-ts'un and Chou-k'ou-tien, we were given small pamphlets explaining the significance of the sites and showing some of the more important finds from each. The little booklets are simply written and well illustrated. The Ting-ts'un brochure is especially well produced and has several full-color plates, in addition to line drawings and halftones. I have seen a few similar brochures on sites outside China and even had a hand in designing one, and I found the Ting-ts'un pamphlet, in particular, an exemplary specimen.

REVIEW

Bearing in mind how short our trip was, and thus how tentative any impressions we received must be, the reader may still find something of use in these personal evaluations. The institutional organization of paleoanthropology and associated pursuits seems admirable on paper. There are enough official institutions and their functions theoretically interdigitate sufficiently to cover most of the essentials of paleoanthropological research in strength. We were assured that funding is no problem: there is abundant money for research, including funding for interdisciplinary studies. Scientists we interviewed at the Institute of Archeology and the Institute of Geology and Paleontology (Nanking) recognized the need for such investigations and expressed regret that other more pressing demands of socialist construction make intensive collaboration in paleoanthropological investigations impractical for the present. The essential scientists simply do not have the time.

The old saw tells us that time is money. But in this case, time is people. There is plenty of money; there are simply not enough trained specialists to satisfy the current demand. And there is no indication that a wave of new talent is on its way to relieve the situation.

To process more new specialists to meet these needs, middle school has been shortened and the university career has been pared radically. Training in paleoanthropology-related specialities has been cut so drastically since the Cultural Revolution that there seems to me to be inadequate opportunity for students to acquire the kinds of minimal competences in those specialities and ancillary natural sciences that we in the U.S. have found to be absolutely essential to young professionals.

The story of Paleolithic cultural developments in China is as interesting as that of any region of the world--in fact, it is more interesting than most just at present, because paleoanthropological research in China has just begun. The pioneers are still alive and

teaching. There is more opportunity for a young paleonanthropologist
in China to make exciting new discoveries that will set current doctrine
on its heels than there is in most of the rest of the world. Paleoanthropology should be an attractive profession for the young generation
in the People's Republic of China. Yet, somehow it fails to draw them.

Although Chinese excavation techniques used at Paleolithic sites
are apparently no worse than the world average, they are not greatly
different from those practiced in the 1930's. We have since learned
many ways of extracting information from archeological deposits that
were not dreamed of then. It has become a cliché that modern prehistoric
archeologists learn more about past ways of life from the dirt they
excavate than from the artifacts and features it contains. Painstaking
study of context, including the spatial position and orientation of recovered finds, provides information on depositional environments and
cultural behavior that is lost if those data go unrecorded. But some
of these productive sources of information are still ignored in Chinese
paleoanthropology. Every professional has an obligation to use the
most thorough data-gathering techniques available. To keep up with new
developments, excavation and recording techniques in the People's Republic must be improved.

Techniques of data analysis are even more in need of revision. Today, paleoanthropological investigations without the aid and participation of many other natural scientists from the fieldwork stage
through all phases of analysis are unimaginable. If there are not
enough trained natural scientists to provide the necessary interdisciplinary collaboration, no major research project, other than the salvage
of sites faced with imminent destruction, should be undertaken. Even
decent site survey demands cooperation between paleoanthropologists,
stratigraphic geologists, paleontologists, and geomorphologists at the
very least.

Quantitative techniques for the description and comparison of assemblages that go beyond simple percentage calculations are also essential tools of paleoanthropological investigation. These methods may
be employed by statistical specialists, but even in that case the paleo-
anthropologist directing a research project must know enough about them
to understand and evaluate in general terms the results the statistician
produces. In my opinion, it will eventually be necessary to re-expand
the current university curriculum to provide these kinds of training.

China is justifiably proud that the masses take an interest in paleoanthropological investigation. But, in an attempt to involve the
people more deeply in the conduct of paleoanthropological research,
there is the danger than an inadequately prepared public will be encouraged to undertake independent investigations, resulting in the destruction of archeological evidence instead of its preservation.

Artifact typology is a fundamental building block of paleoanthropological analysis. Systematic and logical frameworks for artifact classification must be developed or analysis is crippled--interassemblage
comparisons will mislead rather than inform, and the intelligent public
will soon learn to dismiss our results as trivial. Well-founded typology
eases communication between scholar and scholar across international
frontiers and between professionals and the public they serve.

Communication is essential to the health of our discipline. Paleo-anthropology, like other sciences, is stifled by parochialism and isolation. The interchange of delegations such as ours is a heartening sign, which one trusts will continue.

REFERENCES

Andersson, J. 1923a. An early Chinese culture. Bull. Geol. Surv. China 5:1-68.

Andersson, J. G. 1923b. Essays on the Cenozoic of northern China. Geol. Mem. Surv. China, Ser. A, no. 3.

Andersson, J. 1943. Researches into the prehistory of the Chinese. Bull. Mus. Far East. Antiquities, Stockholm, 15.

Andersson, J. 1973. Children of the yellow earth. The M.I.T. Press, Reprint of the 1934 edition.

Black, D. 1922. The Geological Society and Science in China. Bull. Geol. Soc. China I:9-10.

Black, D. 1929a. Preliminary note on additional *Sinanthropus* material discovered in Chou Kou Tien during 1928. Bull. Geol. Soc. China 8:15-32.

Black, D. 1929b. Preliminary notice of the discovery of an adult *Sinanthropus* skull at Chou Kou Tien. Bull. Geol. Soc. China 8:207-30.

Black, D. 1932. Evidences of the use of fire by *Sinanthropus*. Bull. Geol. Soc. China 11:107-8.

Black, D. 1934. On the discovery, morphology and environment of *Sinanthropus pekinensis*. Philos. Trans. R. Soc. London Ser. B 223: 57-120, plates 6-15.

Black, D., P. Teilhard de Chardin, C. C. Young, and W. C. Pei. 1933. Fossil man in China. Mem. Geol. Surv. China Ser. A, XI.

Bohlin, B. 1927. Excavation of the Chow K'ou Tien deposit. Bull. Geol. Soc. China VI:345-46.

Bordes, F. 1968. Le Paléolithique dans le monde. Hachette, Paris.

Boule, M., H. Breuil, E. Licent, and P. Teilhard de Chardin. 1928. Le Paléolithique de la Chine. Arch. Inst. Paleontol. Mem. IV.

Bowers, J. 1972. Western medicine in a Chinese palace. Peking Union Medical College, 1917-1951. Josiah Macy, Jr., Foundation.

Breuil, H. 1932. Le feu et l'industrie osseuse à Choukoutien. Bull. Geol. Soc. China 11:147-54.

Breuil, H. 1935. L'État actuel de nos connaissances sur les industries paléolithiques de Choukoutien (et Nihowan). Anthropologie 45:740-46.

Breuil, H. 1939. Bone and antler industry of the Choukoutien *Sinanthropus* site. Paleontol. Sinica, n.s. D, no. 6.

Chang, H. T. 1922. On the history of the geological science in China. Bull. Geol. Soc. China 1:4-7.

Chia, L. P., T.-Y. Wang, and C. Wang. 1962. Kēhé, an Early Paleo-lithic site in south-western Shansi, Inst. Vert. Paleontol. Paleo-anthropol. Mem. 3.

Chyne, W. Y. (Chüang Wen-ya). 1936. Handbook of cultural institutions in China.

112

Clark, G. 1965. World Prehistory, an outline. The University Press, Cambridge.

Clark, G. 1967. The Stone Age hunters. McGraw-Hill, New York.

Coles, J., and E. Higgs. 1969. The archaeology of early man. Frederick A. Praeger, New York.

Furth, C. 1970. Ting Wen-chiang. Science and China's new culture. Harvard University Press, Cambridge, Mass.

Geological Society of China. 1934. Proceedings of the special meeting on May 11, 1934. Bull. Geol. Soc. China 13:319-325.

Gregory, W. 1947. Minute on the life and scientific labors of Amadeus William Grabau (1870-1946). Bull. Geol. Soc. China 27:31-34.

Houn, Franklin W. (Hou Fu-Wu). 1957. Central government of China 1912-1928. University of Wisconsin Press, Madison.

Li, C. 1927. The Chou K'ou Tien fossil deposits. Bull. Geol. Soc. China VI:337-344.

Licent, E. 1924. Dix années d'exploration dans le bassin du fleuve jaune. 4 vol. Tientsin. La librarie française.

de Morgan, J. 1925. Prehistoric man. Alfred A. Knopf, New York.

Morgan, L. A. 1963. Ancient society. (Reprint of the 1877 edition with introduction and annotations by E. Leacock). World Publishing Co., Cleveland, Ohio.

Movius, H. L. 1944. Early man and Pleistocene stratigraphy in southern and eastern Asia. Pap. Peabody Mus. Am. Archaeol. Ethnol. Harv. Univ. XIX, no. 3.

Movius, H. L. 1956. New Paleolithic sites near Ting-Ts'un in the Fen River, Shansi Province, North China. Quaternaria 3:11-26.

Oakley, K. P. 1964. Frameworks for dating fossil man. Aldine, Chicago.

Pei, W.-C. 1929. An account of the discovery of an adult *Sinanthropus* skull in the Chou Kou Tien deposit. Bull. Geol. Soc. China 8:203-205.

Pei, W.-C. 1932. Notice of the discovery of quartz and other stone artifacts in the Lower Pleistocene hominid-bearing sediments of the Choukoutien cave deposit. Bull. Geol. Soc. China 11:109-146.

Pei, W.-C. 1933. Preliminary note on some incised, cut and broken bones found in association with *Sinanthropus* remains and lithic artifacts from Choukoutien. Bull. Geol. Surv. China 12:105-112.

Pei, W.-C. 1934a. A preliminary report on the Late-Paleolithic cave of Choukoutien. Bull. Geol. Soc. China 13:327-358.

Pei, W.-C. 1934b. Report on the excavation of the Locality 13 in Choukoutien Bull. Geol. Soc. China 13:359-367.

Pei, W.-C. 1937. Les fouilles de Choukoutien en Chine. Bull. Soc. Prehist. Fr. XXXIV:354-366.

Pei, W.-C. 1938. Le role des animaux et des causes naturelles dans la cassure des os. Paleontol. Sinica, n.s. D, no. 7.

Pei, W.-C. 1939a. The Upper Cave industry of Choukoutien. Paleontol. Sinica, n.s. D, no. 9.

Pei, W.-C. 1939b. A preliminary study on a new paleolithic station known as Locality 15 within the Choukoutien region. Bull. Geol. Soc. China 19:147-187.

Pei, W. C. 1965. Professor Henri Breuil, pioneer of Chinese Paleolithic archeology and its progress after him, pp. 251-271. *In* Miscelanea en homenaje al Abate Henri Breuil, E. Ripoll, ed., vol. 2.

Pei, W. C., and L.-P. Chia *et al*. 1958. Report on the excavations of Paleolithic sites at Ting-ts'un, Hsiang-fên Hsien, Shansi Province, China. Inst. Vert. Paleontol. Paleoanthropol. Mem. 2.

Peking Union Medical College. 1921. Addresses and papers, dedication ceremonies and medical conference. Peking Union Medical College, September 15-22, 1921. Rumford Press, Concord, N.H.

von Richthofen, F. 1877-1911. China, Ergebnisse eigener Reisen und darauf gegrundeten Studien (5 vol.). Dietrich Riemer, Berlin.

von Richthofen, F. 1907. Tagebücher aus China (2 vol.). Dietrich Riemer, Berlin.

Teilhard de Chardin, P. 1941. Early man in China. No. 7. Institut de Géo-Biologie, Peking.

Teilhard de Chardin, P. 1968. Letters from a traveller. Harper and Row, New York.

Teilhard de Chardin, P., and E. Licent. 1924. On the discovery of a paleolithic industry in northern China. Bull. Geol. Soc. China 3:45-50.

Teilhard de Chardin, P., and W.-C. Pei. 1932. The lithic industry of the *Sinanthropus* deposits in Choukoutien. Bull. Geol. Soc. China 11: 315-364.

Teilhard di Chardin, P., and W. C. Pei. 1934. New discoveries in Choukoutien 1933-1934. Bull. Geol. Soc. China 13:369-394.

Teilhard de Chardin, P., and C. C. Young. 1929. Preliminary report on the Chou Kou Tien fossififerous [*sic*] deposits. Bull. Geol. Soc. China 8:173-202.

Ting, V. K. 1919. Foreword. Bull. Geol. Surv. China 1:i-iii.

Ting, V. K. 1922. Editorial. Bull. Geol. Soc. China I:1-2.

Treistman, J. 1972. The prehistory of China. Doubleday and Co., Inc., Garden City, N.Y.

Wong, W. 1927. The search for early man in China. Bull. Geol. Soc. China VI:335-36.

Zdansky, O. 1923. Uber ein Säugetierknochenlager in Chou-k'ou-tien, Provinz Chihli. Bull. Geol. Sur. China 5:83-90.

Zdansky, O. 1926. Preliminary notice on two teeth of a hominid from a cave in Chihli (China). Bull. Geol. Soc. China 5:281-84.

Zdansky, O. 1928. Die Säugetiere der Quartärfauna von Choukoutien. Paleontol. Sinica Ser. C, V fasc. 4:1-146.

7

ARCHEOLOGY OF THE LATE AND POST-PLEISTOCENE FROM A NEW WORLD PERSPECTIVE

H. M. Wormington

For all students of the Paleo-Indian period in the New World, sites of late Pleistocene age in eastern Asia are of special interest. We have conclusive proof from many sites that between 11,000 and 12,000 years ago there were people in North America who had highly sophisticated tool kits that included bifacially flaked points and implements made on blades. No date of more than 12,000 years has won universal acceptance, but in recent years sites have been found in North and South America that have led a growing number of archeologists to conclude that there has been human occupation of the New World for a longer period of time. Most estimates range between 25,000 and 40,000 years ago; some archeologists postulate a still earlier period of occupation.

Those sites, believed to predate the fully established stage of Paleo-Indian occupation by a considerable period of time, lack bifacially flaked projectile points, and most are characterized by a level of stone-working technology reminiscent of the lower Paleolithic stage in the Old World. Stone artifacts were produced by percussion, and core and flake tools were usually large and heavy. Choppers and chopping tools were commonly made from pebbles. Such a lithic tradition is one of several present in Siberia in sites which are less than 20,000 years old as well as in some that are not firmly dated but that are believed to be of considerably greater age.

Nothing that I saw in China could be *specifically* equated with Siberian or American finds with which I am familiar. The most that can be said is that a tradition of making crude heavy tools persisted over a long period of time, and this could be the area from which similar traditions spread to Siberia and, ultimately, to the New World. Only one middle Paleolithic site was visited by the Delegation, and I had the opportunity to examine small collections from this and four upper Paleolithic sites. Tools from a fifth were viewed in a closed case, and there were a few casts of tools from the Ordos area in another case and that was not opened.

In view of the limitations of time and restrictions concerning measurements of specimens, there could be no fully objective analysis, and my impressions are essentially subjective ones. Counts of tool types would have been meaningless since only parts of collections were available for study, and there was no way of determining how these samples had been selected.

115

The middle Paleolithic site visited by the Delegation was Ting-ts'un in Hsiang-fen Hsien, southern Shansi Province. It was discovered in the course of construction activities in 1953 and was investigated by members of the Chinese Academy of Sciences (P'ei and Chia, 1958). Some 15 localities located in a 15-km-long section of the east bank of the Fen Ho River were studied. One yielded three human teeth, discussed in the chapter by W. W. Howells. Others produced some 2,000 stone artifacts.

The Ting-ts'un localities were first thought to be of middle Pleistocene age. After reassessment of the stratigraphy and fauna, however, it was concluded that the site was of late Pleistocene age. According to Cheng (1966), 28 forms of fossil mammals were represented in the fossil assemblages of Ting-ts'un. Two varieties of rhinoceros, a species of deer, and a form of elephant represent archaic survivals from the middle Pleistocene. Mammals that are common in the Sjara-osso-gol deposits of later age are represented by rhinoceros, two species each: of horses, elephant, ox, and several species of deer. Remains of dogs, rats, and another species of deer resemble recent forms.

Information concerning the artifacts of Ting-ts'un has been summarized in publications in English by Cheng (1959), Chang (1968), and Aigner (1975). Lithic specimens were produced from big pebbles from which large flakes were struck. Rounded stones with pitted surfaces appear to represent hammerstones used for this purpose. There was preparation of the striking platform. The greater number of flakes had an angle of about 120°. This prevented pebbles from being fully utilized, and many good-sized nuclei remained. Most flakes were large and thick, but there were also some thin parallel-sided flakes. Some flakes with sharp edges could be utilized without further modification; others were retouched along the edges. In general shapes were not standardized. There were choppers and chopping tools as well as pointed specimens of triangular shapes and scrapers. One distinctive form was a sharply pointed trihedral pick.

Chard (1974) has noted that specimens found in the three lowest levels of Hoshino Cave in the northern Kanto District of Japan, dated to the Early Würm, provide evidence of the detaching of flakes from prepared cores, and there are traces of flat bifacial retouch. He believes that the closest affinities are with the Ting-ts'un assemblages.

I examined some 40 specimens from the Ting-ts'un localities in the Institute of Vertebrate Paleontology and Paleoanthropology in Peking and saw five additional specimens in the Shanghai Museum. These included cores and flakes and choppers and chopping tools, thick triangular flakes with retouched edges, and trihedral picks. There were only general resemblances between any of these and specimens from New World sites. Time available for working with collections was so limited that it seemed unwise to duplicate studies undertaken by other members of the Delegation. Ting-ts'un falls within the time period with which I was concerned, but the most detailed examinations of the artifacts found were those done by Leslie Freeman. There are large bifacially flaked specimens and it was desirable that he be able to make comparisons with Acheulean collections with which he is familiar. Descriptions of the artifacts will be found in the chapter by Freeman.

An important late Paleolithic site is Hsiao-nan-hai, a limestone cave that lies some 33 km west of An-yang in northern Honan Province. It was discovered in 1960 as a result of blasting operations while building a reservoir, and it was excavated by the Archaeological Institute of Peking during a 6-week period in which a 10-m^2 pit was dug. Artifacts and fragmentary faunal remains were found in stratified loess deposits. Animal remains are those of very old or very young individuals, and many show evidence of burning. They probably represent remnants of food obtained by hunting. The major publication in Chinese is by An Chih-min (1965), "Trial Excavations of the Paleolithic Cave of Hsiao-nan-hai, Anyang, Honan." Jean Aigner (1972) has published in English an excellent report on the site. It is illustrated with line drawings. The faunal list published by Aigner includes:

- *Struthio anderssoni* Lowe
- *Erinaceus* sp.
- *Pongo* sp.
- *Myospalax fontanieri* (M-E)
- *Rattus* sp.
- *Ursus* cf. *arctos**
- *Meles leucurus* Hodgson
- *Crocuta crocuta ultima* (Matsumoto)
- *Canis* cf. *lupus* L
- *Panthera pardus* (L)
- *Equus hemionus* Pallas
- *Coelodonta antiquitatis* (Blumenbach)
- *Sus* sp.
- *Capreolus* cf. *manchuricus* Lydekker
- *Cervus* (*Pseudaxis*) sp.
- *Bubalus* sp.
- *Gazella przewalskyi* Buchner
- *Capricornis* sp.

Of the artifacts found, 6,360 were made of chert, 680 were of quartz, 9 of flint, 2 of chalcedony, and 1 of limestone. One bone bead was found but it was not *in situ*. There were 397 core and pebble tools, 4 of which were classified as choppers. More than 6,000 flakes were found which showed no evidence of retouch or utilization. Ninety-six flakes had been intentionally modified or had wear patterns indicating usage and were classified as scrapers.

This appears to be a site that would have been suitable for a multi-disciplinary approach of the type that is becoming increasingly common in investigations of Paleo-Indian sites in the United States. Archeologists from the Institute of Archeology, as far as I could gather, collected samples for specialists in other disciplines and consulted them after excavations had been completed, but such scholars were not part of the team involved in the primary investigations.

Ursus was identified as *U.* cf. *spelaeus,* but Kurten (1968) doubts the identification in Chinese sites. (Aigner, 1972, p. 41.)

The Delegation had asked to visit Hsiao-nan-hai, but since it was not accessible by road, our request was not met. Most artifacts were reported to be in the Museum of the Chinese Revolution and Chinese History and were not available for examination.

In the Institute of Archeology in Peking I saw some 50 lithic specimens, but they appeared to represent debitage rather than tools. In the museum in An-yang I examined 30 stone specimens and 94 pieces of eggshell. Chert specimens included a few microblades, small pointed flakes, a few denticulates, and some flakes slightly retouched on one edge. One piece of eggshell had a small depressed dot. It may have been intentionally produced, but I am inclined to believe that it is of natural origin. In a case in the Provincial Museum in Cheng-chou there were a few lithic specimens from Hsiao-nan-hai, some fragments of ostrich shell, and a picture of the cave. Thirteen of the specimens were of chert, and three were of quartz. The case was dimly lighted, and it was impossible to ascertain if there was evidence of retouch. The case label stated that the estimated age was between 10,000 and 20,000 years.

Shih-yü, an open site of upper Pleistocene age in Shansi Province, was excavated in 1963 under the auspices of the Institute of Vertebrate Paleontology and Paleoanthropology. I am greatly indebted to Li Yuan-chang for providing information about the site and translating for me from the report that appeared in *Kao-ku Hsüeh Pao* (No. 1, pp. 39-58, 1972). No plus and minus factors were given, but Shih-yü was dated at about 28,000 years by the radiocarbon method. Over 12,000 artifacts were recovered, and there were many animal bones. Forty percent represented extinct species. The faunal list was as follows:

- *Struthio* sp.
- *Crocuta* sp.*
- *Erinaceus*
- *Panthera tigra* Linnaeus
- *Cervus elaphus*
- *Megaloceros ordosanua* Young*
- *Gazella przewalski*
- *Gazella subgututosa*
- *Bovidae* (genus undetermined)
- *Bubalus* sp. *wansijocki**
- *Coelodonta antiquitatis**
- *Equus przewalski*
- *Equus hemionus*

There are four stratified layers:

- Grey and yellow silt. 18 m thick.
- Grey to white sandy layers. 8.9 m thick.
- Culture layers. Stone artifacts, animal bones, and ashes were found in sandy clay. Grey to black, some brown. 0.9 to 1.5 m thick.
- Grey and brown sand and gravel. The gravel is formed of limestone,

*Extinct species.

sandstone, and some slate. It is very angular and ranges from 2 to 3 cm in diameter. The layer is from 0.5 to 1 m thick.

Artifacts were made of quartz, limestone, silicious limestone, and chalcedony. The collection includes cores, flakes (some quite small), and blades. There are some polyhedral nuclei. In some cases a bipolar technique was used, and there were some pièces esquillées. Scrapers were of three types: sidescrapers retouched on two edges, sidescrapers retouched on one edge, and round disc forms. Some of the implements with retouched sides were denticulate. One small specimen, retouched at the end with a contracting base, was classified as a knife, but the form and nature of the wear pattern suggested that it could have been a scraper. There were some dihedral burins. One of the most interesting lithic implements was a stemmed unifacial projectile point, about 2.5 cm long, with a very delicate retouch around the edges. It was reminiscent of the edge-retouched projectile points found at the site of El Mirador and in the lowest unit at the Hueyatlaco site in the Valsequillo area near Pueblà, Mexico (Irwin-Williams, 1968).

The most famous of terminal Pleistocene or early Holocene sites is the Upper Cave at Chou-k'ou-tien excavated in 1933-1934 by P'ei Wen-chung. It was not accessible during the time of occupation of the area by Sinanthropus, and all of the human skeletal remains removed were fully modern. Studies of fauna and flora have indicated that at the time when the Upper Cave was occupied the climate of northern China was warmer than it is today (Chang, 1968). Some authors have considered the site late Paleolithic and think it may be of pre-Würm Maximum age (Aigner, 1975); others have classified it as Mesolithic (Chang, 1968).

The nature of the fractures on skulls recovered led Franz Weidenreich to believe that the dead represented the victims of deliberate attack. Others think that the bones could have been damaged by rockfalls and that they represent intentional burials (Chang, 1968). The presence of large quantities of hematite scattered around the bones would suggest that this may have been the case. Placement of hematite in graves has a long history in western Europe. Two Paleo-Indian sites in North America have also shown association between human skeletal remains and hematite. The Anzick-Wilsall site in Montana, which contained Clovis points and which is probably some 11,000 years old, produced human bones and hematite (Taylor, 1969; Lahren and Bonnichsen, 1974). Hematite was also found with the Gordon Creek burial in Colorado, dated by the radio-carbon method at 9,700 ± 250 years B.P. (Breternitz et al., 1971).

It was regrettable that it was impossible to see stone tools from this important site. They were reportedly made from pebbles and flakes and included choppers, chopping tools, and scrapers. There is general agreement that the industry, while somewhat more evolved, clearly re-sembles those of the ancient lithic tradition represented in the older Chou-k'ou-tien localities that yielded the remains of Peking man. In a conversation while visiting the Museum at Chou-k'ou-tien, Wu Hsin-chih said that similarities were so great that the suggestion had been made that Upper Cave occupants might have reused some older tools.

Only one chipped stone specimen from the Upper Cave, a small amorphous flake, was on display in the Museum. Other specimens that I examined there included one fragmentary needle about 7 cm long, broken at the base of the perforation, two types of bone beads (polished round specimens about 1 cm in diameter and beads made from bird long bones that had been polished at the ends and that were decorated with small depressed dots in varying numbers), and a perforated bone pendant. Four fragmentary long bones exhibited very fine striations.

A few similar specimens were seen at the Institute of Vertebrate Paleontology and Paleoanthropology in Peking. There was a needle, also broken at the base of the perforation, polished round beads, and bird bone beads with dots. There were also some polished pear-shaped bone fragments with holes at the top and perforated shells that probably served as pendants.

Small collections from two other sites of late Pleistocene or early Holocene age were seen. In an unopened case at Northwest University in Sian nine crude artifacts from Ho-huan included cores, flakes, and a chopper. They had been found in association with bones of rhinoceros and large cervids, *Mergaloceras* and *Canadensis*.

A chopper, similar flake implements, and some hammerstones from the Yellow Cave in the Feng-k'ai District were exhibited in the Kwangtung Provincial Museum. There was no association with extinct fauna, but bones of elephant and rhinoceros were found below the occupational level.

Had it been possible, I should like to have seen more collections of flaked specimens of Neolithic age, for I had been interested in An Chih-min's statement in his presentation at the Institute of Archeology that flaked implements of Neolithic age, like those of the Upper Cave, are comparable with much older specimens from Chou-k'ou-tien. At the Pan-p'o Museum there were crudely flaked choppers and chopping tools and flakes exhibited with well-made polished stone projectile points. Specimens from a site of Neolithic age in the Pa-an District, exhibited in the Kwangtung Provincial Museum, included crude chopping tools and pseudo-Levallois flakes as well as polished stone adzes and axes.

As one who was for some decades active in museum work and who is now deeply concerned with interpretation of sites for students and laymen, I was keenly interested in the museums visited by the Delegation. Localities where portions of excavated sites were preserved for permanent display were particularly impressive.

In the People's Republic of China strong efforts are being made to instruct the public. American museum workers might well find it beneficial to follow the Chinese practice of having labels and exhibits checked by a wide range of nonprofessionals in an effort to determine whether they are fully intelligible to the layman who has no special expertise.

There was some variation in quality of museum exhibits, but on the whole they were very good, although in many cases lighting left much to be desired. There was some impressive use of graphics. In the excellent Shanghai Museum, rubbings of sections of bronze vessels, which brought out details of designs and inscriptions, were shown in conjunction with the actual specimens. In some rooms where pottery was exhibited there were drawings of design elements above the specimens.

In the Provincial Museum in Cheng-chou, the Delegation saw an extremely interesting demonstration of pottery mending. Ceramic fragments were heated with a blowtorch; then a stick of some sort of lacquer was applied to the broken edges and they were pressed together. The mended section was then cooled by being brushed with water on a paint brush, and the pieces were firmly bonded.

In a number of institutions, and particularly at the Chou-k'ou-tien Museum, statues, bas reliefs, dioramas, and paintings were used effectively in stressing that archeology is properly concerned with people, not just with objects, and that the importance of artifacts lies in what they tell us of past human life. Accuracy of some reconstructions may be questioned, but the approach is sound.

Normally, archeological sites are largely or wholly destroyed in the process of excavation and retrieval of specimens. The valuable information gained through excavation may be preserved with proper recording, but the site itself can no longer be seen as it was when the archeological remains were uncovered but still in place. Under these conditions only a limited number of people are able to visit the sites.

Among the most impressive Museum exhibits viewed by the Delegation, particularly from the point of view of a Paleo-Indian specialist, were those that revealed excavated sites enclosed and protected by buildings so that visitors could see areas with features, bones, and artifacts just as they were after archeologists had uncovered them. The sections of these sites visited by the Delegation included house remains of Ta-ho-ts'un, a portion of a Neolithic village at Pan-p'o, a ditch in the Shang Palace foundations with human skulls with evidence of cutting, and a horse-and-chariot burial at Chang-chia-p'o.

These were all of post-Paleolithic age, but it is obvious that some Early man sites in America would lend themselves very well to similar treatment. If portions of some of the most important sites could be enclosed in buildings, a great many people would be able to see them over a period of many years. Such exhibits might do a great deal to show the public how much can be lost through uncontrolled digging, and they would serve as most useful teaching aids for those concerned with training students in the field of archeology.

Had it been possible to enclose a section of the Murray Springs site in Arizona, for example, one could still see not only butchered bones of mammoth and bison and the tools of those who hunted them more than 11,000 years ago, but also the depressions that appear to represent the footprints of those long dead animals. There have been many other Paleo-Indian sites, sections of which would have been well worth exhibiting, that are no longer available. Others are still being excavated, however, and undoubtedly many more will be found in the years to come. Building construction and maintenance are costly, but so are salvage activities in general, and preservation of portions of specially significant sites might well be considered an important form of salvage.

REFERENCES

Aigner, J. S. 1972. Hsiao-nan-hai: An important Hopei Plain camp site. Anthropologie X:39-50.

Aigner, J. S. 1975. The Paleolithic of China. Paper invited for 13th

122

Pacific Science Congress, Vancouver, Canada, August 1975. To be published in the Proceedings.

An Chih-min. 1965. Trial excavations of the Paleolithic cave of Hsiaonan-hai, Anyang, Honan, K'ao Ku Hsüeh Pao, pp. 1-28.

Breternitz, D., A. C. Swetlund, and D. C. Anderson. 1971. An early burial from Gordon Creek, Colorado. Am. Antiq. 36:179-182.

Bryan, A. 1965. Paleo-American prehistory. Pocatello, Occas. Pap. Idaho State Univ. Mus. No. 16.

Chang Kwang-chih. 1968. The archaeology of ancient China, revised and enlarged edition. Yale University Press, New Haven, Conn.

Chard, C. S. 1974. Northeast Asia in prehistory. University of Wisconsin Press, Madison.

Cheng Te-k'un. 1959. Archaeology in China. Vol. I. Prehistoric China. W. Heffer & Sons, Ltd., Cambridge.

Cheng Te-k'un. 1966. New light on Prehistoric China. Supplement to Vol. I, Archaeology in China. W. Heffer & Sons, Ltd., Cambridge, University of Toronto Press.

Irwin-Williams, C. 1968. Summary of the archaeological evidence from the Valsequillo Region, Puebla, Mexico. Manuscript of the Geological Society of America Valsequillo Field Conference, Mexico City.

Krieger, A. D. 1964. Early man in the New World, pp. 23-31. In J. D. Jennings and E. Norbeck, ed., University of Chicago Press, Chicago.

Kurten, B. 1968. Pleistocene mammals in Europe. Weidenfeld and Nicolson, London.

Lahren, L., and R. Bonnichsen. 1974. Bone foreshafts from a clovis burial in Southwestern Montana. Science 186:147-150.

P'ei Wen-chung, and Chia Lan-po. 1958. English resumé studies of Tingtsun Paleoliths, pp. 110-111. In P'ei Wen-chung, ed., Report of the excavation of Paleolithic sites at Tingtsun, Hsiangfenhsien, Shansi Province, China. Inst. Vert. Paleontol. Acad. Sinica Mem. No. 2. Science Press, Peking.

Taylor, D. C. 1969. The Wilsall site: An exercise in frustration. Helena. Proc. Mont. Acad. Sci. No. 29, pp. 147-150.

ARCHEOLOGY AND
HISTORY IN CHINESE SOCIETY

David N. Keightley

Archeology and history are commingled in China. This situation is well justified by the rich supply of archeological finds for the entire historical period, by the attention paid to historical context and periodization in museum displays of artifacts, and by the interest in material culture and in demonstrating the contributions of the Chinese laboring people. This commingling is especially fruitful in the area of Bronze Age studies, where the two disciplines are as inseparable in China as elsewhere. The following discussion, therefore, is focused less upon the role of history itself and more upon the role of history and archeology considered together. The fact that we met no historians (as opposed to archeologists) actually working in the history of Bronze Age China denied us the opportunity to engage in technical discussions of texts and inscriptions. Nevertheless, we did visit the history departments of three universities, were escorted through six major historical museums, and visited numerous sites from all stages of Chinese history. We were given a broad introduction to the practice of history in the People's Republic.

HISTORY IN THE UNIVERSITY

Historians and archeologists cooperate in single university departments, archeology being treated, for administrative purposes, as a branch of history. The professors and lecturers we met were dignified, quietly self-confident, and seemingly satisfied with their roles. In general, the tone of our sessions with scholars, courteous and helpful though they were, was dutiful and formal. This was partly due to a quite natural reticence in dealing with foreigners; one may also encounter it in Taiwan. It may have been partly due to the fact that our presence was viewed in terms that were primarily political rather than academic. But it may also be explained by the fact that academic, technical, and research questions receive lower priority in China than they do in the United States. It would be unrealistic, of course, to expect provincial universities in China to match the research expectations of Harvard or Berkeley. Northwest University in Sian or Fu-tan University in Shanghai, for example, might more properly be compared to state colleges in America, devoted to serving the people and with the faculty's energies reserved

123

primarily for teaching and the passion for "pure research" muted accordingly. But even in research institutes, research is only "pure"
if it can be justified in terms of serving the people; as a result historical scholarship naturally emphasizes education and propaganda, and
research serves the people by vindicating the orthodox view of the past
(see below). Such priorities may explain, for example, the serene, Tao-
ist, *wu-wei* attitude of our hosts in Peking about publishing some of the
newly excavated bone and bamboo documents. There was a willingness to
wait; it would be done in its proper time, when the best interests of the
state and society would be served. There was less of the pressure to
publish, to get on with the next project, that is typical (and not necessarily praiseworthy) among American research scholars. Perhaps the Cultural Revolution injected a sense of relaxation, of fatalism, into the
old academic professionalism.

Partly as a result of such attitudes, and partly as a result of the
formal nature of our visit, we were invited, as we visited universities
and research institutions, to take a somewhat stronger interest than we
would have wished in the *structure* of historical studies. In the universities, the *content* of historical instruction was presented to us
only in general terms, such as the coverage or titles of courses. Text-
books, still being rewritten with the help of workers, peasants, and
soldiers, were unavailable. In general, we were given formal accounts
of programs and objectives. We were introduced at the universities not
just to historians as scholars, but to an administrative and instruc-
tional bureaucracy staffed by historical functionaries, whose main al-
legiance was not to "the discipline," as it would be in the West, but
to the service of the people and the propagandizing (the term is used
with no pejorative intent) of Maxist-Leninist-Maoist historical truth.
The faculty members were professionals in their commitment to these goals,
less evidently so in their commitment to research and the discovery of
new knowledge; again the comparison with state colleges comes to mind.
This concern with history as instruction rather than inquiry is a traditional one (contrast the etymologies of *shih* and *historia*) that has been
adapted, not created, by the present authorities. Nor did we find this
approach particularly disturbing or frustrating. Chinese society is not
Western society, and it would be unreasonable to assume that Chinese
history would be Western history. We were in China precisely to identify
such differences.

The emphasis on presenting the essence of historical truth may also
be discerned, obliquely, from the library resources of the universities
we visited. These conclusions are based upon a small sample--the libraries at Northwest University and Fu-tan University--and focus upon
the specialized field of Shang history; they may not be representative.
It does appear, however, that the more advanced reaches of early Chinese
history are not being pursued at these two major provincial universities
at a technical level. The library holdings of Shang inscriptions were
weak; of a corpus of about 60 volumes of published inscriptions, we saw
no more than 10 to 15. The indispensable reference work, Shima Kunio's
Inkyo bokuji sōrui, was absent. And there was little secondary Chinese
scholarship; only Ch'en Meng-chia's 1956 work Yin-hsü pu-tzu tsung-hsu
was present (in multiple copies). Nor was there any evidence that Shang

history was being read in detail; the volumes we looked at were dusty and had not been checked out for years (since 1962 at Fu-tan). We did see excellent library resources at the Institute of Archeology in Peking, and they presumably exist at the few universities where oracle-bone scholars are active, but at least two provincial universities in China are not as well equipped to teach early Chinese history at an advanced level as are the libraries say at Berkeley, Chicago, Columbia, or Harvard. Primary research would be difficult. Western scholarship was also underrepresented. The only work of H. G. Creel's at Fu-tan University, for example, was his *Birth of China* (1937). It would be a useful form of scholarly communication if more works of Western and Japanese sinologists could be acquired by Chinese university libraries.

On the positive side, though undergraduates were not allowed in the stacks, the library at Fu-tan was open for long hours, 7 days a week. This was in pleasant contrast to the curtailed hours of many American university libraries. The practice of serving the people by sending complete sets of periodicals off to a commune for extended loan seemed of uncertain value, though a higher rate of use may justify the practice.

It would be pointless for us, nonspecialists in modern Chinese education, to dwell further on the teaching of history in China. The fact that all the universities we visited were virtually emptied of students and faculty (harvesting the winter wheat); the fact that we saw no evidence of a formal graduate program; the fact that the ratio of faculty to enrolled students was very small (at Nanking University, for example, there were 60 faculty in the department of history [and archeology] and only about 130 students) because much of the teachers' efforts goes into extension and correspondence teaching; the fact that history majors are admitted to the university only when it is known that a position will be ready for them 3 years later; all these and many more aspects of Chinese education have been well reported in modern Western studies. Indeed, to make a general observation, we found that China's educational institutions as well as Chinese society as a whole had been well reported by Western political scientists, journalists, and travellers.

In fact, one of the anomalies of a trip such as this is that, given the Chinese desire to expose us to society as a whole, and given the trip's fundamental nonresearch orientation, we all were forced to become "experts" about communes, day-care centers, factory wages, the Cultural Revolution, women's liberation, university administration, etc., discovering piecemeal for ourselves things already covered comprehensively in Western monographs. This is existentially (and hence intellectually) invaluable. But we were constantly playing blind men to the Chinese elephant when relatively good photographs of the animal exist back home.

One further observation may be added. In our own limited introduction to Chinese university education, no matter how attractive the "open door" policy, or the stress on practical experience, or on open-book exams and mutual support sounded--and they did sound attractive to many of us--we had no way of evaluating the results. We had no chance to see or talk with students in depth, no chance to discover what happens to students after graduation. The faculty we spoke to naturally praised the new system and its results, but there was no opportunity for independent evaluation. There are times, indeed, when China seems like a vast, mutual admiration society. This is not the result of self-deception but of intense pride. The Chinese are deservedly proud of their institutions, proud of the revolutionary changes that have occurred, and convinced that a new age has arrived. And it is precisely because so many institutions in China--communes, factories, nurseries, apartment complexes, museums, universities, etc.--are thought to be working well that the Chinese wished us to see them (raising the sobering question: how many comparable institutions in America are working so well in the interests of social and economic democracy that we would want to show them to foreigners in this way?). Whatever doubts may exist about the efficacy of the new educational programs, for example, they are presumably overwhelmed by the general *esprit de corps* that pervades Chinese society; they are certainly not discussed with foreigners.

HISTORY IN THE MUSEUM

We saw specialized research museums at the Institute of Archeology in Peking and at the archeological research station at Hsiao-t'un. These contained recently excavated materials extremely exciting to research scholars; not yet intended to serve a propaganda function, the materials were presented in their own right, with no political labels.
   The historical museum in Peking was still closed (reports indicate that it has been reopened on a limited basis as of October 1975), but we visited public historical or archeological museums in Chou-k'ou-tien, Tientsin, Sian, Pan-p'o, Cheng-chou, Nanking, Shanghai, and Kuang-chou (Canton). The mission of the Chinese museums is protection, preservation, collection, research, and education. The fundamental exhibition policy is to serve the people, and, provided one accepts the values and aims of the Chinese state, this is well done. We were universally impressed by the attention and skill that the Chinese have devoted to museum displays; they are models of popular pedagogy. The museum cases and the accompanying explanations convey an impressive amount of historical information. Moving as rapidly as we did--"seeing the flowers from horseback"--and faced with paragraphs of Chinese, the wealth of information displayed was not, perhaps, appreciated at the time. But our color slides, perused in tranquillity, give a good sense of the potential impact on a Chinese viewer with time to spend. Posters, charts, maps, diagrams, reconstructions, paintings, dioramas, etc., tell a clear and effective story: the development of Chinese history through its assigned Marxist stages, from Yang-shao matriarchy, to Lung-shan patriarchy, to Shang and Chou slave society, to the period of imperial feudalism, and on to the Chinese resistance against imperialist aggression. Class struggle and exploitation are stressed, and great attention is paid to peasant uprisings and their leaders. The objects are placed within a specific historical context, and their social and political meanings are explicated in Marxist terms. Where museum displays in America are dominated by the objects themselves, usually with a small, discrete card listing the few essential facts, in China the objects tend to be dominated by their explications. Large posters in every room headline the stages of

society, the lessons to be learned; in addition there are lengthy texts
of historical explanation on the walls and in the cases. No visitor to
a Chinese museum is in doubt about what he is seeing, why he is seeing
it, and what it should mean. And certainly some of our own curators
might learn from the effort that their Chinese counterparts make to supply a historical context.

The differences in technique, of course, reflect profounder differences
in purpose. The Chinese curators care about the past in a way that we do
not. We exhibit the past for its own sake. They do so for the sake of
modern China. And they do so not just for ideological and traditional
reasons, but because the past has played a more evident and agonizing
role in China's present than it has in our own, at least until recently.
China's past does much to explain her slow reaction to the Western impact
in the nineteenth and twentieth centuries. Cartoons about Confucius are
not just about a dead figure; they are about the living hand of Confucian-
ism that, until recently, was very much a reality. As in psychoanalysis,
the past has to be confronted and reinterpreted before the present can be
radically changed.

All museums, actively or passively, play an ideological role. The
Western museum, with its neutral presentation of ancient objects for the
viewer to judge in his own terms, indicates that the past has no living
political meaning but is to be evaluated aesthetically and academically.
By contrast, Chinese museums are overt propaganda classrooms and certain
consequences arise from that political role. They contain, for example,
many nonhistorical, anachronistic items that *dramatize* rather than *document* the past. We saw many modern paintings (to say nothing of the anti-
Confucian cartoons) of what the past must have been like but few ancient
paintings that represent the past in its own terms. The larger-than-life
statues of peasant heroes like Ch'en She (d. 209 B.C.) have no historical
basis and serve to inculcate attitudes rather than impart information.

There is also a uniformity to the explications that, though perfectly
understandable in view of the museum's political functions, leads to monotony. The same inscriptions, with the same tendentious explanations,
are displayed in Sian, Cheng-chou, and Nanking, for example. The same
Stone Age skulls and explanations appear in Chou-k'ou-tien and Tientsin.
Perhaps this is not a real issue in the Chinese case, since it is unlikely that many inhabitants of Sian will visit the Nanking museum. But
it does mean that museums, and the objects they display, are not sources
of new ideas or insights. Further, the explanations about primitive man
in the museum at Chou-k'ou-tien are repeated verbatim (or taken from?)
a popular book, *Lao-tung ch'uang-tsao-le jen* (Labor Made Man) by T'ang
Hsiao-wen. Other examples of such textual duplication could probably be
found. The museum displays, therefore, become a source of repetition
and reinforcement rather than of fresh instruction or new insight. They
are congruent with the orthodox view of history, a feature that diminishes
the uniqueness of the provincial museums and the objects they display.
(This is not to minimize the importance that provincial museums place upon
their regional cultures, but the explanatory framework in which those
cultures are placed is fully familiar.) One reason for the stress on
imaginative reconstructions--paintings of Shang slave rebellions, busts
of anti-literati rebels, dioramas of rent-collecting courtyards--may well

be that only in this area do the curators have a chance to express their individual views of the past--by dramatizing a modern truth.

The museum explanations naturally rely on published Chinese scholarship, and, since the displays tend to emphasize the more political conclusions, it is these aspects of the scholarship that become dominant. The treatment of matriarchy displayed at Pan-p'o is for the archeologists to consider. But similar questions arise about the treatment of slave society and the sometimes questionable use of Shang and Chou inscriptions. The questions involved are partly those of definition and partly technical. Debatable points may be found in museum displays around the world-- curators are no more infallible than scholars--though in the Chinese case the interpretations in question tend to follow a predictable, ideological pattern.

None of these considerations diminish what a Western scholar, especially one who is expert in the field, can learn from the Chinese museums. And the direct exposure to an alien historiographical tradition--like the exposure to the landscape and culture itself--is one of the most salutary aspects of the trip, causing the historian to ponder questions about history and its relation to sociology and politics, and about his own relation to society, that are frequently ignored or treated casually. One may wonder how well Chairman Mao's policy of "using the past to serve the present" is likely to serve the Chinese people in the long run. The relatively simple nature of the labels assigned to periods ("slave society") or artifacts ("made by slaves for slaveowners") means that the richness and variety of China's past tends to be standardized, not just by ideological pressure but by devotion to history as a nomothetic social science rather than a humanistic discipline. Further, one may wonder if the monotony of the predetermined explanations will not deprive history of its ability to stimulate the political consciousness of the masses. But to raise such possibilities may betray a misunderstanding of the role of history in China. History has traditionally been exemplary, and the popularity of oft-told historical tales suggests that their role has been mythic as well as historical. Nontechnical history, precisely because of its familiar, reassuring nature, is likely to remain a fundamental source of legitimacy in the People's Republic of China. Archeology and history, at least in the faces they show the public, are, as Hsia Nai told us, "One of the weapons with which we can struggle against our enemies."

EVALUATION

A visit to the People's Republic of China is likely to affect a historian or other China scholar far more deeply than he or she might have anticipated. One receives an existential sense of the size, reality, and depth of Chinese civilization that no amount of reading can provide. Underlying all the individual insights is the almost spiritual sense of contact with the enduring continuum of Chinese history. To see the Sian region, site of 11 different dynastic capitals; to stand on the tomb of Ch'in Shih-huang-ti; to see the wheat harvest being gathered across Honan in ways that have changed relatively little since the Neolithic--each impression was comparatively small, but the cumulative impact was enormous and unexpected.

For the historian, the opportunity of seeing the land and culture he studies can make an immense professional contribution that will benefit both teaching and research. He can "believe" in China in a fuller way than he did before and can thus teach with greater conviction. As a colleague quipped on our return, "You have seen the past, and it worked." Such trips are profoundly important for the personal development of the scholars involved and for the students and public with whom they will have contact on returning.

For the trip itself, then, I have nothing but strong and positive feelings. In assessing what we saw in China, however, reactions are more complicated and ambivalent. This derives in part from the comprehensive nature of the trip. We sampled more aspects of Chinese society--schools, factories, communes, museums, universities, villages, workers' apartments, nurseries, etc.--than we would have seen as tourists in a comparable month in, say, France. The size of the sample made the experience hard to assimilate, made it hard to have one consistent reaction.

But the ambivalence goes deeper. It is due basically to a tension between existential pleasure and intellectual caution. We do admire modern China. Chairman Mao has stimulated a vast, economically backward, agrarian society to move forward in concert. None are hungry or ill-fed. Given the recent history of modern China, this represents an enormous achievement. Ch'i-li-ying commune was an attractive and bucolic place, a thriving ideal community that lingers in the mind like T'ao Yüan-ming's "peach-blossom spring," a good model (so far as one can judge without talking to the peasants at length and in private) to which the rest of China can aspire. But this progress, this victory over peasant inertia, has required intense ideological pressure, precisely the kind of pressure we saw in the museums, that downplays an interest in technical and academic points of historical scholarship. In admiring the society we have to realize that it has achieved its successes in part by politicizing (and there are many traditional precedents) the kind of pure scholarship we admire and value in the West. The kind of work we do--that most scholars who read this report do--is a luxury in Chinese terms. The ivory tower itself is a luxury. It is explicitly regarded as a symbol of the enemy--academic and hence indifferent to the needs of the masses.

Our ambivalence, of course, was not due only to these technical and professional considerations. Just as Chinese historiography challenged many of our academic assumptions, Chinese society, as we saw it, challenged many of our assumptions about politics and human nature. To the extent that the society works--and it seemed to be working--it encouraged us to be more aware of shortcomings in our own system. In our terms, it was a revolutionary society; and since we were nonrevolutionaries, it was disturbing--for it raised basic questions with great force. To the extent that we left China with uneasy minds, the seeds of a Cultural Revolution had been planted in us. There are no single, simple solutions in human history. Despite--and even because of--their great achievements, the Chinese are caught in the ambiguities of the human predicament in characteristically Chinese ways. But they provide us with a model, both in history and in the present, that urges the profoundest consideration.

PUBLIC ARCHEOLOGY IN CHINA

Kwang-chih Chang

As anthropologists we are well aware of the necessity to understand--
not to mention evaluate--non-Western cultures and societies in their
own terms, since cultural and social behavior has relative as well as
universal dimensions. But as scientists practicing in a Western society, we find it easy to forget that scientific behavior is not exempt
from such conditions, and consequently we sometimes tend to look at and
evaluate foreign scientific behavior in all its multifarious dimensions
against our own conventions and standards, as if these latter were absolute. It is, therefore, necessary to be reminded once again that
Chinese palaeoanthropology must first of all be approached and understood in the terms in which it is practiced in contemporary Chinese
society.

Although on this month-long trip my assignment was to study all
aspects of Chinese archeology, and I have indeed learned much, my information is of uneven quantity and quality with regard to the various
parts of the subject matter. My first-hand information on the substantive aspects of Chinese prehistory and history is highly fragmentary,
and it will in no way enable me to generalize about any period of
Chinese prehistory without taking into account the very abundant corpus
of data that has already been published in Chinese archeological journals
and monographs. On the other hand, the public aspect of archeology in
China has been more systematically perceived by us than any other, and
my notes in this area appear sufficient to enable my readers to share
with me a preliminary appreciation of some of the most important compo-
nents of public archeology in China, the phrase "public archeology"
being used here in the sense in which it is used in Charles McGimsey's
book, *Public Archaeology* (New York and London: Seminar Press, 1972).

Fortunately, the public aspects of archeology are, in my opinion,
among the most important terms in which contemporary Chinese archeology
must be understood. As McGimsey's book has made clear, archeological
pursuit in the United States also has an increasingly important public
dimension. It is important to stress that in China all archeology is
already public. If we imagine for a minute a situation in which
American archeology is totally funded by the federal, state, and local
governments, all archeological relics are designated by federal statute
as national resources, all archeologists are on the public payroll, and
the priorities of training, research, publication, and public education

in the field of archeology are determined by Congress, state legislatures, and the aldermanic councils, then we can begin to understand how things work in China insofar as archeology is concerned.

In the following, I will briefly characterize the place of archeology in Chinese society and describe my data that I gathered on this trip pertaining to the preservation efforts of cultural relics and to the dissemination of archeological information, mainly through museums. Other pertinent aspects, such as research and training and their priorities, are dealt with elsewhere in this report.

PLACE OF ARCHEOLOGY IN CHINESE SOCIETY

It may be useful at the outset to point out several major characteristics of contemporary Chinese society that have everything to do with archeology's "state of the art," even though this can be done here only briefly and somewhat simplistically.

First of all, the Chinese political system is drastically different, and the place of Chinese "scholars" in their society, particularly in regard to making decisions about future plans and current priorities, cannot be directly compared with the roles American scholars play. Here let us take a look at the Constitution of the People's Republic of China, adopted in January of 1975 by the Fourth National People's Congress. Article 1 of this document states that "the People's Republic of China is a socialist state of the dictatorship of the proletariat led by the working class and based on the alliance of workers and peasants." Full-time archeologists may come from workers and peasants, but they must be led by the latter, whom they are also expected to serve. Article 12 states that "the proletariat must exercise all-around dictatorship over the bourgeoisie in the superstructure, including all spheres of culture. Culture and education, literature and art, physical education, health work and *scientific research work must all serve proletarian politics, serve the workers, peasants and soldiers, and be combined with productive labor*" (italics added).

Even though our visit was brief and hurried, I gained the clear impression that these articles in the Constitution are not empty words. In China the archeologists are not meant to be, and are not, society's elite, free and powerful to make the most important "priority" decisions about their profession or about their own services in it; they are meant to be, and are in fact, led by workers and peasants to serve workers and peasants. My impression is that intellectual elitism is one of the main targets of the Cultural Revolution of 1966. If that Revolution has left any profound marks on Chinese society, as it obviously has, then a visitor would be naive in professing to be surprised by the obvious fact that, although China's archeology is being conducted at the scientific and technical level by archeologists, the major decisions with regard to the place of archeology in Chinese society are made by workers and peasants or by those who have a claim to represent them. Archeologists participate in these decisions, but in the roles of workers and peasants or revolutionary scientists thinking and speaking in the interest of workers and peasants.

The fact that archeologists and archeology exist to serve workers and peasants is illustrated by many things we saw and encountered, and the examples that come to mind are the evidently vast investment of time made by senior archeologists in writing popular pamphlets, magazine articles, and museum labels about human evolutionary and historical topics of current interest, and the participation of the archeologists (along with everyone else) in the wheat harvests that we witnessed in Sian, Cheng-chou, and Nanking.

It must also be remembered that "scientific research must serve proletarian politics." Archeology as a "purely academic" pursuit cannot have any prominent place in this society: it must serve proletarian politics in the sense of serving the interest of workers and peasants in their political struggles against their class enemies. In this light the political tone of archeological writings and of museum displays should in no way be difficult to understand. It is because archeology is a political weapon in the never-ending struggle between classes that social history of China is first of all "periodized" into the primitive society, slave society, feudal society, semifeudal and semicolonial society, and socialist society sequence, rather than into some other possible classificatory schemes. From his own point of view, a visitor may wish to engage in arguments about the relative merits of this and other periodization schemes. Such arguments nevertheless miss the point about the societal context of present-day China.

"Self-reliance" and "independence" are also slogans that one frequently sees in China nowadays. These slogans are taken very seriously. In the "Preamble" of the new Constitution we find the following expression of resolution: "We should build socialism independently and with the initiative in our own hands, through self-reliance, hard struggle, diligence and thrift and by going all out, aiming high and achieving greater, faster, better and more economical results." These principles are applicable in agriculture and in industry, but they are also literally observed in archeological work. The Institute of Archeology set up its own Physics Laboratory to do radiocarbon determination apparently without any foreign assistance. There were some difficulties in the early stages, but these have been overcome. The same goes for the matter of methods, techniques, and interpretive models. What some visitors may with reason regard as provincialism is in fact a determined expression of this self-reliance. In my month-long trip through China I never once saw or heard any of my Chinese colleagues asking for professional help in any way. When a visitor volunteered assistance, if it involved foreign personnel and materials it would be declined, but if it involved simply information contained in the written word it was more often than not graciously accepted. (This distinction is one I have made in hindsight, and is not meant to cover every case, but it seems to generally apply.)

PRESERVATION OF CULTURAL RELICS

Among people and things that left a profound impression on me during this trip to China, two images are particularly subject to frequent vivid recall in my mind. One is the smiling face of Mr. Ting Sheng-yao, a dark, slim, middle-aged farmer at Ting-ts'un, the person charged with the responsibility for the preservation of the Ting-ts'un site. The other is a 10 x 10 m pit at the site of Ta-ho-ts'un, in which were exposed 21 human skeletons, buried in this cemetery by the Yang-shao people and now soaked in water that seeped up from underground because water had just been let into the fields surrounding the site in preparation for transplanted rice seedlings. Both images say much about the preservation efforts for cultural relics in China today and the reason for their success.

Mr. Ting symbolizes these efforts at the grass-roots level. A Ting-ts'un Site Preservation Team (Ting-ts'un Pao-hu Hsiao-tsu) was formed in 1954, with the excavation at the site. It now has seven members, all residents of the Ting-ts'un Production Brigade, within whose territorial confines the majority of the Paleolithic localities were found. Members of the team make inspection tours at each of the localities twice a month and clean up each of the areas monthly. Anytime when natural or man-made destruction occurs, the fact should be reported up to the county cultural relics agency. Any finds that become newly exposed should also be reported. We were told that since the onset of the Cultural Revolution more than a hundred specimens (stone implements and mammalian fossils) had been submitted to the county. I understood that the county officials would then send them up to the provincial cultural relics workers, among whom there are specialists capable of identifying the find and determining its importance. When Mr. Ting was proudly showing us the localities--which were only the locations where secondarily derived fossils and stone implements happened to be found in large concentrations--and pointing out to us the freshly painted markers ("Ting-t'sun Locality 54: 100", and so on), the thought occurred to me that nobody could come here and so much as pick up a pinch of dirt without the knowledge and consent of Mr. Ting and his six teammates.

The Cheng-chou burials at Ta-ho-ts'un were exposed and allowed to soak in underground water (which would not hurt the skeletons unless somebody tried to pick them up before the water had subsided and the bones became dry again) because plans were being made to preserve them for permanent display. There was already an exhibition hall at another part of the site in which some house floors and the base of walls were permanently preserved. Some sites of this nature are the Pan-p'o village, a group of chariot and horse burials at Chang-chia-p'o near Sian, and a ditch amidst the Shang palace foundations in which were dumped a number of human skulls, some bearing marks of cutting and other work. Excavations at these sites were stopped at the point where the features were best shown. Then a permanent structure of timber and bricks was constructed over them, placing them under sealed protection from the elements. These buildings are not cheap, and the state must be willing to spend valuable funds to preserve these features in their original conditions. Obviously the money is spent not only to preserve but also to educate, but an archeologist like myself cannot be more delighted to be educated along with the general public through these displays as well as through publications.

These examples stuck in my mind because they suggest to me that the efforts for cultural relics preservation will be successful because the state spares no expenses and the masses are organized for this purpose at the grass roots level. Other evidence of such efforts, of course, abounds. Although we had time to see for ourselves only a limited number of archeological sites, we saw what may be called the cream--a significant number of the most important archeological monuments: Chou-k'ou-tien, Ting-ts'un, Pan-p'o, Ta-ho-ts'un, Shang City at Cheng-chou, Yin Hsün in An-yang, the Imperial tombs of Ch'in Shih Huang, T'ang Kao Tsung and Wu Tse-t'ien, Ming Wan Li (the Forbidden City, the Mausoleum of Dr. Sun Yat-sen, the Forest of Steles, the Chin Shrine in T'ai-yüan, and so forth. All were in a good state of repair. Many of these have been declared Nationally Protected Cultural Relics, meaning that to alter them in any way requires permission from the State Council. (Others are protected at the provincial, municipal, or county level.) At each site a large sign is prominently displayed, bearing the following instructions (in translation):

1. Protect revolutionary relics. Further develop the revolutionary tradition.
2. Protect historical cultural heritage. Construct socialist national culture.
3. Cultural relics and ancient monuments belong to all the people. Protection of cultural relics and ancient monuments is everyone's duty.
4. Protecting local cultural relics and ancient monuments is the glorious duty of every one of the cadres and of the masses.
5. Any monuments, relics, flowers and grasses, and trees within the protected area are not to be destroyed.

And I have little doubt that these rules are observed. (Not to mention, of course, that our own paleobotanist, with our hosts' ready and indulgent consent, took a few tree leaves and grass plants at some of the imperial tomb areas for her botanical collection!)
Our hosts showed every sign of being stung by the talk in the foreign press during the period of the Cultural Revolution about widespread destruction of ancient monuments by rampaging Red Guards, and they became rather sensitive and agitated whenever this topic was mentioned. At the places we were shown, I saw no evidence of any such widespread destruction. In fact, at these places I saw no evidence of any significant destruction of apparently recent vintage. At a few places (Chin Tz'u and Kuei-lin) some of the stone steles bore signs of fresh repairs, but graffiti and vandalism are antiquities' perennial enemies all over the world. Steles suffered damages throughout Chinese history, and I had no reason not to date these damages to decades or even centuries ago. Judging from the publications and from museum labels, Chinese archeology did not stand still during the 1966-69 period, despite the fact that nothing was *published* during this period that I have ever read; on the contrary, many significant new discoveries were made during these years.

DISSEMINATION OF ARCHEOLOGICAL INFORMATION

Archeological data and results of study are published in monographs and
in scientific journals. Most important of the latter are four journals:
Vertebrata PalAsiatica, K'ao-ku, K'ao-ku Hsüeh Pao, and *Wen-wu.* I saw
current issues of all or some of them in Hsin Hua bookstores in Peking
and Shanghai, but I was told that the only way to ensure having copies
of them without interruption was by subscription through the post office.
Both *K'ao-ku* and *Wen-wu* can be quite technical at times, and one might
imagine that the more than 80,000 copies printed of each issue should
satisfy the demand. But I don't doubt that, with its demonstrated interest in archeology, the domestic market could absorb at least twice
that number. I had occasion to visit the library of an ordinary middle
school (one of dozens) in Peking, and I was amazed to see both *K'ao-ku*
and *Wen-wu* on the current rack (like discovering that our high school
libraries subscribe to *American Antiquity*). One day I went to shop at
the East Wind Market, near Peking Hotel where we stayed, and saw three
paperback copies of the new and entirely technical monograph on the
neolithic site at Ta-wen-k'ou (Shantung) at the market's book counters.
I had purchased a hardcover edition of the same book at the Hsin Hua
bookstore and had mailed it home the previous day without giving it a
second thought. But after I returned to the hotel it occurred to me
that I should get a paperback copy as well, which is lighter and could
be carried with me, so as to ensure having the book as soon as I
arrived home. The next day at lunchtime I returned to the book counter
in the East Wind Market to buy a copy of the book. All three copies
were gone!

But even so, in a country of more than 800 million, the technical
publications cannot begin to reach much beyond the archeologists themselves, and the workers, peasants, and soldiers, in whose service the
archeologists toil, necessarily depend on more digested forms of communication for their archeological information. The mass media probably carry important archeological news items, since newspaper articles
are sometimes quoted in archeological writings. As visitors we had no
access to local newspapers and I could not investigate this matter.
In recent months I have come across a significant number of small pamphlets on archeological or archeologically relevant historical topics
(sample titles: *Labor Created Man, Chinese Primitive Society, Slave
Society, Feudal Society*). Some of these were probably written by professional scholars at national research institutes. I was told by a
senior researcher at the IVPP that senior people, more than their
junior colleagues, take on such assignments. (This reminds me of the
fact that at some of our best universities introductory courses for
freshmen are given--not always through their section men--by the most
senior of the professors!)

Museums must play an extraordinarily significant role in this con-
nection. An indication of the importance attached to museums is the
fact that several years ago a decision was made to "bring our heritage
to the masses" and give the ordinary people everywhere an opportunity
to see the real Peking man stone implements, resulting in the scattering
of the Chou-k'ou-tien collection of several thousand pieces of stone

implements to museums throughout China. Among the museums we saw, few
are other than first-rate in terms of the effectiveness of their message-
conveyance roles. The exhibits are topically arranged, and artifacts
on display are, in general, artfully and sparingly placed together with
carefully painted reconstructive pictures and labels of few and large
characters. We were told that museum curators periodically meet in
Peking under the sponsorship of the Cultural Relics Bureau to exchange
information and ideas and to discuss matters such as the differential
specializations of various museums. A brief review of a selection of
museums that we saw follows.

Peking Man Exhibition Hall and Sites

This is a paleoanthropological shrine surely to be enjoyed by both
specialists and the general public. A trail has been constructed so
that a visitor can take a short walk around the hill and see many of
the fossiliferous localities. First opened in 1953, the present exhibition facilities were completed in 1972. Despite the distance from
central Peking, we were told that close to one thousand visitors can
be expected every day. The exhibition hall has three parts: the first
depicts the evolution of the animal kingdom, emphasizing that of the
vertebrates; the second depicts human evolution, using the Chou-k'ou-
tien finds as primary examples; and the final part shows the progress
in paleoanthropological studies in China since 1949. Many paintings and
scale models used in these rooms are extremely well done.

Pan-p'o Museum and Neolithic Site

The Neolithic site at Pan-p'o was excavated in 1954-57. Part of the
residential region of the neolithic village, about 3,000 m^2 in area,
was left in place and covered by a permanent structure, and in 1958 a

Pan-p'o site

museum consisting of this part of the site and several exhibition rooms was established. The exhibits are in two rooms, divided into four parts: production activities; social organization and clan life; culture and art; and inventions. Again the exhibits have been artfully done, and the museum appears to be well patronized. We were told that between several hundred and one thousand visitors come each day.

Honan Provincial Museum

Originally located in K'ai-feng, this museum was established in 1959 in its present buildings in Cheng-chou. Its activities are archeology and exhibition. Most staff members (more than 40, with 40 involved in excavation-type work) are trained locals, although recently some Peking University (archeology) graduates have joined the staff. Between 1966 and 1970, more than one million pieces of archeological remains are said to have been unearthed. A small part of them are at the museum, but most of the new finds remain under local care. As mentioned before, at least two or three trained para-archeologists or archeologists are at work in each county or city, and many more are found in prolific counties. In general, most archeological work is a local activity. The provincial staff is involved only when important finds turn up.

Nanking Museum

Housed in the spacious facilities of the former National Central Museum of the Nationalist government, the Nanking Museum now undertakes archeological work for the province of Kiangsu. Until recently there was a separate Kiangsu Provincial Commission for the Preservation of Cultural Relics, but it has now merged with the Nanking Museum. At the subprovincial level, all districts (*chuan ch'ü*)--Yang-chou, Chen-chiang, Su-chou, and Hsü-chou--and provincially administered municipalities also have their own museums and their own archeological staffs. When a discovery of archeological relics is reported to the provincial Bureau of Culture, the Bureau asks either the local staff or the Nanking Museum to investigate.

The Nanking Museum has the following departments (*pu*): (1) Preservation of Cultural Relics, responsible for the protection, restoration, repair, and retrieval of aboveground and portable, stray relics; (2) Archeology, for excavation, study, and publication of underground relics; (3) Curatorial, for the cataloging, conserving, repairing, and photographing of archeological relics, whatever the source; (4) Exhibition; and (5) Public Relations (Ch'ün Chung Kung Tso, or "the masses work").

More than 10 staff members are currently with the Department of Archeology, most of whom are Peking University and (secondarily) Nanking University (archeology) graduates. Their average age is in the forties. The department routinely accommodates students from Nanking University, who go there to participate in field research and/or to write their theses.

This museum has more than 3,000 m^2 of exhibit space, about 1,000-2,000 of which are devoted to archeology. Most exhibits pertain to the history of Kiangsu, but there are also temporary topical exhibits such as calligraphy and paintings, handicrafts, and new discoveries. We were told that the Department of Exhibits designs the museum's exhibits by first drawing up a draft for internal discussion, for limited publicizing in order to solicit feedback from the masses and for submission to the Bureau of Culture for approval. There are usually two drafts. The first draft contains only an outline, and the second draft includes main and secondary titles and a detailed list of objects to be exhibited. (The objects generally come from the museum's own collection, but casts of objects in other collections can be made and used.) When the drafts are approved the museum constructs the exhibits. They are open to the public only after another period of inspection and modification. The Department of Public Relations then undertakes the task of explaining the exhibits to the masses. Most docents employed by this department are, like in our museums, women. There are more than 200,000 visitors yearly.

Shanghai Museum

Established in 1952, the Shanghai Museum has a staff of 230, divided into three departments (Exhibition, Storage, and Archeology), two offices (administration and reference materials), and a workshop (for repairs and restorations).

It is essentially an art museum, the main exhibits being bronzes and porcelain. I understand that its collection of paintings is outstanding, but at the time of our visit the painting gallery was closed due to the wet season. Again about one thousand visitors are expected each day. Admission charge is 5 fen (about 3¢) per person, but 2 fen for a member of a group. Group visitors are guided by docents.

THE NATIONAL BUREAU OF CULTURAL RELICS

Some delegation members talked with members of this Bureau while in Peking. Formerly an agency under the Ministry of Culture, and since the Cultural Revolution an independent bureau directly responsible to the State Council, the Bureau of Cultural Relics--located at the former site of Peking University at Sha T'an--is the state's primary agent for the administration of its laws and regulations concerning the nation's cultural relics. Under its jurisdiction are three major categories of activities: libraries, museums, and the preservation of cultural relics (underground, aboveground, and portable relics). The administrative structure includes six institutions: the Palace Museum, the National Library of Peking, the Museum of Revolutionary History (still closed at the time of our visit but presumably the major repository of the nation's most valuable cultural relics), the Wen Wu Press (publisher of the journal *Wen Wu* circulation 50,000+), the Research Institute of Scientific Techniques for the Conservation of Cultural Relics (now still at the planning stage), and the Committee for the Organization of Exhibitions of Archeological Finds of the People's Republic of China. (The first three are colloquially called the *San Ta Kuan,* the Three Large Units, and the last three, the *San Hsiao Tan Wei,* the Three Small Units.)

Although the Bureau is not in itself a research institution, it is an extremely important archeological establishment because of its supervisory role over the nation's museums, which undertake much of the country's archeological research. In addition, the Bureau is in a position to promote research and coordinate research resources from diverse areas. The recent interagency efforts to excavate and study the Ma-wang-tui finds are a prime example.

Our hosts at the National Bureau of Cultural Relics were:

- Ch'en Tzu-te
- Kuo Lao-wei
- Chu T'ien (Wen Wu Press)
- Yang Chin
- Yü Hsiao-yao (Editorial Board, *Wen Wu*)

SUMMARY AND CONCLUSIONS

W. W. Howells

Because of the diversity of subjects and the reportorial nature of our
observations, no factual summary is practical. Instead, the following
is an editorial attempt to point out matters of professional understanding, which are made more explicit in some individual reports but which
drew the attention of all or most of us.

SCIENTIFIC OBSERVATION

We were able to examine hominid fossils freely and thoroughly. The
important animal fossils we could see less thoroughly; although more
numerous, they were less available because of lack of curatorial help
or because they were displayed in cases not open for handling, as in
Tientsin. Our hosts were most obliging in explaining materials as far
as special expertise was available--limited partly because materials
had been found and described long ago and in some cases could not now
be located (see Delson), and partly because the scholars concerned were
in the field with the harvesting. This fact, and our hosts' general
desire to accommodate us if possible, were both reflected in their bring-
ing back some specialists from the field to meet us.

Such limitations applied to archeology and geology particularly. We
had rewarding days at Chou-k'ou-tien and at Paleolithic sites along the
Fen Ho River at the Ting-ts'un Production Brigade village; but otherwise
our investigations were somewhat museum bound. This is evident in the
reports of Malde-Brown, Freeman, and Wormington. It will be noticed to
what extent information is seen through the eyes of their own experience,
being heavily referenced to existing literature. It is not that our
hosts were not well informed; they were, but there were not enough of
them. And again, there was the problem of material, which for a given
site tended to be distributed in different institutions rather than cen-
tralized (see Freeman), and which, when stored in a given institution,
was not open for general inspection, although samples might be brought
out for examination.

The failure to see the requested sites was the major disappointment
of the trip. There was a combination of reasons for this. We were told
we had listed too many for our energies and theirs (probably true) and
that transport and accommodations could not be managed. Also, we were

told that there was no one to receive us or that the site was abandoned
and not prepared--probably an important factor in our hosts' view. Finally, major sections of the country were not open to foreigners, although
privileged groups like congressional delegations had visited them. To us,
used to field conditions and not expecting neat, newly prepared sections
at a site, this was not easy to understand. We felt as a group visiting
the United States might feel, with an itinerary covering New York, Chicago,
St. Louis (with a visit to the Cahokia Mounds), Philadelphia, and Washington (with many museums), Niagara Falls, and a National Park or so, but
no Bad Lands, no Southwest ruins, no Indian reservations, no Paleoindian
sites, no Grand Canyon, Appalachia, or Deep South.

PROGRESS OF SCIENCE

Here the rate of return was higher, our hosts being disposed to describe
this at length and to answer questions. Progress comprises the emergence
from foreign-led projects after Liberation (see Malde, Freeman), increase
in number of workers, and involvement of the masses. Implementing all
this are the shifts in education away from training an elite through study
abroad and toward practical training (actually fairly broad) for particular needs and job openings, with a recently reversed discrimination aimed
at favoring the children of the people.
   This would not correspond to what we ourselves might see as progress:
simple advance of information or technical methods. And the aspects seem-
ing foreign to us are the lack of impatience; the insistence on self-
reliance at the expense of satisfying scientific curiosity; and the
compartmentalizing by disciplines and institutions. It is not our place
to criticize. In China paleoanthropology, a part of history, is a social
science in the sense of social orientation (not in our sense--social
anthropology and sociology, by official sanction, do not exist). Nor is
it for us to guess what this may mean in the way of continuity between
older and younger generation, or what it means to the personal interests
of the highly intelligent and wholeheartedly scientific members of both
cohorts.

SCHOLARLY COMMUNICATION

Good will and a friendly atmosphere were gratifyingly evident, but communication cannot be regarded as what would exist between say, Americans and
British. Some impositions have been noted above. For one thing, it became evident that the Chinese really had not understood the strength of
our desire to visit a larger number of actual sites, however neglected
or difficult of access they might be. For another, most of us gradually
became aware of a Chinese reluctance to exhibit behind-the-scenes work,
wanting only to show fully prepared exhibits. At Ta-ho, for example, we
could photograph at will inside the finished museum built over the exposed Neolithic house foundations, which were also beautifully diagrammed
and explained in wall panels; but we could not photograph the recently
exposed skeletons, for which a protecting shed was planned but not ready.

To our minds this was strange. Lack of free access to stored faunal or archeological material, already mentioned, was another manifestation of this.

This seems to be a matter of national character, not of recent politics. Other delegation reports may have suggested that reticence, and unwillingness to allow free inspection, lay in discomfort at possibly unfavorable comparisons with work in other countries. This hardly applies in force to prehistory, although Freeman questions the level of development of some kinds of field recording or cataloging. Instead, our hosts made no bones about not yet having developed their own equipment (for things like dating techniques) as far as Westerners; they plan to do it by themselves in due course.

Nor did they seem anxious for "communication" in the sense of joint research, or letting samples be taken home by us for assay. Quite the reverse: the modern accent on self-reliance and the lack of investigative urgency are strong factors here, and we were explicitly forbidden to remove any samples or to take measurements for our own work.

Our hosts were at home in formal presentations of any kind, whether describing work done, elaborating on museum exhibits, or describing the operation of institutes or the educational process. In all these, of course, the political element fell into place naturally and could be perceived as such, but it was also apparent that this kind of communication is the congenial one, rather than the late-night discussion, unstructured seminar, or common lab or field experience familiar to Westerners, particularly Americans. Another noticeable facet of communication was our failure to elicit questions to any great degree from our hosts about our own work and the fact, noted by Leopold especially, that there appears to be less communication than one might expect between members of the same profession in different centers.

PUBLIC COMMUNICATION

As the authors herein make plain again and again, great importance is attached to displaying history and prehistory to the people through museums. The element of social indoctrination may be important, but the effort goes far beyond this, in the making of museums--ranging from major ones in cities to small buildings over some archeological feature-- and in the care with which materials are arranged and explained. Several times we heard that explanatory panels or other aspects are worked out on a trial-and-error basis in order to let the public receive the most information from exhibits. Wormington and Chang, especially, convey our recognition of the generally admirable level of the public aspect of the museums and of the spirit of conserving cultural relics and preserving sites.

EFFECT OF CHINA ON OURSELVES

We brought home food for reflection, of which possibly too little appears in most reports, Chang and Keightley being the exceptions. Perhaps,

instead of surprise that things were not more a mirror of our own anticipations, we should be surprised that paleoanthropology exists at all
in the post-Liberation atmosphere of devotion to the public needs with
still limited resources. Rather than remark on the status of Chinese
paleoanthropologists, we might wonder what could be their view of us:
self-indulgently picking our own careers and pursuing our chosen research
with fairly plentiful resources and little constraint; having some concern
for our students but not much for involving the masses--in any case, not
doing what we like to think the Puritans came here to do? Naturally the
contact was one-sided, but it would be a boon if we could know more about
what we conveyed to them, as scientists and citizens of our country, while
we enjoyed the richness of their museums and the experience of the country
during a major phase of China's history.

APPENDIX A:

DELEGATION ITINERARY
May 15-June 14, 1976

_____

Thursday, May 15

Arrival in Peking

Friday, May 16--Peking

All day   Institute of Vertebrate Paleontology and Paleoanthro-
                 pology (IVPP)--Full delegation

Saturday, May 17--Peking

All day   IVPP--Full delegation

Evening   Welcoming banquet hosted by Scientific and Technical
                 Association of the People's Republic China

Sunday, May 18--Peking

All day   The Great Wall and Ming Tombs

Monday, May 19--Peking

Morning   Three groups:
                 1. Institute of Archeology
                 2. Institute of Botany
                 3. IVPP

Afternoon   Two groups:
                 1. IVPP
                 2. Peking University

Tuesday, May 20--Peking

Morning   Four groups:
                1. IVPP
                2. Institute of Geography
                3. Bureau of Cultural Relics/
                    Wen Wu Press and *K'ao Ku* Editorial Board
                4. Institute of Archeology

Afternoon   Three groups:
                1. IVPP
                2. Institute of Geology
                3. Peking Library

Wednesday, May 21--Peking

All day   Chou-k'ou-tien - Full delegation

Thursday, May 22--Peking

Morning   Three groups:
                1. IVPP
                2. Institute of Geophysics
                3. National Minorities Institute
                    (Central Institute for Nationalities)

Afternoon   Two groups:
                1. IVPP
                2. Palace Museum

Friday, May 23--Peking to Tientsin and return, by train

All day   Full delegation (except K. C. Chang)
                Rug factory and Natural History Museum
                (K. C. Chang remained in Peking)

Saturday, May 24--Peking

Morning   Summar Palace

Afternoon   Free time

Evening   Banquet for hosts

Sunday, May 25--Peking to T'ai-yüan by plane

                Arrival just before noon
                Lunch, rest, temple, banquet
                Shansi Provincial Cultural Troupe performance

Monday, May 26--T'ai-yüan to Lin-fen by train

                Arrival early afternoon
                Lunch and rest

                All afternoon in Ting-ts'un
                Banquet

Tuesday, May 27--Lin-fen to Sian by train

Morning	Ting-ts'un
Afternoon	Train to Sian. Arrival about 9:00 p.m. Itinerary discussion

Wednesday, May 28

Morning	Shensi Provincial Museum
Afternoon	Pan-p'o Museum and Big Goose Pagoda

Thursday, May 29--Sian

Morning to midafternoon	Ch'ien Ling Tombs (Wu Tse-t'ien/Yung T'ai Princess)
Late afternoon	Chariot Burial at Chang-chia-p'o

Friday, May 30--Sian

Morning	Free time
Afternoon	Hua-ch'ing-ch'ih and Ch'in Shih Huang Ti Tomb
Evening	Banquet hosted by member of the Standing Committee of the Shensi Provincial Revolutionary Committee

Saturday, May 31--Sian to An-yang by train

Morning   Northwestern University

Afternoon   Overnight train to An-yang

Sunday, June 1--An-yang to Cheng-chou by train

Morning   Arrival in An-yang 5:40 a.m.
                        Visit Yin Hsu Archaeological Station

Afternoon   Two groups:
                        1. Yin Hsü and surrounding area
                        2. An-yang Jade Factory and An-yang Straw Products
                            Company

Late   Departure for Cheng-chou
Afternoon   Arrival in Cheng-chou about 11:00 p.m.

Monday, June 2--Cheng-chou

Morning   Cheng-chou City Museum and Shang Palace Site

Afternoon   Honan Provincial Museum and Shang City Wall

Evening   Banquet hosted by member of the Standing Committee of
                        the Honan Provincial Revolutionary Committee

Tuesday, June 3--Cheng-chou

Morning   Ta-ho-ts'un

Afternoon   Yellow River Museum--Full delegation
                        Then two groups:
                        1. Mang Shan
                        2. Yellow River

Wednesday, June 4--Cheng-chou to Nanking by train

All day   Ch'i-li-ying People's Commune

Evening   9:20 p.m. overnight train to Nanking

Thursday, June 5--Nanking

Arrival in Nanking 10:00 a.m.

Afternoon — Boat ride on Yangtze River, tour of bridge, and Sun Yat-sen Memorial

Evening — Banquet hosted by member of the Standing Committee of the Kiangsu Provincial Revolutionary Committee

Friday, June 6--Nanking

Morning — Three groups:
1. Nanking Museum
2. Institute of Geology and Paleontology
3. Free time

Afternoon — Two groups:
1. Nanking Museum
2. Free time

Late Afternoon — All to Nanking City Wall

Saturday, June 7--Nanking to Shanghai by train

Morning — Nanking University

Afternoon — Train to Shanghai--Arrival 7:00 p.m.

Sunday, June 8--Shanghai

Morning — Children's Palace, Shanghai Mansions, Friendship Store

Afternoon — Two groups:
1. Shanghai Zoo and drive around city
2. Workers residence complex

Evening — Welcoming banquet

Monday, June 9--Shanghai

Morning — Fu-tan University

Afternoon — Natural History Museum

Tuesday, June 10--Shanghai to Kwangchou by plane

Morning   Shanghai Industrial Exhibition

Afternoon   Four groups:
                    1. Natural History Museum
                    2. Shanghai Municipal Museum
                    3. Botanical Institute
                    4. Free time

Evening   Flight to Kwangchou - arrival about 10:30 p.m.

Wednesday, June 11--Kwangchou to Kuei-lin by plane

Morning   Two groups:
                    1. Botanical Garden
                    2. Kwangchou Museum and Kwangtung Provincial Museum
                        and drive around the city

Afternoon   Departure for Kuei-lin 12:15 p.m.
                    Lu Ti Cave

Evening   Banquet

Thursday, June 12--Kuei-lin

Morning   Boat ride on Li Chiang

Afternoon   Forest of Stelae; Bonsai Garden

Evening   Variety/acrobatic show

Friday, June 13--Kuei-lin to Kwangchou by plane

Morning   Two groups:
                    1. Botanical Garden
                    2. Scenic Mountains in Kuei-lin

Afternoon   Flight to Kwangchou

Evening   Banquet

Saturday, June 14--Kwangchou to Hong Kong by train

APPENDIX B:

RESEARCH INSTITUTES IN PALEOANTHROPOLOGY

INSTITUTE OF VERTEBRATE PALEONTOLOGY AND PALEOANTHROPOLOGY (IVPP),*
ACADEMIA SINICA, PEKING

The delegation visited the Institute of Vertebrate Paleontology and
Paleoanthropology on 5 separate days--2 days as an entire delegation
and 3 days in small groups. The IVPP's new quarters are located at the
intersection of Hsi Chih Men Wai Boulevard and San Li Ho Street in the
newly developed (post-1949) western suburbs of Peking.

The Institute's ancestor may be said to be the Cenozoic Research
Laboratory, of the Geological Survey of China, established 1929 on the
momentum created by the excavations at Chou-k'ou-tien. In 1951 the
vertebrate paleontological and paleoanthropological activities were
assigned to a newly established laboratory within the Institute of
Paleontology. Two years later, in 1953, the laboratory became an independent department directly under the Academia Sinica. In 1957 the
present Institute was formed.

In 1975, at the time of our visit, the staff of the IVPP numbered
more than 200, including about 80 research workers, organized into four
research laboratories: (1) lower vertebrates through birds, mostly concerned with Paleozoic and Mesozoic vertebrates (20 researchers);
(2) evolution and zoogeography of mammals (10 researchers); (3) Cenozoic
stratigraphy, mammalian fossils, and glaciation studies (20 researchers);
and (4) human and higher primate fossils and paleolithic archeology and
environments (28 researchers in two groups: physical anthropology of
man and higher *primates;* and Paleolithic archeology and prehistoric
environments).

The Institute publishes monographs and the journal *Vertebrata Pal-
Asiatica* and administers the preservational and exhibitional activities
at the Peking man sites at Chou-k'ou-tien.

The primary tasks of the IVPP include research and dissemination of
knowledge in the fields of evolution, human evolution including higher
primates, and Paleolithic archeology. In addition, the IVPP researchers
engage in the study of biostratigraphy, especially as it applies to

---

*Information on the IVPP was compiled from the reports of Kwang-chih
Chang, Eric Delson, and Leslie G. Freeman, Jr.

economic geology, in conjunction with prospecting for mineral resources by geological teams. When discoveries are made in the provinces, the IVPP sends field teams to assist with excavation and with preparation of exhibits in local museums. Studies of the fossils recovered are usually made by a combined team of local and IVPP workers, and the finds then remain in or are returned to the province. With finds of major importance, however, this does not seem to be the case, and almost all primate materials are kept in Peking.

Other tasks of the IVPP include production of casts of fossils for use in exhibitions of evolution, especially human evolution, in local municipal and provincial museums and providing training for the staff of such institutions. The training is usually by means of short courses lasting from 1 to 6 months, dealing mostly with museological rather than research-oriented phases of vertebrate paleontology.

During our visit, the Institute was in the process of moving its facilities to a building nearer the center of Peking. Some specimens currently under study are kept in the new building, while a research museum, the main collections, the library, and preparation/illustration facilities are in the old building. Of these facilities, only the research museum was shown to us. This includes three rooms, organized temporally and utilized by younger workers receiving training and perhaps also by university students, but not by the public. The exhibits included a number of mounted skeletons of reptiles and mammals, and, in the Tertiary room at least, many of the specimens collected since 1949 are displayed in the cases.

No information was immediately available about the size of the collection of fossil vertebrates in the IVPP. Not all specimens are given a catalog number if not illustrated or described, so that a full count probably does not exist. Several different cataloging systems have been in use throughout the years, beginning with the designations of the old Cenozoic Research Laboratory in the 1920's and 1930's. Such older specimens may be numbered with a C (Cenozoic) and an apparently sequential numbering system. Some specimens at Chou-k'ou-tien were numbered in an informal way, indicating the year of discovery and also either the date or site (e.g., 51:8:H1 or 55.5.10). The standard form now in use in Peking assigns a sequential number preceded by a V (for vertebrate) to all published specimens, except for higher primates (Hominoidea) which are numbered PA (paleoanthropology). The "An" numbers familiar to many from the casts of *Gigantopithecus* mandibles are not specimen numbers, but cast numbers with no scientific value. Other specimens may have no formal catalog designation at all, merely a locality number. This is a five-digit number, of which the first two indicate year of collection and the last three are a sequential listing of localities found in a given year. Not all numbers may be used in any year, as numbers are assigned in batches to each field team, which may use between none and all of its allocation. Specimens collected in succeeding years at the same locality are given the number assigned to that locality in a preceding year, but new numbers may be assigned to new or sublocalities found in a large region or "field."

Many of the major finds and researches of the past decade have been reported in *Vertebrata PalAsiatica,* which was one of the first scientific journals to resume publication after the Cultural Revolution. New finds of many lower vertebrates are documented in these issues, as are those of many Cenozoic fossils. Because of the demands on the IVPP staff for assistance to local museums, there is little opportunity to engage in long-term intensive monographic revisions of any taxa. Instead, new field discoveries are analyzed in a preliminary way and published, after which there are more new discoveries to treat in the same fashion. Three special publications of the Institute have dealt with studies of lower vertebrates, mostly Mesozoic reptiles, by groups of authors.

The Institute's Chou-k'ou-tien field station, which is under the direction of IVPP archeologist Huang Wei-wen, includes the famous limestone fissure complex that yielded Peking man in the early decades of this century. Soon after the People's Republic of China was established in 1949, this important site complex was repaired and restored for preservation and research. A small exhibit room was built in 1953 for the public display of finds, and in 1972 the complex was improved with fences and walks, and a large, multibuilding museum was constructed. The fossil localities and the museum make up the Chou-k'ou-tien field station, which serves as a base for continuing interdisciplinary investigations of the site complex. The museum is open only several days each week but receives over 1,000 visitors in that time, including some 2,000 foreign visitors during 1974. It is an excellent example of the high art of Chinese museology.

The division between the IVPP and the Institute of Archeology is one based largely on tradition and convenience. The IVPP handles Paleolithic archeology, whereas the Institute of Archeology handles everything after the Paleolithic. Studies of human skeletons from Neolithic and historic period cemeteries, for example, are essentially done at the Institute of Archeology. But the division is by no means absolute. Because of its abundance in Neolithic and early historic sites, Honan Province has always been a major activity locus for the Institute of Archeology. When a new Paleolithic cave site was found at Hsiao-nan-hai, near Anyang, it was the Institute of Archeology instead of the IVPP that excavated it. Also the training of most of the Paleolithic archeologists at the IVPP is identical with that given their counterparts in the Institute of Archeology.

The people whom we met during our visit to the IVPP were:

楊鍾健　　　Yang Chung-chien
　　　　　　　　Director

張力彬　　　Chang Li-pin
　　　　　　　　Vice Director and
　　　　　　　　Chairman of the
　　　　　　　　Revolutionary Committee

斐文中　　　P'ei Wen-chung
　　　　　　　　Researcher

賈蘭坡　　　Chia Lan-p'o
　　　　　　Researcher

吳汝康　　　Woo Ju-k'ang
　　　　　　Researcher

周明鎮　　　Chou Ming-chen
　　　　　　Researcher

吳新智　　　Wu Hsin-chih
　　　　　　Researcher

邱中郎　　　Ch'iu Chung-lang
　　　　　　Researcher

張森水　　　Chang Shen-shui
　　　　　　Researcher

張銀運　　　Chang Yin-yün
　　　　　　Researcher

祁国琴　　　Ch'i Kuo-ch'in
　　　　　　Researcher

周国興　　　Chou Kuo-hsing
　　　　　　Researcher

蓋培　　　　Kai P'ei
　　　　　　Researcher

顧玉珉　　　Ku Yü-min
　　　　　　Researcher

衛奇　　　　Wei Ch'i
　　　　　　Researcher

尤玉柱　　　Yu Yü-chu
　　　　　　Researcher

155

INSTITUTE OF ARCHEOLOGY,* ACADEMIA SINICA, PEKING

Part of the delegation visited the Institute of Archeology for two half
days. This is the highest national research institute for late prehistoric and historic archeology. Located on Wang Fu Ta Chieh, in the
eastern district of Peking, the Institute was established in 1950 as one
of the original research institutes of the newly proclaimed Chinese
Academy of Sciences. Prior to that time, there was no single responsible archeological organization. University-based historical archeologists working under the auspices of the old Academia Sinica had already
invested much concentrated research effort in the group of sites near
An-yang, while scholars interested in early prehistory as a general rule
worked under the aegis of the Geological Survey. Field archeological
research diminished during the wartime period, 1937 to 1949; however,
it did not cease entirely.

The Institute now has a staff of more than 160, of whom 70 to 80 are
research personnel. There are three research divisions: (I) Primitive
society (mainly Neolithic archeology); (II) Yin and Chou; and (III) Han
through Ming. In addition, there are workers in restoration, conservation, and photography. There is a chemistry laboratory and also a
physics laboratory which began in 1966 to do radiocarbon dating.

The Institute of Archeology maintains a research library and an editorial office responsible for the publications of the Institute, including its two journals *K'ao Ku* (bimonthly, circulation exceeding 50,000)
and *K'ao Ku Hsüeh Pao* (semiannual, circulation of 8,000).

Field research stations are maintained at Sian, An-yang, and Lo-yang.
As necessary, the Institute sends temporary field teams to the countryside to conduct archeological surveys or to engage in excavation. We
visited only the An-yang field station. At Sian we were told that there
was no one currently at the field station, and we did not meet anyone
from the Institute of Archeology while in Sian, where ongoing activities
(e.g., the excavations of the important Yang-shao culture site at Chiang-
chai) seem to be carried out by the staffs of the Shensi Provincial
Museum, the Pan-p'o Museum, and Northwestern University.

At the Institute of Archeology, research designs are both "actively"
formulated to tackle significant archeological issues and "passively"
put together to coordinate with construction projects (e.g., the Sanmen
Gorge Reservoir and Dam Project) and to investigate important chance
discoveries in response to requests from the provinces or localities.
Examples of the significant archeological issues are: (1) the incipient
Neolithic culture, transition from the Paleolithic to the Neolithic, the
origins of agriculture, the postglacial climatic changes; (2) within the
Neolithic period, regional phases of various periods and their mutual
influences, changes in social structure, filling in blank areas, more
intensive application of scientific chronometric methods, pollen analysis, ancient vegetation covers, ancient foods; (3) the process of dis-
solution of the primitive society and the formation of economic classes
and the state; and (4) history of urbanism in China.

*Information on the Institute of Archeology was compiled from the re-
ports of Kwang-chih Chang and Leslie G. Freeman, Jr.

The people whom we met during our visit were:

夏　鼐　　　Hsia Nai
　　　　　　　Director

安志敏　　　An Chih-min
　　　　　　　Division I

王世民　　　Wang Shih-min
　　　　　　　Division II

芦兆荫　　　Lu Chao-yin
　　　　　　　Division III

仇士华　　　Ch'ou Shih-hua
　　　　　　　Physics Laboratory

蔡蓮珍　　　Ts'ai Lien-chen
　　　　　　　Physics Laboratory

莫润先　　　Mo Jun-hsien
　　　　　　　Editorial Board
　　　　　　　K'ao Ku

INSTITUTE OF BOTANY,* ACADEMIA SINICA, PEKING

This Institute, which was known formerly as the Merrill Institute of Botany (pre-Liberation), has a total staff of 300 workers, organized into seven research laboratories. We visited only the Paleobotany Section and the Herbarium.

The Paleobotany Section includes 19 research workers organized into the following divisions: (1) Paleozoic Paleobotany; (2) Mesozoic Paleobotany; and (3) Cenozoic Paleobotany.

The people whom we met were:

徐　仁　　　Hsü Jen
　　　　　　　Director
　　　　　　　Paleobotany Section

孔昭宸　　　Kung Chao-ch'en
　　　　　　　Cenozoic Palynology

*For more detailed information on the Institute of Botany, please see the report of Estella B. Leopold.

INSTITUTE OF GEOLOGY,* ACADEMIA SINICA, PEKING

The Institute of Geology is organized into eight laboratories: (1) Tectonics; (2) Geology of the Deep Crust; (3) Modelling Laboratory, (4) Engineering Geology; (5) Petrology and Rheology; (6) Sedimentation and Stratigraphy; (7) Isotope Geology; and (8) Geochemistry.
   The people whom we met were:

葉連俊   Yeh Lien-chün
           Director
           Section on Sedimentation
           and Stratigraphy

周昆叔   Chou K'un-shu
           Botanist

INSTITUTE OF GEOGRAPHY,† ACADEMIA SINICA, PEKING

Research work at this Institute includes land analysis, projects in environmental geology and applied hydrology, physical geology, fluvial geomorphology, climatology, and palynology. There is a pollen laboratory, where interpretation of pollen spectra is undertaken. There is also an agricultural experiment station.
   The people whom we met were:

左大康   Tso Ta-k'ang

沈玉昌   Shen Yü-ch'ang

INSTITUTE OF GEOLOGY AND PALEONTOLOGY,†† ACADEMIA SINICA, NANKING

This Institute was founded in 1950 with a staff of 20 and has now grown to a staff of 200, of whom about 160 are research workers. There are six divisions: (1) Palynology; (2) Paleobotany; (3) Lower Paleozoic Invertebrates; (4) Upper Paleozoic Invertebrates; (5) Mesozoic and Cenozoic Invetebrates; and (6) Sedimentary Rocks. Research is centered on applying paleontology and stratigraphy to practical matters of geological surveys, mineral prospecting, and engineering works.

*For more detailed information on the Institute of Geology, please see the report of Harold E. Malde.

†For more detailed information on the Institute of Geography, please see the reports of Estella B. Leopold and Harold E. Malde.

††For more detailed information on the Nanking Institute of Geology and Paleontology, please see the reports of Estella B. Leopold and Harold E. Malde.

The people whom we met were:

劉金陵   Liu Chin-ling
              Palynology

王惠基   Wang Hui-chi
              Cenozoic Gastropods

穆恩之   Mu En-chih
              Graptolites

APPENDIX C:

TRAINING IN THE FIELDS OF
PALEOANTHROPOLOGY AND ARCHEOLOGY

TRAINING OF PALEOANTHROPOLOGISTS*

Fu-tan University of Shanghai is one of the primary educational institutions in China offering training in physical anthrolpology. Most of the
junior specialists that we met at the IVPP in Peking had been trained at
Fu-tan. The principal teacher there for many years was Woo Ting-liang,
who worked with Pearson and others at the Galton Laboratory in London.
Woo died in 1969.

With a total of 3,500 full-time students and an additional 6,000 enrolled in short-term courses, Fu-tan has a faculty of 1,900 teachers and
administrators and 2,000 workers in the large factories run by the university. There are also 16,000 students enrolled in correspondence
courses. They live in the four neighboring provinces and receive their
texts and study materials by mail. An experimental branch university
with 100 students is located in a nearby commune.

Physical anthropology is taught as a specialty within the Biology
Department. The planned 3-year curriculum for the Biology Department
includes such basic sciences as physics, inorganic and organic chemistry
and biochemistry, mathematics (including mathematical statistics), and
vertebrate zoology. Physical anthropology students take the following
courses: primatology and paleoanthropology (80 hours); anthropometry
and osteology (80 hours); genetics and blood groups; statistics; race;
and human anatomy (60 hours).

Facilities include two laboratories and a skeletal collection comprising 800 skulls. The anthropology laboratory has 200 skeletons from
the disecting room, in individual boxes, plus about 60 individual skulls
from excavations; eight sets of anthropometric instruments made in China
in close conformity with Swiss instruments; a fairly full set of casts
of fossil hominids and a number of monkey and ape skulls; and a display
of metal shoulder and hip prostheses, plus X-rays showing clinical before-
and-after cases of insertion. Evidently graduates (who learn X-ray techniques along with anatomy) are expected to be able to act as advisors to
surgeons.

*The information on training of paleoanthropologists was compiled from
the reports of Kwang-chih Chang, Eric Delson, Leslie G. Freeman, Jr.,
and W. W. Howells.

The anatomy laboratory and dissecting room had a wide variety of anatomical materials ranging from standard supply-house plaster models to a variety of well-executed preparations of the pelvis, limbs, a sectioned head, joint capsules, etc., as well as arterial or nervous systems, or the complete central nervous system from the brain stem down.

At Fu-tan there is little staff research, partly for lack of materials, since all fossils are in Peking and the skeletal collection is in storage. Blood group or genetic studies are not being done now, for the blood work is being carried out at the Academy of Medical Sciences in Peking. Some practical anthropometry--human engineering--is done by the staff here and also at a design institute in Peking. Staff effort is in teaching the regular curriculum plus short courses and correspondence courses.

TRAINING OF ARCHEOLOGISTS*

Archeological workers in the People's Republic of China are being trained in two kinds of programs: university programs and short-training schools. The latter program will be described first.

Short-Training Schools

The short-training schools are of two different types, one for part-time and one for full-time archeologists. The program for part-time archeologists is a recent experiment. It is conducted at localities where large-scale, ongoing excavations are taking place (such as the Ch'u town in Chiang-ling in central Hupei) and is open mainly to worker-peasant-soldier interns. After a short period in which these interns learn the essentials of archeological concepts and operations, they return to their worker-peasant-soldier careers. They are then responsible for the protection and preservation of local antiquities and constitute a ready pool of experienced excavators whenever archeological excavations are carried out in their localities.

The short-training schools for full-time archeologists are open to archeological workers in museums or county or provincial cultural relics commissions. Generally speaking, these workers have not, and will not, attend college. One school is run jointly by the Institute of Archeology and the Bureau of Cultural Relics (and, at one time, Peking University). Since 1953 it has graduated four classes of students, and many of the graduates have assumed archeological leadership positions throughout China.

University Programs

The principal training ground for China's archeologists, however, is the

*The information on training of archeologists was compiled from the reports of Kwang-chih Chang and Leslie G. Freeman, Jr.

universities. We learned that there are eight universities that offer
a specialization in archeology: Peking, Kirin, Shantung, Hsi-pei (Northwest) Nanking, Szechuan, Amoy, and Chungshan Universities. What is
meant by university training is actually undergraduate training, but
Chinese undergraduate education has always been much more professionally
oriented than in the West, and it is during the undergraduate period that
a student in China is trained to become competent in a specialized profession.

In Chinese universities the archeology specialization falls under the
history department. Before the Cultural Revolution, the length of time
required in the specialization was 4 years, although in some places it
had increased to 5. Now, however, the curriculum covers 3 years. While
the different universities presumably have different curricula, the eight
share the following characteristics: (1) all emphasize Chinese archeology; (2) all emphasize practical work, meaning excavations or the actual
study of collections; and (3) all emphasize basic training in the funda-
mentals of archeology, leaving specialization (in Paleolithic, Neolithic,
Shang-Chou, Han, and so forth) to a final stage or, in most cases, until
after graduation. What distinguishes the eight universities from each
other is their location and their local archeological resources. They
tend to draw students from their respective areas, although some (e.g.,
Peking) are more national in student origins.

To discuss university training of archeologists in China requires a
discussion of university education in general, focusing on changes made
after the Cultural Revolution. After 5 years in elementary school and
5 years in middle school, a Chinese youth spends 2 to 3 years in the
countryside, in a factory, or in the army to engage in practical work.
After this time, the youth may apply to enter a university in a specialization, but his acceptance depends upon the recommendation of his co-
workers and the leadership of his work unit. We were told that many
students apply to the archeology specialization because of their participation in archeological excavations near their schools or work units.
Candidates for archeology programs in the universities also come from
museum workers and other governmental employees engaged in cultural relics work.

The matching of acceptable candidates with available university slots
is done on a national scale by a special commission of the Ministry of
Education. Each year, organizations engaged in research and teaching
such as local and provincial museums, regional Commissions on Cultural
Relics, the Bureau of Cultural Relics, and universities and research
institutes report on their future needs for trained workers to the Ministry of Education. The Ministry then draws up a national plan for training and notifies each university as to how many vacancies for prospective
specialists are available. The university may negotiate this figure with
the Ministry if the number suggested is not suitable, and in practice the
university often offers to train a specific number of specialists before
the Ministry quota is assigned. That was the case with the 1974-75
entering class at Nanking University; the university suggested that it
could admit ten new students and the Ministry agreed to that number.

Of the eight universities with archeology programs, we visited only
three: Peking, Hsi-pei, and Nanking.

Peking University

Peking University's archeology specialization is the oldest (since 1952) and probably the most influential. Professor Su Pai is currently in charge; other professors include Lü Tsun-eh and Li Yang-sung. Currently, eighty students are enrolled. Unfortunately we did not have time at the university to go into further detail.

Hsi-Pei University, Sian

Hsi-Pei University has a Department of History with a faculty of 61. It is divided into two specializations: history and archeology, with the archeology specialization having a faculty of 11. Professor Ch'en Chih is the director and is an outstanding archeologist of the Han and T'ang periods. We met only one other member of the archeology faculty, Mr. Wang Shih-ho, a specialist in primitive society archeology.

At Hsi-pei there were 70 archeology students as of June 1975--25 in the first year and 45 in the third. (There were no second year students.) They came from Shensi, Kansu, Chinghai, Ninghsia, Shansi, and Tibet. Most were recommended through cultural relics agencies, to which they were expected to return after graduation. They came here because they were from the local area, but also because Sian is rich in Han and T'ang relics.

Required courses are: (1) primitive society archeology, (2) Yin and Chou archeology, (3) Ch'in and Han archeology, and (4) Sui and T'ang archeology. Electives include: ancient history of China, ancient history of the world, ancient Chinese, ethnology, history of the Mongols, history of the Uighurs, and history of the Tibetans. Japanese is the preferred foreign language for the archeology students, who also take history and geology courses, but not statistics. Reading and research courses on special topics are also offered, depending on student interest.

For their courses, self-study on the students' part is emphasized. Notes with references for further reading are circulated before each topic comes up, and students prepare largely through their own efforts. A course is usually organized around topics. For example, the course on Ch'in-Han archeology comprises the following topics: the Han city in Sian; Han handicrafts, especially the development of iron technology; excavations of burials; study methods. At the end of each course the students are required to submit *tsung chie*, or a "summary of important issues." This could take the form of a final examination or a term paper. At the end of the program the student must write a graduate essay, which could be a report of a piece of practical archeological work.

Nanking University

Nanking University's archeology specialization was established in 1972 in the history department. The senior professor is Chiang Tsuan-ch'u, who was formerly with the Nanking Museum. We also met two younger instructors, Liu Tse-ch'un, a Quaternary archeologist, and Ch'in Hao, a specialist in Sui and T'ang archeology. Altogether there are 10 archeology faculty members, as opposed to 50 for history, and 30 archeology students, as opposed to about 100 history students. All ten students who matriculated in 1974-75 were cultural relics workers from Kiangsu, Kiangsi, Anhwei, Hupei, and Honan.

Courses may be grouped in three categories: (1) basic archeology (Paleolithic and Neolithic archeology, Shang and Chou archeology, Warring States, Ch'in, and Han archeology, Wei, Ch'in, the Six Dynasties, and subsequent periods) is a 2-year course, taught by a majority of faculty members; (2) topical courses (epigraphy, ancient architecture of China, ancient art of China); and (3) courses of archeological techniques (field archeology, archeological drawing, surveying, photography, conservation). These are all required courses. Other required courses include the general history of China and the general history of the world. Foreign languages are optional, with English the preferred foreign language. There is no statistics requirement.

Each academic year is divided into two semesters, each having 20 weeks. Classes of four periods are in the morning, from 7:30-11:30. Students study or take tutorials in the afternoons. During each semester, half the time is spent at the university and half in the field. In addition, for 3 weeks each year students must go to the villages or factories for productive labor. If there is an archeological excavation at the village where a student is working, he may be assigned to that excavation.

APPENDIX D:

A VISIT TO A CHINESE VILLAGE AND ARCHEOLOGICAL
SITE (reprinted from *The National Research
Council in 1976: Current Issues and Studies*)*

A paleoanthropology delegation of eleven American scholars--archaeolo-
gists, anthropologists, geologists, botanists, and China experts--visited
the People's Republic of China between May 15 and June 14, 1975. Their
trip was sponsored by the Committee on Scholarly Communication with the
People's Republic of China[†] and the Chinese Scientific and Technical
Association. Traveling a total of some 5,500 kilometers by train, plane,
and car during their 4-week stay, the Americans visited research institutes, museums, and universities in such cities as Beijing (Peking),
Tianjin (Tientsin), Xian (Sian), Anyang, Chengzhou, Nanjing (Nanking),
Shanghai, and Guangzhou (Canton). The delegation also had the opportunity to see a number of Paleolithic, Neolithic and Bronze Age sites. It
is hoped that what follows--an account prepared by the delegation of its
visit to the Ding Cun Paleolithic site--will give a sense of a "typical
day" during the trip.

Ding Cun (Ding village) in southwest Shanxi Province is on the banks
of the Fen River some 37 kilometers south of Lin Fen, the district seat,
where we stayed. This region--some 600 kilometers southwest of Beijing
as the crow flies (or perhaps we should say as the *bugou* flies, a bird
which arrives a few weeks before the wheat harvest and whose haunting
cry charmed us throughout Shanxi)--is traditionally associated with the
capital of one of the legendary sage emperors who are thought to have
ruled China in the third millennium B.C. It is a region that foreigners
rarely visit--only groups from Korea, Cuba, and Albania had previously
visited Ding Cun--so that during the course of our stay our convoy of
cars and minibuses frequently drove through streets lined by crowds of
smiling, clapping onlookers, some of whom had stood for long periods in
the rain and the dark waiting for a glimpse as we drove by. It was a
curious experience to find ourselves the center of such seemingly un-
merited attention.

*National Academy of Sciences, Washington, D.C., 1976, pp. 175-179.

[†]The Committee was established in 1966 by the American Council of Learned
Societies, the national Academy of Sciences, and the Social Science Research Council.

164

We arrived by steam train at 2:50 p.m. on May 26 after a comfortable 5-hour ride down the Fen River Valley through a fantastically eroded loess plateau and were immediately driven to our hostel, a three-story cement structure, set back in a courtyard behind a guarded gate that was soon surrounded by an expectant crowd. After some refreshment, we set out by 3:50 p.m. for Ding Cun itself, speeding along a paved road lined with young poplars, as our drivers insistently blared their way through a variety of bicyclists, carts, trucks, and buses. The road ran parallel to a terraced landscape that descends in dissected loess to the Fen River. As elsewhere in Shanxi and Hopei, the yellow dust in the air obscured the sun, giving the sky a leaden look and penetrating hair, ears, clothes, and cameras.

Turning off the highway and traveling about 2 kilometers down a dirt road (specially smoothed for us, as we later discovered) that ran toward the river, we arrived at the small, central plaza of Ding Cun, dominated by a large wall painting of workers of the world singing the "Internationale," the words painted beside it. At that time, we saw none of the village population. The village itself was immaculate. It consisted of a complex of houses and walls built of brick and rammed earth, the walls frequently whitewashed (and painted with slogans--e.g., "For industry study [Da Qing]"; "For agriculture study [Da Jai]"; "The whole country studies the People's Liberation Army"), and all divided by narrow alleys and an occasional ornamental gate. From an upper balcony we were given a panoramic view of the village with its gray tile roofs; every level plot of ground terraced into the eroded loess plateau surrounding the village was under careful cultivation, much of it in winter wheat awaiting harvest. We then descended on Ding Cun's barefoot doctor and her aide, both women in their early twenties, who showed us the impressive rural pharmacy, examination room, and fully adequate supply of Western medicines (including antibiotics such as sulfonamides, penicillins, and tetracyclines; drugs such as procaine and adrenalin; and vitamins B_1, B_6, B_{12}, C, and K_3 in both injectable and oral form), as well as its large supply of traditional Chinese herbs. Of particular interest was a birth control chart on the wall indicating the number of births and deaths for the most recent years and the number of peasants using various forms of contraception. The barefoot doctor (whose surname was that of the village, Ding) won our hearts with her confidence and aplomb in answering our questions.

Next we crowded into several classes in the elementary school where we saw children doing fractions and learning how to read (since it was now about 5:30 p.m., we guessed that the children had been kept in class specially for us). The wide-eyed younger children were remarkably well-disciplined as the teachers led them through their recitations and as they sang a song and then applauded us. One of the great pleasures of visiting China was to see the friendly and totally charming Chinese children; we left that classroom, as we were to do many others, with broad smiles on our faces.

We next visited the quarters of city youths who had completed Middle School and had "volunteered" to serve for 3 or more years in Ding Cun to help the peasants and to learn from them. Three or four lived in a room; the rooms were sparsely furnished, with volumes by Marx and Engels (in Chinese) by the beds. After a trip to the kitchen where we saw *man tou,* the north China "bread," being made, we returned to the long meeting room, with its whitewashed walls, where we sat with our hosts at two long rows of tables, under bare electric light bulbs, with the portraits of Chairman Mao at one end of the room and of Marx, Engels, Lenin, and Stalin at the other. Our hosts were the local cadres attached to the Revolutionary Committees, Bureaus of Cultural Affairs, as well as the Ding Cun Cultural Relics Preservation Team. It was typical of the care with which we were treated that two members of the Institute of Vertebrate Paleontology and Paleoanthropology (IVPP) had come by train from Beijing in order to show us the site. Another member of the IVPP, who spoke English, traveled with us throughout China.

As we sipped tea and wine and nibbled on wine-soaked dates (a local product), we were given a detailed account of the Ding Cun production brigade and the history of the archaeological site. We learned, for example, that the peasants earn about 1 *yuan* (57 cents U.S.) a day; that the average household savings were 150 *yuan*; that there were 950 people in the Ding Cun production brigade, with 140 big animals and 224 pigs; that over 100,000 trees had been planted; that illiteracy has been eliminated; that each house has electricity; that the population has doubled since 1949; that private household plots do exist, but that they are now cultivated collectively; and so on. We were told that, thanks to the leadership of Chairman Mao, life had improved immensely since liberation, and the evident prosperity of the village supported this convincingly.

Tired after our train ride and tour of the village, we were glad when the orientation session was brought to a close around 7:30 p.m. and we rode back to Lin Fen in the dark through the usual curious crowds, some running beside the minibuses for a longer look. Dinner with our Lin Fen hosts was a staggering banquet of local delicacies (such as golden ingot eggs). Another of the great joys of touring China is the cuisine, and the dinner that night in Lin Fen was superb.

Pressed for time, we breakfasted at 6:30 the next morning (surviving a minor misunderstanding about Western tastes--heavily sugared "coffee-tea" served as one drink) and were back in Ding Cun by 8:00. We left the vehicles soon after leaving the highway and walked at our leisure down the dirt road, which at this point paralleled a ravine deeply eroded in the loess. The steep walls, about 60 meters high, provided excellent exposures of the loess and its varied soils, some of which we examined close at hand in the roadside banks. We passed through the village where we could see the villagers--our first glimpse of the village population--held back at the far end of the street and walked down through the fields to the archaeological localities, which lie scattered on the western banks of the Fen River. The localities were of great interest to us because of their postulated age (Late Pleistocene) and the association of stone tools, fossil animal bones, pollen, and human fossils, which might permit rather detailed reconstructions of past climates, environments, and human adaptations.

The first group of sites was in a cultivated area along the single track of the Taiyuan-to-Xian railway. Prompted by finds originally made by peasants in 1953, local archaeological teams have found some 2,000 stone instruments, 28 species of fossil mammals, 30 molluscan species, and several kinds of fossil fish. (We had already examined some of these finds in the IVPP in Beijing.) These came from consolidated sand and gravel that lies gradationally below the loess, about 15 meters above the present river. Because of cultivation and grading, the deposits that produce these artifacts and fossils were now covered, but we saw enough to comprehend their geologic character.

We then walked south for more than a kilometer along the railroad to Locality 100, famous among paleoanthropologists as the place of discovery of three human teeth, again from alluvial deposits, gradational below the loess. The geologists in our delegation agreed that this geologic section could be matched in general attributes with Late Pleistocene stratigraphy elsewhere in the world. During this archaeological ramble along the loessic banks we were accompanied by our hosts from Lin Fen, Ding Cun, and the IVPP. A case of *qi shui* (the Chinese soda pop) and a box of glasses had been carried down to the riverbank and Chinese and Americans all sat and drank beneath a tree. The barefoot doctor, who was gathering medicinal herbs as we walked, took the occasion to correct a mistranslation in the previous day's discussion that had given us an erroneously high figure for infant mortality in the village; it was clear that our questioning on this point the day before must have provoked discussion.

As we walked back through the fields toward Ding Cun at about 11:30 a.m., large numbers of peasants, male and female, bearing their hoes and other tools on their shoulders, sallied out of the villages and marched past us towards the fields, well-dressed, smiling, and occasionally clapping.

We drove back to Lin Fen at a leisurely pace, lunched, and, still coated with the yellow dust, caught the 3:00 p.m. train for Xian, the same train on which we had arrived just 24 hours earlier. And some 20 minutes later we were rolling past the archaeological sites where we had been so warmly received and had learned so much.

Ding Cun is undoubtedly a special village that has been prepared for foreign and Chinese guests, a printed color brochure, in Chinese, describes the site, and over 7,000 Chinese have now visited it. But the opportunity to stroll down dirt lanes in the Chinese countryside, to examine the loessic strata, and to see the site of major paleolithic finds, all in the company of Chinese experts, was a rare and agreeable one that permitted important scientific and social learning to take place. We saw the archaeological sites and obtained new insights for dating and evaluating the finds. But we saw more than that. The village of Ding Cun was not just the gateway to the archaeological site: it was, in the Chinese view, the necessary experience through which scientists must pass in order to understand that their work exists for, and is supported by, the people. This blend of scientific and social experience was typical, not just of our day in Ding Cun, but of our entire month in China.

APPENDIX E:

NOTES ON CHINESE LOESS*

Francis H. Brown

_____

INTRODUCTION

As early as 1866, Pumpelly had visited the loess areas of China and made
them known to Western scientists. He considered the loess to be lacustrine in origin, deposited by the Yellow River. His hypothesis was accepted by other early workers until it was flatly contradicted by von
Richthofen (1882), who considered the loess to be eolian in origin.
Pumpelly (1879) accepted the idea, as did Bogdanovich (1892), Loczy
(1893), Obruchev (1900), Wright (1902), and Tafel (1914). Although
these authors accepted the eolian hypothesis of the origin of loess in
China, they were divided on the problem of the source of the detritus.
Willis (1907) doubted that wind was capable of transporting so much material and inclined toward a fluvial origin.

   Much the same debate has gone on about the genesis of loess in the
lower Mississippi Valley of the United States. Some workers (e.g., Swineford and Frye) favor the eolian hypothesis, while others (e.g., Russell)
have strenuously opposed it.

   Among Russian geologists we again find opinions divided, but not along
neat lines. With the typical penchant for obfuscation of some Russian
geologists, many different processes are supposed to be responsible for
the formation of loess, including one process termed loessification (see
for example Pavlinov, 1959).

   Chinese workers also are divided as to the origin of the loess--some
accept the eolian hypothesis, while others "[attribute] to the loess an
alluvial lacustrine genesis. But this opinion has not much currency"
(Chang, 1959). While the latter opinion may not have much currency,
Yang (1959, p. 123) states that "loess formation was explained, not very
convincingly, by the action of wind." Later (p. 125) he goes on to say
that "the main factor in loess formation were [sic] currents of water."

   Some of the debate about the origin of loess is promulgated by inclusion of different materials and formations into what has been called
loess in China. Other parts of the debate are furthered by differing

*The information in this article is based on published material, rather
than on observations made during the visit to China of the Paleoanthropology Delegation.

168

concepts of what is meant by loess. Among those authors who have written most clearly about the genesis of loess are Obruchev (1959), Richthofen (1882), and Kes' (1959).

DEFINITION OF LOESS

As a working definition of loess we may take that of Flint (1957), whose definition is almost identical with that of Scheidig (1934). Loess is a sediment, commonly nonstratified and commonly unconsolidated, composed dominantly of silt-size particles, ordinarily with accessory clay and sand, and deposited primarily by the wind (Flint, 1957). Scheidig (1934) would add that a rude vertical parting is common at many places. Other definitions may be found which incorporate mineralogical and chemical characteristics of loess (e.g., Thorp, 1945, p. 264), but these addition-al characteristics may vary widely from one loess to another, and even within the same loess, and do not help the definition materially.

In papers I have read, Chinese workers use such terms as loess, loessic rocks, eolian loess, proluvial loess, loesslike loan, etc., but nowhere have I found these terms well defined.

Obruchev (1945) recognizes two types of loess: typical or primary loess; and clay-like loams, sandy loams, and sands which are grouped to-gether as secondary loess. Primary loess is an eolian formation, while secondary loess is either the result of deposition of primary loess by water or is an alluvial fine-grained earthy formation that acquired its loesslike characters by weathering and soil-forming processes. If pri-mary loess loses its typical properties *in situ,* Obruchev designates it altered or degraded loess.

In addition, Obruchev (1945) distinguishes cold and warm loess. Cold loess is associated with glaciers and derived from barren glacio-fluvial deposits and till. Warm loess, on the other hand, is created in deserts and semiarid continental regions.

THEORIES OF FORMATION OF LOESS

There are at least 50 theories that have been advanced to explain the accumulation of loess. This is not the place for discussion of all of them, but the following have been put forward to explain the loess of China.

The Eolian Hypothesis

Most geologists consider the majority of loess to have been transported and deposited by the wind. It is necessary for sediment to be exposed at the surface of the earth without a protective cover of vegetation. Central Asia is such a region, and the best conditions for deflation are a dry continental climate with moderate or strong winds. Thus according to the eolian hypothesis, the loess of China is composed of wind-trans-ported material from Central Asia (northern China and Mongolia).

170

The Eluvial Hypothesis

According to this hypothesis, loess forms by eluvial alteration (alteration *in situ*) of proluvial sediment. Proluvial sediment, or proluvium, is a term applied to mudflow and flash-flood deposits of a bajada-type alluvial fan. In this view, loess is a soil, and the characters that it possesses are a result of comminution *in situ*. In its most extended form, this hypothesis is identical with a process termed loessification by L. S. Berg (1916), or Huangtuization by Sakai (1967), in which any rock becomes loess *in situ* under the proper conditions. What the basis for this hypothesis is I do not know.

Fluvio-Lacustrine (Marine) Hypothesis

As mentioned earlier, Pumpelly (1866) first considered loess to be a sediment deposited in extensive lakes in western China but accepted von Richthofen's idea that loess of Eolian origin by 1879. Still, in 1902, Wright stated that "deposition of loess is now taking place...all along the Chinese side of the Yellow sea," and he also believed that much of the loess of China was deposited in standing water. Wright, however, does not entirely discredit the eolian hypothesis and felt that "ample credit must still be given the wind as an agency which is still at work distributing the loess." Workers in Russia who have considered loess to be primarily alluvial in nature are Sobolev, Pavlov, Gerasimov, and Markov, although details of their concepts of loess formation differ.

According to the fluvio-lacustrine hypothesis, loess is formed when running water that carries much silt in suspension spreads out in shallow lacustrine basins. The reduction of velocity on reaching the basins allows the silt to settle. Loess deposition, according to another variation of this hypothesis, may also take place in deltas and valleys of rivers descending from mountainous regions. Most workers who subscribe to this theory seem willing to allow some of the loess to have been transported by wind, but they flatly deny that the typical properties of loess are features that result from primary eolian deposition.

PHYSICAL PROPERTIES OF LOESS

Macroscopic Features

The principal macroscopic features of loess are evident in its definition. Loess is nonstratified and nonconsolidated; in many places it has a rude vertical parting. Layers of carbonate concretions may occur, and these are often called loess dolls or loess kindchen in the literature. Sakai (1967) states that these concretions are called Sha-chiang or Shih-chiang in northern China. Within deposits of loess there may be erosional boundaries or buried soils. Occasionally lenses of gravel and sand are observed.

Steep cliffs and vertically walled gullies characterize loess-covered country, and the steep drop from a loess plain to the bottom of one of these gullies results in erosion by piping and gives rise to karstlike features. We observed some of these pipes at Mang Shan near the Yellow River. The steep walled gullies were seen everywhere in the loess country.

Granulometry

The mean grain size of particles in loess is small, generally between 4.5ϕ and 6.5ϕ* (-1ϕ to $+4\phi$ are sand sizes; 4ϕ to 8ϕ are silt sizes; 8ϕ are clay sizes). Thus the mean grain size of loess is silt. Median grain sizes fall between 4ϕ and 6ϕ, in the silt range as well. Skewness of cumulative curves for loess is invariably positive, meaning that there is a fine tail. The skewness values lie between 0.4ϕ and 1.2ϕ in general, which means that, according to Folk (1968), loess is strongly fine skewed. While loess is often said to be well-sorted material, graphic standard deviations range from about 0.35ϕ to 1.33ϕ, which means that the material within one standard deviation of the mean is well sorted. If the Inclusive graphic standard deviation is used however, the range of this parameter is from about 1ϕ to 2.5ϕ, which results in loess being classed as poorly sorted. The difference arises because the Inclusive graphic standard deviation considers all sizes within three standard deviations of the mean, and the higher values reflect inclusion of much of the fine tail that generally comprises less than 20 percent of the sample and is therefore missed in the Graphic standard deviation computation.

The grain size distribution of loess can be expressed in many ways, but for comparative purposes I use here the method of traingular plots in which sand, silt, and clay are computed as percentages. This is the only method I have found by which it is possible to directly compare size analyses of Chinese loess with loess from other parts of the world. In Figure E-1, the analyses of loess presented by Chang (1959) are plotted together with loess from other parts of the world (Europe, Argentina, and the United States). The Chinese loess is most similar to European loess on a diagram of this type, although some samples fall within the range of American loess. Only Argentine loess, which is more sandy, appears at all distinct.

Mineralogy of Loess

Liu and Chang (1962) have published very complete analyses of the coarse fraction of Malan loess from many different localities in China and report 48 different minerals in the heavy fraction (density greater than 2.90 gm/cc) alone. They report six varieties of pyroxene, eight amphiboles, four mica minerals, five varieties of the epidote-zoisite group, two chlorites, wollastonite, sillimanite, apatite, garnet, kyanite, staurolite, sphene, barite, serpentine, eleven iron titanium oxide minerals,

*The ϕ scale is related to the millimeter as follows: $\phi = \log_{10} D / \log_{10} 2$, where D is the particle diameter in millimeters.

172

FIGURE E-1
Comparison of analyses
of loess from China,
North America, Europe,
and Argentina.

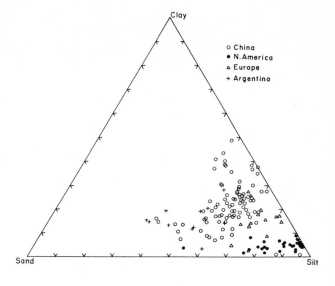

tourmaline, topaz, and zorcon. Quartz and feldspar make up 80 to 90 percent of the fragments, and carbonate minerals are also present. They
state that the fine fraction (<0.001 mm) contains illite, montmorillonite,
kaolinite, geothite, limonite, quartz, and calcite.

The mineralogy of loess in Kansas has been studied by Swineford and
Frye (1951), who report that the silt size fraction is composed of quartz
(ca. 50 percent), feldspars, volcanic glass shards, carbonate minerals,
and mica. Loess from Europe likewise contains quartz, feldspars, muscov-
ite, biotite, carbonate minerals, and in addition metamorphic and igneous
rock fragments.

The light mineral composition compares favorably between Chinese and
Western loess, but there are no analyses of the heavy mineral fraction
of loess from the Western world which can be compared with the exceptionally complete analyses of Chinese workers.

Chemistry

Comparative analyses of loess from China and other parts of the world are
presented in Table E-1. The Chinese analyses are taken from Liu and Chang
(1962), the Argentine analyses from Terruggi (1957), and the average
Peoria loess from Swineford and Frye (1951).

Chinese loess is lower in silica and alumina, slightly higher in iron,
and distinctly higher in lime than loess from other parts of the world.
In other respects the chemical composition appears similar.

Fabric

Matalucci et al. (1969) have studied the fabric of loess both petrograph-
ically and by using its dielectric anisotropy. They have found that

TABLE E-1 Chemical Analyses of Loess

Compound	1[a]	2	3	4	5	6
SiO_2	71.36	63.54	56.00	58.83	59.10	53.92
TiO_2	--	0.84	0.50	0.68	0.64	0.58
Al_2O_3	12.57[b]	15.65	11.48	9.64	10.35	9.22
Fe_2O_3	3.12	5.11	3.98	3.02	3.52	3.82
FeO	--	-	1.20	2.14	1.57	1.24
MnO	-	-	0.18	0.18	0.15	0.05
MgO	1.62	1.56	3.42	2.33	2.28	2.07
CaO	2.94	2.75	8.64	8.19	7.64	11.10
Na_2O	1.54	1.90	1.73	1.78	1.69	1.02
K_2O	2.68	1.83	1.95	2.55	2.56	2.23
P_2O_5	--	-	-	0.16	0.16	0.13
H_2O^+	0.49	4.72	-	3.85	3.88	4.77
H_2O^-	-	-	-	1.07	1.44	1.87
S	-	-	-	0.50	0.50	0.51
CO_2	-	-	-	4.99	4.49	7.20

[a](1) Average Peoria loess: (2) average Argentine loess; (3) average Malan loess; (4) Malan loess Lü-Liang; (5) Li-Shih loess Lü-Ling; (6) Wu-Ch'eng loess Lü-liang.

[b]Includes TiO_2.

174

orientation of elongate grains of quartz and feldspar can be used to
determine the direction from which the loess came. No comparable data
exist for loess in China, but it would appear to be a fruitful area for
study.

DISTRIBUTION OF LOESS IN CHINA

In a brief but remarkably informative paper, Liu and Chang (1962) have
reviewed the distribution, stratigraphy, granulometry, mineralogical
composition, and chemical composition of Chinese loess. Figure E-2 is
adapted from their Map I and shows the known distribution of loess in
China.

Liu and Chang (1962) document several features of the distribution of
the loess. The mean grain size of a particular loess decreases from
north to south. This could be taken as evidence that the loess was derived from the north. Loess is found at higher levels and is thicker on
the north and west slopes of mountains than on the south and east slopes.
Again this is consistent with a northerly source for the loess. These
authors give the total area covered by loess as 440,680 km^2, with 72 percent of this area in the middle Yellow River valley. The average thickness of loess is stated as about 100 m (80-120 m), and the maximum
thickness noted is 175 m.

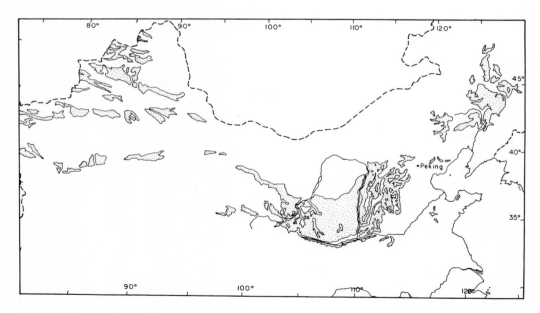

FIGURE E-2 Distribution of loess in the People's Republic of China.
From Liu and Chang (1962).

STRATIGRAPHY OF LOESS IN CHINA

According to Liu and Chang (1962), the standard stratigraphic profile
for loess in the middle Yellow River region can be taken as the profile
at Wu-ch'eng, Shansi. Here four different layers of loess are recognized, and their names and stratigraphic description are as follows:

4. Malan loess (10 m). Light gray yellow in color. Even distribution unconformably covering an erosion surface on the Upper Li-Shih loess.
3. Upper Li-Shih loess (51.5 m). Gray yellow to yellow in color. Contains seven buried soil horizons. Unconformably covers an erosion surface on the lower Li-Shih loess.
2. Lower Li-Shih loess (42 m). Yellow to light brownish yellow in
color with 14 poorly developed buried soil and weathering horizons. Dis-
conformably covers the weathered surface of the Wu-Ch'eng loess.
1. Wu-ch'eng loess (17.5 m). Reddish yellow in color. Contains six
beds of buried soils and weathering horizons. Unconformably overlies
Pliocene boulder beds.

The Malan loess is considered to have been deposited during the late
Pleistocene; the upper Li-shih loess, during the late middle Pleistocene;
the lower Li-shih loess, during the lower middle Pleistocene (equivalent
to Chou-k'ou-tien Locality 13); and the Wu-ch'eng loess, during the early
Pleistocene (Villafranchian). All of these age assignments are based on
faunal evidence.
Other divisions of the loess have been proposed by Obruchev (1959),
and Kes' (1959) among others, but that of Liu and Chang (1962) is the
only one, so far as I know, that is based on a single type section where
each of the beds can be seen, and therefore it seems best to follow their
division and attempt correlation with loess in other parts of China by
whatever means possible. If Liu and Chang (1962) are correct, this has
already been accomplished over much of the middle Yellow River region,
and, with time, correlation with loess in other parts of China should
be effected.
As nearly as can be stated, the fourfold division of the loess used
by Liu and Chang corresponds to that of Obruchev (1959) and Kes' (1959)
as follows:

Liu and Chang	Kes'	Obruchev
Malan loess	Yellow loess	
Upper Li-shih loess	Loess with buried soils	Yellow loess
Lower Li-shih loess		
Wu-ch'eng loess	Red loess	
	Pink clay	Sanmen Formation
	Red clay	Hipparion clay

FAUNA AND FLORA OF THE LOESS

References to fossils collected from the loess of China are scattered and
not always reliable. Obruchev (1959) gives one of the better summaries,

but I do not know if his nomenclature is current. He lists not only vertebrate elements of the fauna but also invertebrate fossils. Other invertebrate fossils are tabulated by Sakai (1967). Pollen profiles in the standard section at Wu-ch'eng are described by Liu and Chang (1962). Fourteen genera of angiosperms (*Juglans, Carpinus, Quercus, Ulmus, Morus, Acer, Ephedra, Salix, Corylus, Typha, Humunus* [sic], *Clematis, Convolvulus, Artemisia*) are listed as well as three families (Chenopodiaceae, Crayphyllaceae, Compositae) not identified to the generic level. Two genera of gymnosperms (*Abies* and *Pinus*) are listed as well as the family Cupressaceae.

RELATION OF LOESS TO EARLY MAN

If Chinese loess is defined to encompass only the Malan loess, then a chronology of the loess will be applicable only to the later stages of cultural evolution of man in China. This appears to be the viewpoint of Aigner (1972). If on the other hand the loess is defined more broadly, as Liu and Chang (1962) have done, then loess deposition has taken place at intervals during most of the time that man has lived in China.

If the loess horizons were ascribed to absolute time intervals, they would provide excellent stratigraphic markers over most of the Yellow River valley and would be of great importance to determining not only relative but also absolute times of human occupation in this area and beyond. Ho (1969) has demonstrated that the "cradle of Chinese Neolithic culture" was on the loess highlands. I know of no absolute dates on the loess, but some comments on how such dates might be obtained follow.

SUGGESTIONS FOR DETERMINING ABSOLUTE DATES OF THE LOESS

Potassium-Argon Dating

Pavlinov (1959) states that "in the district of Tatung...in one wide valley where typical deluvial-proluvial loess merges with alluvial loessic formations, no less than 20 small volcanic cones are known, consisting of basalt, volcanic breccias and welded tuff. The volcanic material...occurs upon typical loess.... The sheets of basalt...are in ...turn covered by the younger loess."

This seems to be an ideal situation in which to determine an absolute date on the loess sequence by potassium-argon dating of the basalt.

Radiocarbon Dating

This method should be applicable to bones, organic material, and ostrich egg shells found in loess but might yield only limiting dates for the older deposits of loess. Even these would be welcome.

Paleomagnetic Reversal Chronology

If some of the loess is as old as early Pleistocene, as is suggested by
Liu and Chang (1962), then we can expect the older loess to be at least
1, and possibly 2, million years in age. Therefore even a superficial
study of the loess should turn up some levels of reversed polarity, and
with a little more work a number of polarity boundaries might be recognized. This method of investigation would seem to be the most straight-
forward for dealing with the loess and should be applicable to loess in
every part of China, thus possibly being a valuable tool in correlation
of various layers.

REFERENCES

Aigner, J. R. 1972. Relative dating of North Chinese faunal and cul-
    tural complexes. Arctic Anthropol. 9:36-76.
Berg, L. W. 1916. The Origin of loess. Izv. Russ. Geog. Obshch.
    vol. 52.
Bogdanovich, K. I. 1892. Geolocical researches in Eastern Turkestan.
    In Trudy Tibetskoi ekspeditsii, vol. 2. St. Petersburg, 168 pp.
Chang, Tsung-hu. 1959. The genesis and formation process of loess in
    the Lungtung region of northwestern China. In Loess of Northern
    China, trans. by A. Gourevitch. U.S. Department of Agriculture, 1964.
Flint, R. F. 1957. Glacial and Pleistocene geology. John Wiley & Sons,
    New York. 553 pp.
Folk, R. L. 1968. Petrology of sedimentary rocks. Hemphill's, Austin,
    Texas.
Ho, Ping-ti. 1969. The loess and the origin of Chinese agriculture.
    Am. Hist. Rev. 75:1-36.
Kes', A. S. 1959. The question of the origin of loess in Northern
    China. In Loess of Northern China, trans. by A. Gourevitch. U.S.
    Department of Agriculture, 1964.
Liu, T. S., and C. Y Chang. 1962. The loess of China. Acta Geol.
    Sinica 42:1.
Loczy, L. 1893. Beschreibung der geologischen Beobachtungen und deren
    Resultate die wiss. Ergeb. Reise Gr. Bela Sechenyi Ost-Asien 1877-
    1880. 1:307-845.
Matalucci, R. V., J. W. Shelton, and M. Abel-Hady. 1969. Grain orienta-
    tion in Vicksburg loess. J. Sediment Petrol. 39:969-979.
Obruchev, V. A. 1900. Inner Asia, Northern China and Nan-Shan. Report
    on the Expedition of 1892-1894, vol. 2. St. Petersburg.
Obruchev, V. A. 1945. Loess types and their origin. Am. J. Sci. 243:
    256-262.
Obruchev, V. A. 1959. Loess of Northern China. In Loess of Northern
    China, trans. by A. Gourevitch. U.S. Department of Agriculture, 1964.
Pavlinov, V. I. 1959. Some data about the genesis of Chinese loess.
    In Loess of Northern China, trans. by A. Gourevitch. U.S. Department
    of Agriculture, 1964.

Pumpelly, R. 1866. Geological researches in China, Mongolia and Japan
    during the years 1862-1865. Smithson. Contrib. Knowl. no. 202, p. 143,
    Philadelphia.

Pumpelly, R. 1879. Relations of Secular rock disintegration to loess,
    glacial drift and rock basins. Am. J. Sci. Arts, vol. 27.

Richthofen, F. F. von. 1882. On the mode of origin of the loess. Geol.
    Mag. 9:293-305.

Russell, R. J. 1944. Lower Mississippi valley loess. Bull. Geol. Soc.
    Am. 55:1-40.

Sakai, E. 1967. The Huangtu Formation and the loess of North China.
    In T. Ogura, ed., Geology and mineral resources of the far east, vol. 1.
    University of Tokyo Press, Tokyo.

Scheidig. 1934. Der Löss und seine geotechnischen eigenschaften. Th.
    Steinkopff, Dresden und Leipzig.

Swineford, A., and J. C. Frye. 1951. Petrography of the Peoria loess
    in Kansas. J. Geol. 59:306-322.

Swineford, A., and J. C. Frye. 1955. Petrographic comparison of some
    loess from Western Europe with Kansas loess. J. Sediment Petrol.
    25:3-23.

Tafel, A. 1914. Meine Tibetreise. Eine Studienfahrt durch das nord-
    westliche China und durch die inner Mongolei in das ostliche Tibet,
    vol. 1, Berlin.

Terruggi, M. E. 1957. The nature and origin of Argentine loess. J.
    Sediment Petrol. 27:322-332.

Thorp, J. 1945. Significance of loess in classification of soils. Am.
    J. Sci. 243:263-270.

Willis, B. 1907. Research in China, vol. 1. p. 353.

Wright, B. 1902. Origin and distribution of the loess in northern
    China and Central Asia. Bull. Seismol. Soc. Am. 13:127-138.

Yang, Chieh. 1959. The genesis of loess deposits in northern China.
    In Loess of Northern China, trans. by A. Gourevitch. U.S. Department
    of Agriculture, 1964.